KINGSLEY AMIS

WHAT BECAME OF JANE AUSTEN?

And Other Questions

Penguin Books

D1328822

Penguin Books Ltd, Harmondsworth,
Middlesex, England
Penguin Books, 625 Madison Avenue,
New York, New York 10022, U.S.A.
Penguin Books Australia Ltd, Ringwood,
Victoria, Australia
Penguin Books Canada Ltd, 2801 John Street,
Markham, Ontario, Canada L3R 1B4
Penguin Books (N.Z.) Ltd, 182–190 Wairau Road,
Auckland 10, New Zealand

These pieces first appeared in the following periodicals:
Encounter, *New Statesman*, the *Observer*, *Harper's Magazine*,
Playboy, *Spectator*, *Sunday Telegraph* and *Twentieth Century*.
The author and publishers are grateful
for the permission of the editors to reprint.

First published in Great Britain by Jonathan Cape Ltd 1970
Published in Penguin Books 1981
Copyright © Kingsley Amis, 1970

Set, printed and bound in Great Britain by
Cox & Wyman Ltd, Reading
Set in Linotype Lectura

To Violet and Tony Powell

CONTENTS

PREFACE

I have shortened a few of the pieces reprinted here, so as not to cover the same ground twice; I have lengthened a few more, by restoring editorial cuts, incorporating material contributed elsewhere, adding remarks that happened not to have occurred to me the first time round, or (in the case of my note on John le Carré) taking subsequent developments into account. But I have nowhere materially altered what I first wrote, though I have corrected a number of stylistic errors.

WHAT BECAME OF JANE AUSTEN?

There is something to be said for the view, held by rational critics as well as by mere going-through-the-motions appreciators, that *Mansfield Park* is the best of Jane Austen's works. Although there is some loss of high spirits, that invigorating coldness prevails, so that we can believe at times that we are reading an eighteenth-century novel, and the dialogue reaches new heights of flexibility and awareness, so much so that there are some distinct anticipations of the modern novel. Further, we have in Mrs Norris the most hauntingly horrible of the author's horrible characters, and in Sir Thomas Bertram the most fully and firmly drawn and – but for his final obduracy towards his elder daughter – most sympathetic of her patriarchs. And negatively, it might be added, there is less concern here with 'the amorous effects of "brass" ' (in Mr Auden's phrase), with the minutiae of social obligation, with distinctions between a Tweedledum labelled 'well-bred' and a Tweedledee labelled 'coarse' – with some of the things, in fact, which render parts of Jane Austen's other work distasteful.

Correspondingly, however, defects which are incidental elsewhere become radical in *Mansfield Park*. Not even *Pride and Prejudice*, which plainly foreshadows much of the Henry Crawford theme in the later book, exhibits as glaringly the author's inclination to take a long time over what is of minor importance and a short time over what is major. Nor does *Persuasion*, despite the sneering vulgarity with which the

11

character of Mrs Clay is treated, embody to any comparable degree the Austen habit of censoriousness where there ought to be indulgence, and indulgence where there ought to be censure. These are patently moral 'oughts', and it is by moral rather than aesthetic standards that *Mansfield Park*, especially, is defective. Although it never holds up the admirable as vicious, it continually and essentially holds up the vicious as admirable, an inversion rendered all the more insidious by being associated with such dash and skill, and all the more repugnant by the co-presence of a moralistic fervour which verges at times on the evangelical.

It must be said at once that the book succeeds brilliantly whenever it aims to hold up viciousness of character as vicious. Mrs Norris is very fully visualized in domestic and social terms, but these are the lineaments of a moral repulsiveness, and it is a superb if unintentional stroke of moral irony whereby she alone shows charity towards the disgraced and excommunicated Maria. Sir Thomas, again, represents an essay, carried out with scrupulous justice, on the case of the humane and high-principled man whose defects of egotism and a kind of laziness (to be seen running riot in the character of his wife) betray him into inhumanity and are shown as instrumental in the disasters visited upon his daughters. More important still, the unworthiness of Henry and Mary Crawford is allowed to emerge with an effect of inevitability that is only heightened by the author's freedom, almost audacity, in stressing their sprightliness and even their considerable share of right feeling. This is an achievement which changes in ethical outlook have left undimmed and which testifies to a unique and enviable moral poise.

All these, however, are relative triumphs. The characters mentioned, especially the Crawfords, exist less in their own right than in order to show up by contrast the virtues of the central pair, not only in the status of persons but as embodiments of rival ideologies and ways of life. In both capacities the hero and heroine are deficient. The fact that as social beings they are inferior to the Crawfords, that Henry and Mary are good fun and the other two aren't, is a very large part of the author's theme and is perfectly acceptable, even though this particular disparity sometimes goes too far for comfort and further, one cannot help feeling, than can have been intended: to invite Mr and Mrs Edmund Bertram round for the evening would not be lightly undertaken. More basically than this, Edmund and Fanny are both morally detestable and the endorsement of their feelings and behaviour by the author – an endorsement only withdrawn on certain easily recognizable occasions – makes *Mansfield Park* an immoral book. Let us consider first the less heinous of the two offenders.

Edmund's kindness to Fanny entitles him to initial respect, and the bantering form it occasionally takes recalls his far livelier forerunner, Henry Tilney of *Northanger Abbey*. But it is not long before Edmund is shocked by Mary Crawford's complaint – in company, too – that her uncle's rather ill-judged alterations to a cottage of his resulted in the garden being messed up for some time. Soon afterwards he conducts, with the untiringly sycophantic Fanny, a post mortem on this affront to his 'sense of propriety'. This readiness to be shocked, in itself shocking, is not in evidence when, a few chapters later, the pair of them launch into a canting pietistic tirade against Mary's brother-in-law in her presence. Nor does the vaunted sense of propriety exclude boorishness – in reply, for instance, to a perfectly amiable suggestion from Henry Crawford about possible improvements to the Parsonage. But it is his objections to the proposed private theatricals that finally establish Edmund as repulsive, and are thus worth setting out in some detail.

Any such amusement, he considers, is 'open to some objections' – though without divulging these – and in this case 'want of feeling' would be involved, because Sir Thomas is at sea and might get drowned round about now. (The reasonable argument, that Sir Thomas would object to his house being disordered – as in the event he does – is not stressed.) It further transpires that the play proposed, *Lovers' Vows*, is so vicious that merely to rehearse it 'must do away all restraints'. Such scruples, as Mrs Q. D. Leavis notes in her Introduction to the latest reprint of the novel,* are 'well grounded in conventional notions of decorum'. But we are right to expect from Edmund something more intelligent, more liberal, more manly than that, and a cursory reading will show that *Lovers' Vows* is in fact innocuous rubbish. This being so, his eventual reluctant consent to participate, which we are invited to see as the tragic overthrow of a noble mind worked on by Mary Crawford, becomes a squalid and ridiculous belly-flop, and his consequent humiliation is deserved in two senses, since it is earned –

* *Mansfield Park* (Macdonald, 1957).

can we really be reading Jane Austen? – not by being too priggish, but by not being priggish enough.

If Edmund's notions and feelings are vitiated by a narrow and unreflecting pomposity, Fanny's are made odious by a self-regard utterly unredeemed by any humour – is this still Jane Austen? – or even lightness. She is mortified by being excluded – at her own obstinate insistence – from the theatricals. She pities herself and does others the kindness of hoping that they will never know how much she deserves their pity. She feels that Henry's addresses involve 'treating her improperly and unworthily, and in such a way as she had not deserved'. She indulges in righteous anger a good deal, especially when her own interests are threatened. She is disinclined to force herself to be civil to those – a numerous company – whose superior she thinks herself to be; such people she regards with unflinching censoriousness. She is ashamed of her own home in Portsmouth, where there is much 'error' and she finds 'every body underbred', and how relieved she is when the 'horrible evil' of Henry lunching there is averted. Significantly, the climax of her objections to her mother is that Mrs Price is too busy to take much notice of Miss Price from Mansfield Park. And, in the closing stages, her 'horror' at the wretched Maria's elopement is such as to exclude pity in any word or thought.

This indictment could be greatly extended, notably in the direction of the 'moral concern' Fanny feels at Mary's power over Edmund. The tendency of all this can perhaps be fixed by pointing out that the character of Fanny lacks self-knowledge, generosity and humility, the three 'less common acquirements' which her girl cousins are, near the outset, stated to lack and which, by implication, are to be demonstrated as existing in her. Instead it is a monster of complacency and pride who, under a cloak of cringing self-abasement, dominates and gives meaning to the novel. What became of that Jane Austen (if she ever existed) who set out bravely to correct conventional notions of the desirable and virtuous? From being their critic (if she ever was) she became their slave. That is another way of saying that her judgement and her moral sense were corrupted. *Mansfield Park* is the witness of that corruption.

1957

14

Until about twenty years ago, Peacock was still getting his fair share of literary attention, in quantity at any rate: the big scholarly Halliford edition was still coming out in the 1930s, and at that time the bell-etristic belt was kept rolling merrily along with stuff about his connections with Wales and his friendship with Shelley. More recently there has been a recession in this line, while no modern critic that I know of has thrown more than a passing glance towards Peacock's work. It may be that the obvious joviality of most of that work, coupled with an absence of complexity and of the dark night of the soul, has put off some possible investigators; others may have decided, with some show of reason, that any friend of Shelley's could be no friend of theirs. However this may be, when we pick up the nice new Macmillan reprint of *Maid Marian* and *Crotchet Castle*, we find old George Saintsbury still occupying the Introduction, just as he did in the printing of sixty years ago.

Now there is clearly much to be said for this arrangement and for Saintsbury himself, who was debarred by nature from writing anything not worth reading, and is typically judicious here in his account of Peacockian ingredients and formulas. He goes as far and as amiably as most university students, and many general readers, will probably require. Talents far more extraordinary than his, on the other hand, would have been needed to prevent much of what he says from dating, in particular a mysterious remark about Peacock's letters to Lord

Broughton being inaccessible 'for another half-dozen years', which time has robbed of topicality. And talking of dating, was it really necessary to reproduce here F. H. Townsend's truly horrible illustrations to the old edition, with their olio of Rossetti and 1890s *Punch*? If book illustration is coming back, as some signs indicate, surely someone on the payroll of the *Radio Times* or of some hot-drink manufacturer could have been called in to replace Townsend? It wouldn't have been much trouble, any more than it would have been much trouble to announce the identity of the 'G' who indefatigably footnotes the anachronisms of *Maid Marian*.

It may reasonably be objected that this doesn't really matter, that this reprint has made two of the novels more easily available (in a pleasant binding) and that's what counts. I agree in a way. At the same time, if criticism is any use at all, I do feel that the expense of printing a new Introduction, at any rate, could reasonably have been borne and that a small cheque could have coaxed somebody a bit younger than Saintsbury into turning out a few thousand words which might have done something towards re-examining Peacock, towards seeing how he stands up to recent changes in taste and critical approach. Such an effort, such a revival of interest, would be worth while, I think, if only because its subject is almost the only nineteenth-century novelist free of what one might call the puffing and blowing so sadly common in the fiction of his age – and of our own.

The first thing, of course, would be to throw out the notion, popular with Saintsburyite devotees of the printed word, that all Peacock's novels are good, that although *Maid Marian* may not be everybody's cup of tea and *Melincourt* drags here and there, the whole thing is much of a muchness. It would be more reasonable to argue that what we really have is a wild disparity between different books and sometimes between parts of the same book, and an uncertainty on Peacock's part, never resolved or else resolved in the wrong way, about what he was trying for and what he was good at. There is no point, at this date, in glossing over the tedium of a great part of his work, in failing to recognize straight away, for example, that *The Misfortunes of Elphin* is not superior enough to *Maid Marian* to make much odds and that both are fatally injured by whimsy and quaintness, by cumbersome ironizing on modern life and, especially in *Elphin*, by those erudition exercises which will wring a repeated groan from any but the

16

most addicted reader. This last defect, no doubt the result of Peacock's being what we have been taught to call an autodidact, comes near to ruining whole areas of nearly all the novels, not only through the mouths of those awful old gasbags the Reverend Doctors Folliott and Opimian, but in the author's personal commentary as well. It could be suggested, though, that none of this is really radical, and that the real trouble is to be found somewhere in Peacock's very conception of his own talents. He was never at his best, I think, as a pure satirist, or anyway not as the sort of satirist he spent most time on trying to be: the persecutor of learned fools who condemn themselves by their own utterances.

A line must be drawn somewhere between the living and the faded parts of his work, but merely to draw that line between living and faded targets of ridicule – between, say, the Shelley bits in *Nightmare Abbey* and Mr MacQuedy's political economy in *Crotchet Castle* – would not be quite adequate. To throw in a reflection on Peacock's inordinate capacity for simple diffuseness and repetition would have the advantage of helping to get *Melincourt* and *Gryll Grange* out of the way (where they belong), but would be little use on the harder questions. What can we turn to next, then? To plot versus no plot? No: the answer that appeals to me is that Peacock was only at his best in farcical-sentimental comedy with a satiric background. The moment the satirist holds the stage he makes a dive for the lectern, and the reader, unfortified with cold fowl and Madeira, spreads a handkerchief over his face.

With *Headlong Hall*, accordingly, the obvious point to make is not that there is something intrinsically absurd about picturesque gardening which helps on the satire, but that the whole business leads up to, and is justified by, the demolition which blows Mr Cranium into the lake; similarly, Mr Escot is not just a deteriorationist, but a deteriorationist comically in love. And in *Nightmare Abbey*, again, although all the raillery about romanticism has the advantage of bearing on something fairly durable in ideas and conduct – and Mr Hilary's objections to the ideology with 'quarrels with the whole universe for not containing a sylph' are much more penetrating than most raillery – yet we can all agree that it would have little force if it were not made to focus upon Scythrop, whose antics are constantly being pulled across the border into farce, the domain where the amatory and moral themes of the book, remaining recognizable and indeed perfectly serious, are finally clinched. And in *Crotchet Castle* – who wouldn't consent to liquidating that whole tribe of after-dinner lecturers for the sake of a few more pages of the matchless Clarinda taking the stuffing out of Captain Fitzchrome? Those scenes show Peacock in possession of something he never quite found again: a delightful airy felicity which looks back to Congreve and forward to Wilde:

'Do you know, though Mammon has a sort of ill name, I really think he is a very popular character; there must be at the bottom something amiable about him. He is certainly one of those pleasant creatures whom everybody abuses, but without whom no evening party is endurable. I daresay, love in a cottage is very pleasant; but then it positively must be a cottage *ornée*: but would not the same love be a great deal safer in a castle, even if Mammon furnished the fortification? ... A dun is a horridly vulgar creature; it is a creature I cannot endure the thought of: and a cottage lets him in so easily. Now a castle keeps him at bay. You are a half-pay officer, and are at leisure to command the garrison: but where is the castle? and who is to furnish the commissariat?'

Passages like that, together with almost the whole of *Headlong Hall* and *Nightmare Abbey*, entitle Peacock to his place as a minor master – and as somebody far more energetically original than the chorus of drowsy Victorian and Edwardian eulogy would imply. That enchanting urbanity, which gave him command of a whole range between witty seriousness and demented knockabout, was something which disappeared from the English novel almost before it had properly arrived.

1955

THE POET AND THE DREAMER

Acquaintance with school examination scripts and with the tastes (or professed tastes) of young people entering the university will suggest that Keats is still the teacher's favourite poet. After all, Shakespeare, Milton, Wordsworth and the rest of the train require interpretation, textual or ideological: Keats can be read without a glossary and he believed simply in Beauty. This immediacy of appeal is reinforced by the straightforwardly romantic subject-matter of the verse and by the engaging personality, tragic life and high aspirations of the poet; nobody, it seems unmistakable, was ever more of a poet than Keats. Most adolescents of any sensitivity will respond with an enthusiasm they may still recall when, bloody but unbowed after their struggles with pass degree, diploma, appointments board and head teacher, they in their turn face the task of implanting tolerance for poetry in the twelve-year-old mind.

Any favourable attitude towards any verse must be better than none, and yet the results of an early inoculation with Keats may prove an obstacle to further literary development. If Keats is to be the ideal poet, ideal poetry too readily becomes a tissue of affectionate descriptions of nice things interrupted by occasional complaints that the real world is insufficiently productive of those nice things, and if any pupil should wonder what the dales of Arcady have got to do with him, then the answer is that poetry deals with 'the world of the imagination', i.e. not with the real world. Those who undertake to break down such a preconception are likely to suffer from conscience trouble. Is it worth the risk of removing one enjoyment and not managing to substitute a 'better'? Might it not be safer to push the chaps on with their Keats and with the poems that can, with whatever distortion, be assimilated to Keats: 'Christabel', 'Oenone', *Paradise Lost* (first two books only, of course), snippets from *The Faerie Queene*?

A rational reading of Keats, whatever the long-term result, is initially destructive. An uneasy suspicion of this is discernible even at the height of the cult in the late nineteenth century. Sidney Colvin, noting a 'dissonance' – or, more accurately, a piece of poetical fudging – in the 'Ode on a Grecian Urn', remarks consolingly that 'it is a dissonance which the attentive reader can easily reconcile for himself: and none but an attentive reader will notice it.' The attentive reader will have little time for Colvin's book,* the recent reissue of which, seventy years after its first publication, motivates some depression. One imagines it already winging its way to the shelves of school libraries, where its adulatory portraiture and innocent assertion of its subject's greatness will inspire another legion of essays maundering about the way 'the poetry seems to throb in every line with the life of imagination and beauty' in that sugary erotic extravaganza 'The Eve of St Agnes'.

Even in his best poems Keats devotes himself too uncritically to 'the world of the imagination'. Even the 'Ode to a Nightingale', though containing passages which must delight the most jaded, is full of frigidities, of appeals to the remote and merely fanciful. What else are the references to hemlock, Lethe, the Dryad (tautologously described as 'of the trees'), Flora, the blushful Hippocrene (seen as a kind of Greek red sparkling Burgundy, and apparently sedimented at that), Bacchus and his pards (brought in to effect a translation into poetese of the unpoetical notion of getting drunk)? Such entities are, as Jeffrey observed of the subject of 'Hyperion', 'too far removed from all the sources of human interest'. And to string together counters of this kind, to use 'Olympus' faded hierarchy' as correlatives for what are evidently the most passionate feelings, was a favourite procedure with Keats, as can be seen from a glance at the 'Ode to Psyche' (Phoebe, Vesper, Dryads again) or the 'Ode on Melancholy' (Lethe again, Proserpine, Psyche again).

* *Keats* by Sidney Colvin (Macmillan, 1957).

Poetry was for Keats a matter of 'O Poesy', of Apollo, the Muses and inspired bards. This connects with his attitude to the actual business of writing. According to Mr Robert Graves (I cannot track this anecdote), Keats used to dress up in poetic robes and laurel crown to encourage the afflatus. And if Apollo did come through on the line with a personal call, the divine message was not to be tampered with; poetry must come as naturally as leaves to the tree. Keats was too intelligent to believe this all the time, but when he revised his verse at all the task was always scamped and he never became a conscientious craftsman. Shoddily worked sonnets would be thrown off and dispatched to friends the same day, to reappear unaltered in print; he knew *Endymion* needed radical rewriting, but 'I am tired of it' and 'it is not in my nature to fumble' – in other words, to take undue trouble.

Endymion, as the *Quarterly Review* soon pointed out, was scattered with awkwardnesses forced upon, or rather suggested to, the poet by the exigencies of rhyme. Such faults reappear throughout the whole of Keats's work, partly because of his habit of selecting forms that require several rhymes to the same sound. These forms were chosen capriciously, without regard to their appropriateness or to his own capacities, on occasion merely because they happened to have been used by poets he happened to admire. It was only an admiration for *Paradise Lost* that eventually took him to blank verse, where common sense might have taken him before 1818. Even the Odes, written for once in original stanza forms, are disfigured by *Endymion*-like crudities: the 'deceiving elf' of the 'Nightingale', for instance, an incarnation into which 'the Fancy' is recklessly crammed to save having to 'fumble' with the rhyming line, and the two analogous defects of the first stanza – 'emptied ... to the drains' (sc. not 'poured down the drain' but 'drained, drunk off') retained to rhyme with 'pains', and 'melodious plot' (so glaringly inappropriate, with its connections with cultivation) retained to rhyme with 'happy lot'.

It is in the middle stanzas of the poem – I take it as fairly representing the mature Keats – that its merit chiefly lies, in the unforgettably entrancing picture of the wood itself, and in the poet's confession, of an unwonted sobriety in style, that he finds himself 'half in love with easeful Death'. Here, by chance, there are no technical flaws, and here too, of set purpose, the classical lumber is stowed away. That English strain which Dr Leavis rightly notes as characteristic of Keats at his finest comes to the fore. In addition, the poet is talking about himself, not a Delphic simulacrum of himself, and has something to say about human existence, not a wish-fulfilling caricature of it. But it is only here, and in the induction of the revised 'Hyperion', that Keats fulfilled for more than a line or two his often-made promise to treat of 'the agonies, the strife of human hearts', to become one of those 'to whom the miseries of the world are misery, and will not let them rest'.

To exalt into greatness one whose achievement was actually that of an often delightful, if often awkward, decorative poet may have, as was suggested above, harmful consequences. Any presumption that Keats might in time have become a major artist is cast in doubt by the fact that it is unpromising theories about poetry that derive from defects of character, quite as much as bad influences and the results of illness, which vitiate his existing work. The kind of writer he might have become is indicated in his letters:

> Imagine the worst dog-kennel you ever saw, placed upon two poles from a mouldy fencing. In such a wretched thing sat a squalid old woman, squat like an ape half-starved from a scarcity of biscuit in its passage from Madagascar to the Cape, with a pipe in her mouth and looking out with a round-eyed, skinny-lidded inanity, with a sort of horizontal idiotic movement of her head: squat and lean she sat, and puffed out the smoke, while two ragged, tattered girls carried her along. What a thing would be a history of her life and sensations!

But that was not the kind of subject that 'a glorious denizen' of Poesy's wide heaven could undertake.

1957

POSTSCRIPT 1970

This now strikes me as a rather clever undergraduate essay (pretty good, that is to say, compared with most of the undergraduate essays I remember). I would not want to withdraw or mitigate any of the nasty remarks about Keats's technical shortcomings and their connection with a self-indulgence deeply embedded in his mind and heart, and to this day I find it genuinely curious that anybody should have written (as M. R. Ridley did) a whole volume called *Keats' Craftsman-*

ship: surely a candidate for that old shortest-books series along with *Canadian Wit and Humour*, *Great Marxist Humanitarians* and *The Vein of Humility in D. H. Lawrence*.

However, I neglected to celebrate, or took for granted, that tremendous originality and audaciousness which went far beyond any mere 'decorative' quality and, by making poetry personal, so to speak democratized it. When Keats opened the Nightingale ode by writing, 'My heart aches,' he was writing about his own heart and nobody else's. Earlier poems in the first person had had the flame of some other character invisibly prefixed to them, normally an idealized or anyway carefully trimmed version of the poet, often, indeed, the Poet, which figure does a good deal of the talking in Wordsworth's anecdotal and autobiographical verse. Keats's ability to cut through all that – an ability which must have sprung from the same root as his self-indulgence – made it possible for anybody at all to identify with him in the process of reading the poem. The results of that 'democratization', like others, may not have been altogether happy, but, like them, they were inevitable. Whatever the detail of Keats's performance, this achievement is such that no one who has never thought him the greatest poet in the world, no matter for how brief a period, has any real feeling for literature.

STORK, STORK, LONG-LEGGED STORK

It is fitting, as they say, that the 150th anniversary of Hans Andersen's birth should have been celebrated in this country by the appearance of his autobiography in a new translation plus a new biography.* His work was early translated into English, and on his visit to England and Scotland in 1847 he found himself already well known – well enough known, at any rate, to be invited to a flare-up at Lord Palmerston's, where he was very soon surrounded by the most eminent ladies of England, and even in Edinburgh many people went to the lengths of styling him the Danish Walter Scott. Much of his reputation at that time depended upon his novels and travel books, now forgotten, but the fairy-tales had quickly gathered a wide audience among both adults and children. The tales have gone on being read, one supposes, ever since; it is a shock to find, on re-reading them, how many of them one knows in some detail.

A modern Andersen, presumably, would have outdone Kafka, or so it could be argued after looking through 'The Red Shoes', say, or 'The Shadow'. A glance at Andersen's early life is likely to give grounds for a similar reflection. Few literary childhoods can have been such a forcing-frame for neurosis, so rich in trauma. The birth itself, on a bed converted from the staging on which a defunct count had lain in state,

* *The Mermaid Man: the Autobiography of Hans Christian Andersen.* Translated by Maurice Michael (Arthur Barker, 1955). *Hans Christian Andersen* by Rumer Godden (Hutchinson, 1955).

24

even perhaps suggests Poe rather than Kafka, and other circumstances make the standard bullying father, possessive mother, bad time at Harrow upbringing look like a free-expression school outing. Quite apart from the hopelessly crazed grandfather, the father who went mad before he died, the stepfather, and the mother who took to drink and went mad, there was all the business at the local asylum, where the grandmother looked after the garden. Here Andersen, as a child of six or seven, used to listen to the songs and talk of the less violent cases, was crammed with superstition by the old women who came to spin in an outbuilding, and was attacked – though without actual physical harm – by a naked madwoman. It is no real surprise to find him describing himself at that period as living 'in the grip of fantasy'. Later, there was the half-humorous mass sexual assault at the clothing factory where he worked, and later still he was to be put to school among children years younger than himself, with a headmaster who sent him along to witness a public beheading as a useful experience, and who told him, on saying good-bye, that he would surely end in the madhouse. But before this Andersen had set out from his native Odense* for Copenhagen with ten rix-dollars in his pocket. He was then fourteen.

It was after an initial period of writing tragedies and poems and walking into prosperous literary drawing-rooms to recite them, to sing and to ask for money, that Andersen was bundled off to school by the directors of the Royal Theatre. After coping with the headmaster and his flighty wife, he went off to wage an unsuccessful battle with the drama and to found a career as a novelist. The state soon began grant-

* Not so long after writing this I happened to be in Odense and of course visited the Andersen Museum. One of the chief exhibits, the writer's bed, was behind plate glass, a recent installation devised, so the curator told me, to prevent any repetition of the behaviour of the actor Danny Kaye, who, on a visit connected with his role in a film of Andersen's life, had snatched up and donned the great man's top-hat, opened his umbrella and thrown himself on to the bed in question. This had – reasonably, I think – irritated the Odenseans. However, my main recollection is of a contemporary portrait of Andersen which resembled, to a really quite alarming degree of exactitude, our own John Osborne. As a firm believer in the principle that physical resemblances are an index of deep psychological and other affinity, I offer this piece of observation to future assessors of Mr Osborne's art.

ing him travel bursaries, and the events of this period are what give his autobiography most of its life, though it would be a pity to miss one Copenhagen detail, a review of his third novel by Kierkegaard, the latter's first published work, as a matter of fact, and so long and, more important, so 'Hegelian', that only he and Andersen ever got through it. On the whole, however, it is the picture he provides of early-Victorian London which will appeal most to English readers, together with some teasing glimpses of the great figures of the day: Liszt, for instance, 'a juggler with notes who dumbfounded your imagination'; or Dickens, whom Andersen evidently bored stiff; or Hugo, who received him in dressing-gown, drawers and elegant boots, and who wrote his autograph, out of prudential considerations, right at the top of the paper.

Between them, the autobiography and the biography afford all the evidence needed to build up a clear impression of what kind of man Andersen was. One would be justified, on the other hand, in treating with great reserve most of Miss Godden's opinions and generalizations. Her book is readable enough as pure information, and its reviewer cannot help feeling a little churlish in pouring cold water on what is so clearly aimed at the not very literary 'general' reader. But it seems almost obligatory to object to her trick of imputing inner feelings to her characters, her stream of sentimental instruction on the nature of 'the artist' and 'the true poet' – whose chief difficulty, we are told, lies in balancing dreams and living, and to whom a social life is death – and, all in all, her systematic buttressing of the ignorant prejudices which are likely to afflict the 'general' reader in his attempt to get closer to literature. Though she can hardly miss seeing the manic-depressive pattern in Andersen's behaviour, and cannot avoid illustrating his childlike vanity and silliness, she tries to draw a veil of romantic bardolatry over his frantic self-advertisement, his lifelong habit of lachrymose despair at the slightest opposition, and his similarly unending demand for love, admiration and fame. Perhaps in consequence, she fails to emphasize what are equally real, and equally childlike, qualities in him. His immense determination, his fascination with the outward details of life (which made him an excellent travel-writer), his irreverence, his loyalty and lack of malice, his great fund of disinterested affection.

Any account of Andersen's fairy-tales must inevitably, I suppose, start from the verity that, being in so many ways a child himself, he was just the boy to write children's stories. A useful addition to this can be made by an approach only slightly more sophisticated: Andersen is a real gift for the school which finds in art a re-enactment of personal conflicts and obsessions. Seen from this angle, 'The Swineherd' becomes a symbolical attack on the triviality of the women who laughed at his huge head, straggling hair and stork-like legs, and ends, with the phrase 'I am come to despise thee', in a symbolical rejection. Again, the heroine of 'The Little Mermaid' possessed, quite irrelevantly from the story's point of view, a beautiful voice, and in an attempt to win her Prince suffered her tongue being cut out; it is hard to forget that Andersen was unhappily in love with Jenny Lind. And we all know who the Ugly Duckling was and what it went through before 'it realized its happiness in all the splendour that surrounded it'. Hidden and neglected merit finally revealed and rewarded is perhaps the central theme of the stories, and it is here, of course, that their obsessional origin ties up with their appeal to children. It took a man like Andersen to remember, or to re-evoke, childhood's dreadful impatience with the unregarding world and to dramatize it in terms that childhood can understand. To read of the immense care he lavished on his tales, to remember how scrupulously he preserves the repetitive element that children love, and how boldly he anthropomorphizes trees, needles and fire-tongs, makes it tempting to believe that he knew exactly what he was doing, that he was consciously offering up his own prolonged childhood. And yet he seems to have regarded the whole business as a sideline; the tales were written as a diversion from the serious concerns of a novelist and poet, or else to raise money, and although good at entertaining children there is little evidence that he was fond of them. Was he perhaps secretly ashamed and frightened of being childish? He need not have been. It made him an insufferable companion, but how many great writers have been any better?

1955

27

THE COCKNEY'S HOMER

'Dickens gone! The "Spectator" says he beat Shakespeare at his best, and instances Mrs Gamp as superior to Juliet's nurse. This in a critical newspaper!'

Meredith (in a letter of 1870)

The task of scholarship might be broadly defined as that of explaining and illustrating how a given literary work appeared to its original readers. This will involve perhaps in the first place some kind of linguistic study, backed up by such things as the relating of the literary work to its analogues. A further useful supplement to understanding, and one which may greatly alter perspective, can be provided by the comparatively unfamiliar method of investigating the behaviour of an original audience. What, for example, did Dickens's Victorian readers think of him, and he of them? In an outstandingly able book* Professor George H. Ford has expounded the answers to these questions, as well as tracing the course of Dickens's posthumous career, which has thrown up some very odd Dickensians indeed. He writes easily and wittily in the way we have come to expect from modern American scholars, as distinct, unfortunately, from some of their British colleagues. As well as covering its ostensible subject, his book is an excellent general introduction to Dickens's work.

The relation between Dickens and his readers, as we are shown, was not as simple or as close as is commonly thought. To have his work described as 'puppy pie and stewed cat' was no more than he eventually came to expect from his less urbane detractors, who were not few, and it often happened that a journalist or critic, having

* *Dickens and His Readers: Aspects of Novel-Criticism since 1836* (O.U.P., 1955).

awarded an earlier work a *satisfecit*, packaged up with a list of recommendations for the future, would later round on the author for not having done as he was told. Reviewers, it seems, have not changed much; then as now, too, highbrow readers displayed what Professor Ford calls restlessness, a tendency to drop a writer once he becomes established and to turn their talent-detectors elsewhere. 1847, which saw the appearance of *Vanity Fair*, *Wuthering Heights* and *Jane Eyre*, must have been an *annus horribilis* for Dickens. On his own side, the public's wish was not inevitably his command: his fondness for low scenes and low characters, the growing bitterness of his satire after 1850, his attacks on the Victorian home in *Our Mutual Friend*, all ran counter to contemporary preference, and the shift after *Pickwick* to the unamiabilities of *Oliver Twist* was an early but not a lonely example of his readiness to abandon a wildly successful formula for an untried one.

Despite all this, it can hardly be maintained that many things in *Dombey and Son*, for instance, were not a direct concession to the taste of the day. The important question is, whose taste? London cabmen might have wanted to get Dickens to take up their cause in his next novel, but the pressure they could bring to bear on him was limited; it was the intelligentsia who got themselves a death-scene *ordinaire* in the opening number of *Dombey* and a Little-Nell-type death-scene in episode five. The reactions to the death of the original Little Nell have provided some of Professor Ford's most remarkable pages. Among the roll-call of those detected sobbing like a child at the relevant time were Daniel O'Connell (who went further and threw the book out of the window), Macready and Jeffrey – the Jeffrey who had shown himself so notably impervious to some earlier features of romanticism and who was to sob as heartily over 'that sweet Paul' as over 'that divine Nelly'. Others demonstrably unmanned were Sydney Smith (repenting, no doubt, of having found the name 'Boz' somewhat vulgar), Hood, Carlyle, Landor ('indeed [Dickens's] women are superior to Shakespeare's. No one of our poets comes near him') and FitzGerald, who copied out all the parts of the book which featured Nell so as to construct 'a kind of Nelly-ad or Homeric narration', and yet, it might be added, was going to turn against Tennyson in the 1860s for alleged popularizing sentimentality. The account can be rounded off by reference to Poe (then presumably engaged on 'The Murders in the Rue Morgue'), who thought Nell's death should have been omitted as 'excessively painful' to the reader.

Any suspicion that the above particulars have here been rehearsed for fun must be banished by consideration of the fact that nothing Dickens ever wrote aroused such passionate regard as the passing of that divine Nelly. There was passionate disgust too: Swinburne found her as real as a child with two heads, Ruskin thought her death 'a diseased extravagance', carried out 'for the market, as a butcher kills a lamb', and almost certainly Dr Arnold would have noted as a consequence an exacerbation of the 'decrease of manly thoughtfulness' at Rugby for which he had blamed the publication of *Pickwick*. But all in all there can be few episodes which throw a stronger or more curious light upon the early-Victorian heart. One would welcome a history of the propriety of weeping on the part of adult males in public, beginning round about Achilles and winding up with the renascence exemplified by two fairly recent war-films. In both *From Here to Eternity* (American) and *The Cruel Sea* (British) tears were to be seen coursing unregarded down heroic cheeks. Perhaps Professor Ford has a promising pupil he could put on to the project for a Ph.D.

It is not as a tear-jerker, however, that Dickens will nowadays be recommended or even deplored. Discussion has shifted to remote sectors, most notably, perhaps, that of symbolism. To impute Dickensian lineage to Dostoievsky is no longer the thing; he has been turned out by Kafka, and to compare *Bleak House* with *The Trial*, though of questionable import, is not altogether absurd. It would be hard to say the same of Mr Auden's suggestion, almost Dickensian in its expansive hilariousness, that 'Mr Pickwick represents, in his early stages, a pagan god wandering imperviously through the world; later, through suffering, the god is transformed into a human creature.' Stuff like this can be considered as, in part, modish attempts to defend Dickens from the charges of vulgarity, lack of artistry and what-not which some kinds of reader have brought against him. These charges have been remarkably persistent: there is a good deal in common between Bagehot's censure of Dickens as a laugh-jerker as well as a tear-jerker ('it is not the function of really artistic productions to contribute to the mirth of human beings') and Mrs Leavis's allegation that both in comedy and in pathos he 'stands primarily for a set of crude emotional exercises'. The simplest way of meeting these objections is to admit their justice and then dismiss them as irrelevant in view of Dickens's abounding vigour. He certainly has vigour, and vigour is certainly a rare and desirable quality in the novel of the last 150-odd years. It is clearly right, as Mr V. S. Pritchett among others has recommended, to swallow Dickens whole, fantasy, vulgarity, weak motivation, improbabilities and all, if one can. But can one? My own experience in reading Dickens, and I doubt whether it is an uncommon one, is to be bounced between violent admiration and violent distaste almost every couple of paragraphs, and this is too uncomfortable a condition to be much alleviated by an inward recital of one's duty not to be fastidious, to gulp the stuff down in gobbets like a man. What, for me, cancels out all that humour, all that movement, all that triumphant concentration on external detail, all that magnificent variety, is the ubiquitous, obsessive repetition, the inability to leave anything, good or bad, alone – what Saintsbury called 'that damnable iteration'. Sometimes this method produces cumulative effects of great power, as in the chain of references to the whiteness and regularity of Mr Carker's teeth; much more often, in my view, it fills the reader with an exasperated ennui. It was a splendid idea to introduce, in Mrs Dombey's death scene, the ticking of the physicians' watches; it was maddening folly to introduce it three times. The same characteristic produces the aura of insubstantiality which can afflict even the more successful minor portraits. They are not so much too flat as too small; their one or two leading traits reappear too often, and reappear unchanged, and go on reappearing. This doesn't happen to Mrs Gamp, but I think it does happen to Mr Jingle. And yet it would be ungracious not to admit, in conclusion, that Professor Ford's book, more than any piece of Dickens criticism I can remember, breeds a determination to sit down to the novels again and see whether this time they can't be subdued into greatness.

1956

FOUNDING FATHER

The year 1963 should not be allowed to pass without some salute to the not very successful Paris lawyer and part-time verse dramatist who, a century ago, brought out a novel* that initiated a new literary form. 1863 also saw the appearance of *Romola* and *The Water Babies* – the publication of *Salammbo* in the previous year is the best I can do with the French scene – but none of these, perhaps, nor even Mill's *Utilitarianism*, another exact contemporary, has had such a durable effect. The historians may point to Swift, More, Lucian of Samosata as predecessors, and Wells was unarguably a far greater writer. Nevertheless, it was Jules Verne who set science fiction going.

The physical context and the scale of gadgetry were to be widely varied in his later books, but in other respects *Five Weeks in a Balloon* shows Verne's method already firmly settled. He introduces his favourite trio of intrepid adventure types. In this instance they are Dr Fergusson, the eccentric, obstinate, absurdly omniscient and resourceful scientist who designs, builds and skippers the dirigible; Kennedy, the honourable but hot-tempered man of action with his rifles and pistols; and Joe, the brave, loyal servant who is allowed to provide some comic relief, though never of a sort that might threaten Fergusson's dignity (or raise much more than an indulgent smile). Girls are soppy and don't come into it: this is a boy's world. To say so is not to denigrate

* *Five Weeks in a Balloon* by Jules Verne (Arco Publications with Bernard Hanison, 1962).

it, for an adult's world that was not also a boy's world here and there, now and then, would be a chilly place.

The airborne voyage across Africa with which the story mainly deals is preceded by a short scene at a London Geographical Society meeting. This is satirical in tone and did not appear in earlier English translations, though to the modern eye it could hardly be more innocuous. Kenneth Allott, in his excellent biography, suggests that this mundane opening, a favourite device of Verne's, was aimed at reassuring Parisian sophisticates who might have balked at unleavened romance.

However this may be, anything so ambitious is dropped with the balloon's first load of ballast, and all the way across the Dark Continent enthusiastic earnestness flourishes unchecked. In the intervals between Fergusson's lectures on history, geography and science the travellers incur adventures, described with innocent energy, see remarkable sights, decked out in profuse but largely unevocative detail, and deliver volubly wooden harangues:

' "We are in the midst of the desert!" said the doctor. "Look at this immensity of sand! What a strange spectacle! What a singular freak of Nature! . . . The wind is afraid to breathe; it has gone to sleep." '

It is hard to imagine any sort of equivalent to these verbal postures in mid-twentieth-century idiom, nor should we feel happy with them, I think, if they could be devised. Verne's flavour is of the later nineteenth century and, to a great degree, of his original Victorian translators. The present version (part of a monumental new complete edition) successfully retains this flavour while correcting some earlier ineptitudes.

One settles down to read or re-read Verne with an eagerness based on ruminating about him, rather than on any notion of what he is actually like to read. He displays that curious property – shared perhaps with Dickens? – of making his effect not so much when the book is open as after it is shut and put away, so that each novel starts to improve in retrospect the moment one starts to forget it. At any rate, he arouses an expectation that is never properly fulfilled. It is not that the style and narrative method are a barrier; they are part of the fun. And although Verne had no interest in character, his people always endear themselves, so much so as to cast doubt on the first clause of this sentence. The trouble is partly that the adventures, which sound all right in summary and feel all right in memory – a typhoon, an attack on the gas envelope by gyrfalcons, the rescue of a French missionary from the sacrificial stake – are never brought to the pitch of real suspense. We know much too certainly that if Fergusson hasn't got the answer, Kennedy or Joe will come up with it rather too soon.

The most obvious chances of drama and excitement are missed. When Joe, imprisoned by tribesmen in a town on an island in Lake Chad, wakes up to find that a cataclysm has submerged tribesmen, town and island, he might have been pardoned a momentary sense of puzzlement, even alarm. *Mais non!* In a trice the worthy fellow has taken his courage in his hands and seized a sort of boat, roughly hewn out of a tree-trunk, that chances to be drifting past!

This kind of insensitivity is connected with a rather deadening scrupulousness about probability and fact. The Africa seen by the Fergusson expedition is altogether too much the Africa of reliable contemporary report, of Livingstone and Burton and Speke. One may learn to dislike irresponsible sensationalism by dipping into the science fiction of our own time, but a shot of it here* would have done a world of good. Any number of well authenticated anthropophagi are no substitute for a handful of men whose heads do grow beneath their shoulders.

Again, Verne's balloon travelled four thousand miles, but a real one had gone eight hundred miles four years earlier, and a straight multiplication factor of five is hardly enough for a tale of wonder. (The immediate source of the novel, Poe's *Balloon-Hoax* of 1844, featured a non-stop flip from North Wales to South Carolina.) A similar conservatism saw to it that that supposed marvel, Captain Nemo's *Nautilus*, was behind the submarine technology of its era in every respect but its electrical power supply; and a voyage to the Moon that omits a landing on the Moon is a dud, never mind the author's excuses about the impracticability of returning to Earth.

All this might matter less if Verne's science were consistently real science. But it is not. The account of the cruise of the *Nautilus* is riddled with errors and contradictions of fact and principle, all of which could have been put right by a session with an encyclopaedia of

* And in the kind of avant-garde 'Science fiction' that has become modish since this was written.

the day or even half an hour's chat with a reasonably informed school-master. The Moon projectile was fired from a gun at an initial acceleration which would have instantly killed its occupants – and then the author had the cheek to complain bitterly when Wells got his characters *off* the Moon by using a (then wildly fanciful) gravity insulator. And at least Wells was not the sort to saturate his readers between whiles with a polytechnic course in the theory of gravitation.

Verne got his fingertips on to some of the great myths of our time – the wonderful submarine, the ship so huge that it becomes a floating island, the moon voyage, the monstrous explosion – without ever showing the ability to grasp them. And yet, in more than one sense, this inability hardly matters. The response to his example was not immediate. But its volume was tremendous. It was inevitable that the first science-fiction magazines in the late 1920s should have depended heavily on reprinting his work, no more than fitting that for years there should have been a drawing of his tomb at Amiens on the title page of *Amazing Stories*. Again, up to a point a myth works without the intervention of style and treatment and, as I have said, is more durable than these in the memory.

But only up to a point. An author who cannot be read without continuous disappointment is only half an author, however much the larger that half may be. It is tempting to urge of Verne, as others have urged of Dickens, that he should be swallowed whole; but how do you do that?

1963

PATER AND OLD CHAP

Although it could never rate as one of the books of my life, I can fairly claim some degree of personal involvement with *Sorrell and Son*.* Many years ago a young person of my acquaintance, aware that I was fond of a good read, gave me a copy for Christmas. I knew in advance just what to think of the thing, for it featured prominently in that trenchant study of the abolition of literature, Mrs Leavis's *Fiction and the Reading Public* – a work which, like the Moonlight Sonata, has its part to play in everybody's education. I started on *Sorrell and Son* as a joke, taking time off every so often to inscribe *scholia* of facetious or obscene import. After a time I packed that up, but went on reading in order to find out what happened next.

Many and good, certainly, are the reasons for wanting to defile the pages of Warwick Deeping's masterpiece. The dinning interchange of 'old chap' and 'pater' between the Sorrells tries the nerves sorely, especially in such favourite combinations as 'I understand – old chap' or 'You are a brick – pater'. Entities like 'the brutal glow of her handsome strength' and 'the big, wise heart of the man' are invoked with a readiness not matched by any very readily acceptable demonstration of their presence in the appropriate cases. And we have to put up with, for instance, the 'unconventional' clergyman who enjoys 'amusing himself with Einstein's theory', and the girl with whom Sorrell junior cracks a bottle of Château Ducru ('*Bien, monsieur*') and who has, fittingly enough, 'something French in the logic of her emotions'.

* First published by Cassell in 1925.

36

It would be a sentimental error, however, to conclude that a novel with things like that in it must be worthless, and in fact there is much here that is neither inept nor meretricious. The initial situation – Sorrell is an unemployed ex-officer, is divorced, has a young son to bring up – is genuinely interesting and it is skilfully assembled and got off the mark. The narrative is rich in incident, exploiting the advantages of being a double success story: the father rises via hotel porter to hotel manager with a directorship, the son becomes a promising surgeon. If the characters are often off the peg, a sure instinct governs the timing of their first appearances, and at least two of them – a bullying head porter and an eccentric medical man – are firmly realized in visual terms.

A strong visual sense is also at work in the otherwise rather grimly mechanical bouts of scene-setting that come along whenever anyone goes anywhere new. It accompanies an interest in detail, in what sort of houses people live in and what they see out of their windows and how they divide up their day, which is not impaired by adjacent crudities and would be appropriate – or ought by rights to be appropriate – to writers more intelligent than Deeping. The long episode at the Pelican Inn, where Sorrell rises to fame, may be horribly sullied by the presence of the wise-hearted hotel owner (' "This is our show. I take it that we are all keen on making a success of our show" ') but the machinery of that success is not fudged and the Pelican is visualized down to the last purple-and-old-rose cushion-cover.

It is tempting to match the author of this work with some of the novelists Mrs Leavis classes as among the saved – to compare him with T. F. Powys in point of fidelity to fact, say, or pit him against Virginia Woolf as regards the ability of each to describe an event in terms that make it clear what actually took place – but this would lead outside our present scope. Better to admit at once that if we are curious to know why Sorrell and Son has sold a million copies, and has recently been thought worth reprinting by Pan Books, then it will not quite do to list the literary merits of the thing and ask for the next question. The significance of the book, and much of the hilarity it offers the sophisticated, resides in the nature of the (mainly social) passions it serves to inflame or placate.

The ideal, though by no means the only possible, reader of Sorrell and Son is a middle-aged white-collar worker in the industrial suburbs who feels menaced by a falling real income, a decline in status and the emergence into power and affluence of uncouth persons who sneer at what he feels he stands for. This predicament is probably more common in 1957 than it was in 1925, and yet a second wave of popularity for the book seems unlikely, not merely because such a reader demands a contemporary dress for his problems, but because reaction to these problems has become more self-conscious. Our Wimbledon or Solihull malcontent would find no difficulty in agreeing that 'the wrong people have got the money' nowadays, but he would probably be chary of endorsing the view that working people 'exuded a perfume of stale sweat', or admiring the 'shrewdness' of the young lady who says:

'"... Poor old father has forgotten how to grind the faces of the poor ... Poor old pater has always been trying to see his beastly workmen's point of view. They are all over him now like a lot of dogs. I'd teach 'em."

"How?"

"With a whip, old Kit-bag, a whip."'

There is an almost appealing quality about the honesty of that and many similar passages, about all the talk of the 'barbarians' and their 'savage and resentful cries', about the religiose intensity that can affirm 'snobbery is the footstool at the feet of reverence', and can view death as a class-oriented selection board 'letting the finer spirits through, and throwing the baser back upon the muck-heap'. And there is a taking simplicity in the quadrilateral view of society whereby those below you are divided into 'that class – in the mass' and the select few who give you the respect due to a gentleman, while those above you are either 'kind' because 'well matured' or 'bored and wearily superior'. I do not share these attitudes, but there is something to be said for them as against, for instance, more up-to-date Pharisaisms about mass culture.

However that may be, it will be seen that the social antagonisms of a considerable stratum are dramatized in these pages; the more rabidly inclined, indeed, are likely to derive from them a guilty excitement akin to that engendered by pornography. Kindred prejudices, some dated, some still rampant, are accommodated. There is a persistent thread of anti-Americanism; there is continual deprecation of the 'highbrow' and 'clever'; 'sex is nature' and like eating your dinner, but by a deft synthesis it also includes 'the mystery of woman'; Freud and all that needn't be taken seriously, we aren't abnormal – 'the

38

abnormality could be looked for on the Continent'; people with money and fame, like film stars, are unhappy and want to be like you and me. To round it off nicely, savage things are said about the Commissioners of Inland Revenue.

The neatness with which all this is tailored for one kind of reader tempts another kind to think in terms of efficient market research, but any such imputation would be unfounded. *Sorrell and Son* fully upholds the traditional claim of the best-selling novelist that he writes straight from the heart. Only an ingenuous author, indeed, could have drawn so plainly the sexual triangle comprising Sorrell, his son and the divorced wife. The mother's efforts to capture the son go beyond maternal possessiveness into a swingeing Jocasta complex, while the bond between father and son approaches the marital, and idealized marital at that. A rapturous wish-fulfilling dream of perfect filial love lies at the core of the book, involving absolute rejection of the mother and absolute devotion to the father, and hinting at a disturbance in the author of dimensions normally reserved for figures of pan-European stature.

It seems appropriate, on all grounds, to end on a less clinical note. The trouble with books of this kind is not that they are frightfully corrupt and bad all the time; *pace* Mrs Leavis, that seems inevitable, and the bad passages are full of interest. I should have been sorry to miss episodes like the one where young Sorrell deals out a licking to a rotter stated but not (unhappily) shown to go in for 'obscene and husky humour', and I pondered fruitfully on the statement that Sorrell senior 'was more than a sex-man'. No: the trouble begins when *Sorrell and Son* threatens to start being good, when it starts demonstrating that loyalty is important, that there comes a time when a man must put his pride in his pocket, that any kind of job should be done as well as possible. It is the bad teaching of good lessons that can be painful.

1957

'*What an education for me! To find such things taken as natural*'
– *Bartle in* Darkness and Day.

People seem to be getting more and more inclined to turn writers into cults. There can be no harm in this, as common sense will show, and the vocal devotee, or literary barker, occupies a familiar and on the whole honourable place in recent literary history: one thinks of what Mockton Milnes did for Keats's work, and what Richard le Gallienne did for Meredith's, and what almost everybody one runs into has done for Lawrence's. This, of course, is fine, and only becomes irritating in proportion as the middleman ignores, or pretends not to mind, or tries to turn into virtue, that large area of weakness which, wherever it may lie, invariably accompanies the kind of talent that some people will want to turn into a cult. Such unwillingness, or inability, to give one's hero less than ten out of ten for everything results occasionally in the utter alienation of more temperate admirers – for example I often feel I will never pick up a book by Orwell again until I have read a frank discussion of the dishonesty and hysteria that mar some of his best work. While as for the author of *Lady Chatterley's Lover* . . . No: not wanting to have my windows smashed by Lawrence vigilantes I will sidestep that one and come to Mr Robert Liddell's contribution* to the cult of Miss I. Compton-Burnett.

To put it like that may convey a sneer, which is not my intention, for Miss Compton-Burnett is by any standards a considerable novelist and

* *The Novels of I. Compton-Burnett* (Gollancz, 1955).

Mr Liddell an acute and conscientious critic. It is even very doubtful whether one should speak of a Compton-Burnett cult in the same breath as a Lawrence cult. After all, writers who put in a lot of time ordering the human race about make the best demigods, and no zealots are likely to attach themselves to one who not only never deviates from fiction as the organ of her beliefs, but who habitually declines the small indulgence of generalizing commentary within that fiction. Nevertheless, although an able piece of exposition, and valuable as a groundwork for discussion, Mr Liddell's book allies itself with some of the cult-like chat one sees and hears, by always finding the flattering name for the equivocal quality, so that, for example, it is the 'brilliance' of Compton-Burnett dialogue which completely carries the day over occasional 'woodenness', while the fact that it is 'stylized' is seen as just a thing about it, not as a possible defect that survives superficial reading. Mr Liddell has made an exhaustive list of some of the things which Miss Compton-Burnett does, and one must admire his industry in having among other things collected and put into alphabetical order all the sixty different kinds of tone in which her various characters are described as speaking; but he seems to me to be dodging some of the hard questions, even, perhaps, to be ignorant of the objections of the Compton-Burnett method which need answering, or at least formulating.

The latest novel* affords as handy a starting-point as any. One of the things to say about it is that it is not as good as its predecessor, *The Present and the Past* – hardly an audacious pronouncement, but of the kind which should be made more often about this author: when an artist's work seems at first blush to be homogeneous and of consistent merit, then the critic must work extra hard to establish internal differences. Anyway, the main crux of *Mother and Son* involves – one is immediately tempted to say 'as usual' – infidelity, bastardy, deception and revelation. Julius Hume, hearing that his wife Miranda has only a short while to live, and wanting there to be no secrets between them at such a time, reveals to her that the three children he has been bringing up in their home are not, as was given out, the issue of his dead brother but of himself. The shock kills Miranda on the spot. It is later revealed, by an improbable accident involving a hidden letter,

* *Mother and Son* (Gollancz, 1955).

41

that she had deceived her husband in a similar way. Around this familiar centre are grouped other elements equally familiar: Miranda is one of the basic types of Compton-Burnett 'tyrant'; nothing like as monstrous as horrible old Aunt Matty in *A Family and a Fortune* (though in both cases the tyranny involves a paid companion), and without the priggish moralizing note of Horace Lamb in *Manservant and Maidservant*, but with the customary venting of malice upon those rendered defenceless by their position in the household; in particular, of course, the children, who are reminded with dreadful frequency that their presence, indeed their continued existence, depends on charity. Other familiar elements include the arrangement of children-and-tutor, or children-versus-tutor, scenes, with the children winning hands down; the introduction of a secondary household apart from the main one, where the concerns of the latter are debated and partly directed; and the important part borne in the plot by improbabilities – in addition to the hidden letter already mentioned, which strongly recalls an incident in *Darkness and Day*, there are two crucial over-hearings. The companion, Hester Wolsey, happens to be in the room unnoticed when Julius makes his fatal confession to Miranda, and also happens to be standing about unnoticed when the letter is found and read aloud.

Despite all these things, it would be wrong to imply that the book is a tissue of repetitions, that it is no more than a 're-make' of earlier successes. In particular, the character of Rosebery Hume (the 'Son' of the title), which is the best thing in the book, is without parallel anywhere at all: soft, priggish, self-centred and weak, and yet possessed of a silly integrity, a fat-headed concern for justice, which makes him in the end extremely sympathetic. The secondary household, moreover, carries us outside the range of family relationships, offering instead a lively and astringent sketch of the emotional manoeuvrings of two spinsters, their companion-housekeeper and their cat. At the same time, the book in general brings a feeling of recognition, of having seen a great part of it done before, which only the most thoroughly addicted reader will unreservedly enjoy. In the present connection there are, I think, two main kinds of repetitiveness in Miss Compton-Burnett's work: that of character and that of incident. The first of these has been often enough noted, especially as regards the tyrannical heads of households. 'Some readers', says Mr

Liddell, 'have . . . complained that they do not remember or distinguish them after they have closed the books,' and if Mr Liddell says this we can take it as strongly established. His answer is that he personally finds no difficulty here, claiming that he 'could unerringly assign any speech to the right speaker'. No doubt; but Mr Liddell is a devotee, and even if he were not he has written a whole book about these novels. I much prefer the conclusion of Miss Pamela Hansford-Johnson (in her British Council and National Book League pamphlet) that 'Miss Compton-Burnett has not a sufficient *diversity* of types within her range of experience for the number of her novels. We can group her characters with such ease that eventually the memory entangles them . . .' (Italics in original.) If this is true, it affords the right way of approaching a question sometimes raised by reviewers, that of the narrowness of this author's range in general; but, more interesting, perhaps, it seems to argue a poverty of invention that goes very strangely with the exuberant inventiveness to be found in every line of the dialogue. The second kind of repetitiveness – that of incident – tells the same story, and with rather more damaging implication, for although each successive revelation of illegitimacy, each piece of eaves-dropping, each whiff of incest, each discovery of a vital letter or photograph will hardly do more than make the non-addicted reader grit his teeth in an effort to go on taking the thing seriously, he may yet be moved to reflect that these devices, 'melodramatic' or not, form the only method by which a Compton-Burnett plot is carried on and indeed determine the whole shape of her books.

This author's entire strategy is comprised in first setting out a few scenes of talk, which may be of any length and come in any order; and then, a good long time after the initial situation has been established, somebody listens at a door or finds a letter, a switch is thrown and a new situation takes immediate charge, though without causing or re-vealing any significant change in the characters involved. (Miss Hans-ford-Johnson rightly notes that where there is such change, it is implausible: Horace Lamb is the example here.) There is something almost lazy about this procedure; it exempts the author from having to construct any chain of incident such as is likely in fact to determine change and progress in human lives, substituting a mere arbitrary framework, within the divisions of which no development is called for. One danger of such a method is that large stretches of any given book

43

are liable to escape being clipped together by these devices and will hence be called upon to justify themselves. Miss Compton-Burnett is too gifted not to be able to pull this off time and time again – one immediately remembers such things as the marvellously invigorating battles between the governess Mildred Hallam and her two young charges in *Darkness and Day*. But the author fails to make the Miss Buchanan scenes in *Manservant and Maidservant*, for instance, anything more than a pendant, a simple addition, to what goes on in the rest of the book: a skilful and amusing addition, again, but so disproportionately large that one began to be troubled lest Miss Buchanan would drop a letter or a photograph revealing her to be somebody's mother. An inferior book like *Two Worlds and Their Ways* can turn into padding, into addition, before it is much more than half over, though the virtuosity of the dialogue, as always, remains undiminished to the end, while even a masterpiece like *The Present and the Past* is too long by some twenty pages. One might sum up these points by saying that the real objection to the author's method is not that her books are held together by melodramatic, or improbable, or re-duplicated events, but that they are not so held together.

My second main line of argument can also take *Mother and Son* as its starting-point. When Julius tells Miranda his secret, she says:

' "Our time is over; we have only the past that we have seen. What am I to say to you, Julius, in my last hour, on the brink of the grave? That I forgive you, my husband. What else can I say? What other word can pass lips so soon to be closed? And I say them fully. But I thank God that I have not dealt with you, as you have dealt with me." '

Having said this, she dies, and Rosebery at once says:

' "Father, she is dead! She is gone from me, my mother! Why have you done it? Why did you think of yourself? Why could you not keep your secret? What did it matter, your personal burden, the weight on your own mind? Why did you put it on her in her weakness and age? It was for you to spare her, not to think of easing yourself. You have done an ill thing." '

It is not enough, agreed, to say about this that real people never talk (or talked) like that at a moment like that, and certainly not answered by pleading, with Mr Liddell, that real people in the Compton-Burnett period expressed themselves better than we do, and that these are clever people too. If one asks what sort of people do talk like that, one might mention, again with Mr Liddell, people in verse drama, and he has produced an astonishing effect by interlarding Euripides (in English, of course) with Compton-Burnett stage-directions. But this is irrelevant, because Miss Compton-Burnett — and I hope to obtain agreement here — is not writing verse drama, where the conventions are utterly different. (The temptation to regard these novels as Attic tragedies must be resisted at all points: why suggest that the servants in some of the books provide a choric commentary? We don't want a chorus.) The other kinds of people who talk as Miranda and Rosebery do are people in other novels, some of them not too good novels — there is a perilous resemblance to the kind of way some of Mr Charles Morgan's characters go on. And that is fatal. There may be times for people in a book to talk like people in a book, but at moments of emotional crisis it is best avoided. It is often avoided in Miss Compton-Burnett's better novels, and this is an important way in which they establish themselves as better.

There is really not as much in common as all that between this general type of Compton-Burnett dialogue, such as usually occurs in duologue and in what Mr Liddell calls 'the great tragic speeches', and the other, more familiar type where a larger number of characters sit round a table and indulge in communal dialectics. Reviewers have noticed an unrealistic level of aphorism in these exchanges, most conspicuous where children or servants participate, but again to point this out is not quite adequate on its own. What is striking is less what the characters say than the remarkable number of kinds of thing they do not say. To imagine what would have to happen before a Compton-Burnett character could say: 'You bore me' or: 'What a pretty dress' or: 'Give me a kiss' or: 'Oh my God' is an instructive experience. The majority of these conversations are marathon tennis-matches in which the ball always lands in court. Any given return may be a smash, a screw-shot or a plain lob to the base-line — very occasionally it may come off the wood — but no ball ever rebounds from a player's head instead of his racquet, or gets angrily kicked into the net, or is chucked over the wire into the cabbage-patch. Quite a lot of the time the players are virtually interchangeable, maintaining as they do a close verbal and syntactical continuity in their collocations, and holding their favourite idioms in common: two examples are the extended 'that' substitution ('Nurse is at a loss. She often finds herself that') and the cliché critique introduced by some such formula as: 'Why do people always talk as if *x* were a good (or bad) thing?' And in most of the novels one could count on the fingers of one hand, or even on its thumb, the number of times anyone refuses to play.

I think I can probably fudge up a couple of comments on this policy of rigorous limitation and exclusion in dialogue. The first one is just that it takes an almost overweening audacity to discard at the outset the most powerful card in the hand of the novelist interested in character drawing, that of differentiation by mode of speech. It is true that some characters are thus differentiated – Dulcia Bode (*A House and Its Head*) and Cassius Clare (*The Present and the Past*) are good instances – but on the whole the lack of variety is enervating, much more so than any lack of realism. A butler and cook who are no more than overarticulate can perhaps be accepted, but a butler and cook who reproduce the conversational techniques of their master and mistress are merely ventriloquial. Here, too, I think, lies an important source of the repetitiveness of character discussed earlier: how is one to differentiate two tyrants, or two governesses, or two children, or two footmen, who talk the same? And this applies within books as well as between them. To keep separate in the mind the schoolgirls of *Two Worlds and Their Ways* requires a concentration – during reading – incommensurate with the reward offered, and in several other novels the issue is thickened and impeded by similar 'doubling-up' of characters. My second comment is just that the danger in stylizing the procedure of dialogue in this way, and in thus tending inevitably to reduce the status of the individual character, is that of finally turning the whole thing, not indeed into a solemn game, but into a frivolous game. Loss of seriousness is for some reason the dragon that lurks in the path of the writer who opts for other modes than a selection of the language really used by men. To read almost any piece of Compton-Burnett 'communal dialectics' is to experience a pleasure as intense as most available literary pleasures, and yet page after page, sometimes scene after scene (the servants' conversations in *Darkness and Day* provide the most extreme example), is marked by the triviality inseparable from fantasy.

There are two things which decisively rescue a great part of Miss Compton-Burnett's work from this danger. One is her comic sense; the other a dyad composed of her hatred and her pity. To any of her readers, not only her devotees, her comedy will hardly need illustrating, though her liking for subject-matter generally considered tragic may obscure the importance and extent of the wonderfully amusing passages in even the more harrowing books, such as *Manservant and Maidservant*. Her hatred and her pity, her hatred for cruel irresponsible spite and sentimental righteous folly, her pity for their victims, for the downtrodden servant, the hounded companion and above all the child goaded to tears in the name of love and duty – these things too need no emphasis. The relevant point here is that these two passions are realistic passions. They work not through, but alongside and apart from, an arbitrary method of construction and a technique of dialogue which is too often de-individualizing and at times undisciplined. Miss Compton-Burnett is a writer of the wildest internal contradictions and not the least of these is her ability to turn out novels – two or more of which are masterpieces – that conceal under great homogeneity of tone a conglomeration of all but incongruous elements.

The above may seem a sufficiently left-handed tribute to a writer I enjoy and admire. I do not think it really is. Our most original living novelist will not best be served by having an affectionate bloom rubbed over such flaws as, by reason of its vitality, her work inevitably bears. It is only after those flaws have been probed that they can be understood and finally dismissed.

1955

PHOENIX TOO FREQUENT

Hardly a week passes without the canon of Lawrence and Lawrentiana seeming to grow fuller and more overwhelmingly definitive. This latest effort* is a miscellany of essays, articles, reviews and extracts from letters, and is in effect a partial reprint of *Phoenix*, plus most of the *Studies in Classic American Literature*. Mr Anthony Beal's compilation is a good one, running to well over four hundred large and well-printed pages. No Lawrence selection, however, will completely satisfy everybody, and I for one could lament the omission of the lively essay on Franklin. I feel too that no convention would have been flouted if a couple of poems had gone in, 'Fate and the Younger Generation', say, and 'Now It's Happened', which provide between them a more trenchant, and far shorter, critique of the Russian gang than anything their author wrote in prose. A slightly larger deficit is an editorial one: whether we like it or not, Lawrence has become something of a classic, and there are some reticences in this publication which may puzzle second-generation Lawrentians. We are not told, for example, the provenance or date of the first piece, 'Autobiographical Sketch', and there are some passages which deserve, but do not get, an explanatory note: I ought not to have to consult the *Letters* to find out who 'Bunny' was. In addition, some authorial slips of the pen are so evident that even I, with my modest training in textual criticism, could

* *Selected Literary Criticism* by D. H. Lawrence. Edited by Anthony Beal (Heinemann, 1956).

proffer a plausible conjecture. But all in all this is an important volume which tells us a great deal about Lawrence's ideas and the kind of man he was.

To begin at the beginning, we now have ample material on which to base an estimate of his qualities as a literary critic. His gifts in this direction have been often enough recited: his utter and transparent honesty, his indifference to academic and journalistic procedures, and above all what Dr Leavis describes as his 'power of distinguishing his own feelings and emotions from conventional sentiment'. It is this which makes his accounts of Dostoievsky and Fenimore Cooper (to take two diverse examples) so startling and yet for the most part so unquestionable, and which even at this date carries a residuary tremor of the enormous impact Lawrence made on his contemporaries. These abilities are matched by stylistic ones: his syntax and method of paragraphing and so on, which in his best work never decline into mannerisms, were the outward signs of that unparalleled spontaneity.

And yet, despite all his entertaining lessons in critical informality, one need not be pedantic or grey-souled to detect, in many places, the kind of tabloid garrulity that lies in wait for people who talk their prose. To be sure, many of the shorter pieces reprinted here must have been written in a hurry, with no eye to more than ephemeral publication. But even outside such contexts there can be found much prolixity, much incoherence, much clumsiness, much too much repetition – it is true that repetition is an essential part of the Lawrence method, but the effect is diminished every time the needle gets stuck in the groove; often the same groove. Now admittedly, this or any other kind of mannerism need not incapacitate a critic, and many will think it a small price to pay for the insights which accompany it. We should be wrong to demand that a critic must stay on the point all the time; it is enough if he remains in orbit around it. We start objecting, I think, when he takes off in a widening and receding spiral. This is what Lawrence is always doing, and the direction of his departure is obvious enough. Starting with the curiously Paterian aim of discriminating his own impressions, of retailing what boil down to 'the adventures of a soul among masterpieces' (or fiascos), he takes wing for the realm where the soul just has adventures, or just is. It is his own soul, of course, sometimes *in vacuo*, more often held up to its own advantage against the soul of modern man, the mob soul, everyone else's soul.

One can pass over, although not without embarrassment, Lawrence's readiness to puff his own work ('Read my novel. It's a great novel. If *you* can't see the development – which is slow, like growth – I can'), and possibly too his constant threatening of mankind with mass insanity, his revelations of the great pornography conspiracy, even the wonderful give-away where he announces that 'a man who is *emotionally* educated is as rare as a phoenix'–who *can* he be thinking of? Much more unpleasant and damaging is his recommendation, apparently as a practical measure, of the kind of theocracy, or hierocracy, in which the 'mass' (those who can't distinguish between property and life) bow down to the 'elect' (who can, and are 'natural lords' anyway). But perhaps Lawrence thought he was one of the mass. Ah, but again, he said he felt himself the superior of most men he met. If there is a challenge, he says, between another man and himself 'I feel he should do reverence to the gods in me, because they are more than the gods in him. And he should give reverence to the very me, because it is more at one with the gods than is his very self.' Truly, we are dealing with a man of 'terrifying honesty'. And what are we to do, all the rest of us, the mass? Can we become superior too? Hardly, because it's all a matter of feeling, you see. Thinking – including presumably, thinking about what Lawrence said and wrote – won't help. It only makes matters worse. Some are born to sweet delight. Very few.

It may be objected that I have confused an account of Lawrence's extraneous beliefs with an account of his criticism. They are really inseparable; certainly they were for Lawrence, and clearly he wanted them to be. The paranoid outburst quoted above comes as the anticipated coda to one of the Fenimore Cooper essays – in places a highly readable and instructive essay. An examination of Poe gets mixed up with an examination of the Holy Ghost (Lawrence pattern). *The Scarlet Letter* provides thematic material for a tone poem on blood-consciousness versus mind-consciousness. A penetrating discussion of Hardy's novels has for decoration and episodic matter the usual religiose pseudo-psychologics with their Love and Law, Stability and Mobility, and this Absolute and that Absolute. No. Far more than all the sixth-form smartness, the ignorant dismissals of science and philosophy, the shuffling of the meanings of words, the footling but detachable theses about rooks and amoebas having a sense of wonder, and rocks and so on having 'a *form* of sentience', and (on a different tack) America being likely to institute polygamy – far more than all that, and it is plenty, the dovetailing of criticism with private obsession makes seven-eighths of this collection valueless as criticism, however valuable as a holy book for Lawrentians. And this was the stuff, I suppose, on which Dr Leavis based his assessment of Lawrence as 'the finest literary critic of our time'. Thank Heaven that is untrue.

The foregoing will have left undamaged Lawrence's status as one of the great denouncers, the great missionaries the English send to themselves to tell them they are crass, gross, lost, dead, mad and addicted to unnatural vice. I suppose it is a good thing that these chaps continue to roll up, though in this case I wonder whether as much silly conduct has not been encouraged as heartless conduct deterred. However that may be, it is a chilling disappointment to take an actual look at the denunciations and be confronted not only by egomania, fatuity and gimcrack theorizing, but bitterness and censoriousness too. It might even be more intelligent to leave Lawrence on his pinnacle, inspiring, unapproachable and unread.

1956

THOMAS THE RHYMER

*A Prospect of the Sea** stands a good chance of being the last volume of Dylan Thomas's previously uncollected work to appear. It includes, to be sure, some or all of the prose pieces from *The Map of Love* (now out of print), but there seem to be others from the same period which are here reprinted for the first time, and undoubtedly the last four pieces in the book, dating from 1947–53, are new to hard covers. I should explain that the small patches of uncertainty in that last sentence result firstly from my not having thought to bring my copy of *The Map of Love* abroad with me (and if I were ever to look for it on my return I doubt if I should find it); and secondly there is the mysterious failure of Dr Daniel Jones, the editor and arranger of the volume, to indicate which of the earlier stories here reprinted originally appeared in *The Map of Love*. Just what Dr Daniel Jones's editorship and arrangership can have entailed is indeed a fascinating question; I can hardly believe that he would have tinkered with the texts, he clearly wasted little time over correcting the proofs, and yet, Thomas himself having chosen – 'before his death', we learn – what stories and essays he wanted preserved, the only task left to Dr Daniel Jones would seem to have been that of tearing the stories out of *The Map of Love*, *Picture Post* and so on, and sending them off to the printer, which hardly seems to merit the name of editorship, does it? But perhaps it was the toil of arranging the stories in order which

* *A Prospect of the Sea* by Dylan Thomas (Dent, 1955).

52

earned Dr Daniel Jones his place on the title page. After all, if my maths is correct, there were more than 10^{12} combinations to choose from.

With this out of the way, it can be asserted with utter finality that here is a volume which every admirer of Thomas's poems will want to possess, for most of the qualities of the poems are to be found in it. In spite of this, the book seems to me to be worth having. Two or three of the pieces in it echo that other Thomas – not ranting, canting Thomas the Rhymer, but comparatively disciplined, responsible Thomas: the Thomas of the *Portrait of the Artist as a Young Dog*. The stories in that volume, with their humour and truth to fact, are in my view by far the most interesting and re-readable things that their author ever wrote. The last piece, particularly in the present collection, a most energetic and amusing account of an outing to Porthcawl which never got there, is slightly tainted with the Rhymer's fancifulness and yet succeeds in confirming the suspicion that it was as social chronicler, not as 'bard', of his native South Wales that Thomas really excelled. Another piece, 'How to be a Poet' (1950), full of shrewdness and revealing a remarkable gift for parody, gives some hint of the skill with which, if he had lived and had the inclination, he might have chronicled certain aspects of London life. A third effort, 'Conversation about Christmas' (1947), recalls *Under Milk Wood*, which will recommend it to some; and a fourth, dating from 1952, has at any rate a clearly drawn setting and a detectable narrative.

These latter qualities, together with many others, are more or less completely missing from the eleven earlier stories which make up nearly three quarters of this short book. Their typical vein is the near- or quasi-surrealist, 'apocalyptic' one common in their period and, I should say, rejected in most of their author's later verse. Reading them in bulk is not an easy task. To begin with the characters and situations, so far as these words are applicable, are not among those which many people in full possession of their faculties will find interesting or important. What we mainly get are nightmares, or nightmarish reveries, or nightmarish 'experiences' (the distinctions are often exceedingly difficult to draw) of fools, madmen, the dying and creatures which are called children but behave like nothing on earth. Even this fairly tenuous connection with reality or with anything recognizable is frequently dropped, giving place to a sort of verbal free-for-all in which anything whatever may or may not be mentioned or seem to be mentioned. For long stretches very little can be extricated beyond a general air of bustling wildness allied to a vague sexiness or religiosity of subject-matter — if, again, 'subject-matter' is the proper term. The style is that blend of answerless riddle, outworn poeticism and careful linguistic folly which those immune to the spell of the Rhymer will salute with a groan of recognition.

It is sometimes nice to follow up the denunciatory with the mildly analytic. Here is a reasonably representative quotation ('the story so far' is that Marlais, a poet, has had a dream in which some orchards caught fire and he met a couple of female scarecrows who are sisters. When he wakes up he knows that they are his lovers. Now read on):

'Put a two-coloured ring of two women's hair round the blue world, white and coal-black against the summer-coloured boundaries of sky and grass, four-breasted stems at the poles of the summer sea-ends, eyes in the sea-shells, two fruit-trees out of a coal-hill: Poor Marlais's morning, turning to evening, spins before you. Under the eyelids, where the inward night drove backwards, through the skull's base, into the wide, first world on the far-away eye, two love-trees smouldered like sisters. Have an orchard sprout in the night, an enchanted woman with a spine like a railing burn her hand in the leaves, man-on-fire a mile from a sea have a wind put out your heart: Marlais's death in life in the circular going down of the day that had taken no time blow again in the wind for you.'

A number of queries eventually present themselves. As far as points of detail are concerned, what are four-breasted stems and where are the poles of the summer sea-ends? What eyes are to go in what sea-shells and where are the two fruit-trees to be put? What are the nature and location of the wide, first world and whose is the far-away eye? What is a love-tree? Under what circumstances can a going down be said to be circular? And so on. More generally and perhaps more relevantly, what is the significance of the procedures described in the first and last sentences and to what order of events can they be attached?

A reader who finds he must ask such questions will not get very far with poor Marlais or his biographer. The fact that any answers to the questions must be either highly fanciful or highly debatable (or both) appears to me to dispose of the passage quoted and, by implication, of a great deal of the Rhymer's method – if, yet again, 'method' is the name for multiplied whimsy. Of course, this line of attack, like all anti-Rhymer inquiries, lays itself open to the charge of being purblind, cold, narrowly intellectual and even anti-poetic. This objection may diminish in force when an attempt is made to demonstrate how the passage can be read without bafflement and with positive pleasure. What is required of the reader is to permit a response, without ever getting too near identifying its sources, to such matters as the vague love-token romanticness of the women's hair, the vague Picassoan *outré*-ness of the four-breasted stems, the vague Daliesque thrill of eyes in seashells, the vague beauty-in-pit-dirt, *How Green was My Valley* aura of the fruit-trees out of the coal-hill, and above all the very emphatic suggestions of wondrousness and oddity in which the parcel is wrapped up. It might be observed that syntax as much as vocabulary gives this last effect, but that would not be a suitable kind of observation in this kind of reading. I think that it is reading in this way which is really anti-poetic and that it would commend itself only to those who hanker after something sublimer than thinking. That something Thomas wasted his talent and integrity in trying to provide. No ode to his memory could distil a more sombre meditation than that.

1955

AN EVENING WITH DYLAN THOMAS

In the spring of 1951 Dylan Thomas accepted an invitation to give a talk to the English Society of the University College of Swansea. The society's secretary, a pupil of mine, asked me if I would like to come along to the pub and meet Thomas before the official proceedings opened. I said I would like to very much, for although I was not at this time an enthusiast for his verse, I had heard a great deal, in Swansea and elsewhere, of his abilities as a talker and entertainer of his friends. And after all, the fellow was an eminent poet and had written at least one book, the *Portrait of the Artist as a Young Dog*, for which my admiration had never wavered. I arranged with my wife and some of my friends that we would try to get Thomas back into the pub after his talk (we anticipated little difficulty here), and thereafter to our house for coffee and a few bottles of beer. I got down to the pub about six, feeling expectant.

Thomas was already there, a glass of light ale before him and a half circle of students round him. Also in attendance was a Welsh painter of small eminence whom I will call Griffiths; in the course of the evening he told us several times that he had that day driven all the way down from his home in Merionethshire on purpose to meet Thomas, whom he had known, he said, for some years. Except for Griffiths, I think we all felt rather overawed in the presence of the master, and the conversation hung fire a little for some time. Thomas looked tired and a bit puffy, though not in any way ill, and if, as I was told later, he had already been drinking for some time he gave no sign of it. He was in fact very sedate, perhaps because of the tiredness or, what would have been perfectly explicable, through boredom. He was putting the light ales down with regularity but without hurry; I congratulated myself on having bought one of them for him. There was some uninspired talk about his recent visit to America. Then he announced, in his clear, slow, slightly haughty, cut-glass Welsh voice: 'I've just come back from Persia, where I've been pouring water on troubled oil.'

Making what was in those days my stock retort to the prepared epigram, I said: 'I say, I must go and write that down.'

He looked round the circle, grinning. 'I have,' he said.

After a few more remarks about Persia had been exchanged, Griffiths, who had been getting restless, shifted his buttocks along the leatherette bench, raised his bearded chin and asked: 'What about a few of the old limericks, Dylan?'

Thomas agreed, though without the slightest enthusiasm. I thought it possible that he was not greatly attached to Griffiths, who now began to recite a long string of limericks, bending forward along the seat and addressing himself exclusively to Thomas, indeed at times fairly hissing them into his ear. The content was scatological rather than obscene, with a few references to vomiting and dirty socks thrown in.

Thomas went on apparently ignoring Griffiths, sitting there placidly drinking and smoking, gazing over our heads and occasionally wrinkling his parted lips, no doubt a habit of his. When he did this he lost his faintly statuesque appearance and became a dissolute but very amiable frog. All at once he roused himself and told some limericks back to his associate. They barred a few more holds than the other's, but not many. They were, however, distinctly funnier. The only one I remember cannot be reproduced here, on grounds of possible offence to the Crown. Griffiths said he had heard it before.

After some minutes of this antiphon, the secretary, speaking I think for the first time since introducing me, told us it was time to get along to the meeting. Thomas jumped up and bought a number of bottles of beer, two of which he stuffed into his coat pockets. He gave the others to Griffiths to carry. 'No need to worry, man,' Griffiths kept saying. 'Plenty of time afterwards.'

'I've been caught that way before.'

The bottles were still in his pockets – he checked up on this several times – when in due course he sat rather balefully facing his audience in a room in the Students' Union. About fifty or sixty people had turned up: students and lecturers from the college mainly, but with a good sprinkling of persons who looked as if they were implicated in some way with the local Bookmen's Society. With a puzzled expression, as if he wondered who its author could be, Thomas took from his breast pocket and sorted through an ample typescript, which had evidently been used many times before.

His first words were: 'I can't manage a proper talk. I might just manage an improper one.' Some of the female Bookmen glanced at one another apprehensively. The rest of the talk I forget *in toto*, except for a reference to 'crewcut sophomores from the quarterback division', and something about the fierce, huge matrons who, according to him, infested American literary clubs. His theme, in so far as he had one, was indeed his experiences while lecturing on and reading poetry in the United States, and his tone was one of pretty strong contempt. Aside from this, much of what he said seemed good sense and was phrased as such, but rather more was couched in his vein of sonorous whimsy, well tricked out with long impressionistic catalogues, strings of compound adjectives, and puns, or rather bits of homophone play – the vein he used in his broadcasts. Stopping this rather than concluding it, he said he would read some poems.

The one that sticks in my mind most was 'Fern Hill', which he recited with a kind of controlled passion that communicated itself to every person in the room. For the most part, though, he read the work of other poets: Auden's 'The Unknown Citizen', Plomer's 'The Flying Bum' (the Bookmen got a little glassy-eyed about that one) and Yeats's 'Lapis Lazuli'. His voice was magnificent, and his belief in what he read was so patent as to be immediately infectious, yet there was something vaguely discomforting about it too, not only to me. Although obviously without all charlatanry, he did here and there sound or behave like a charlatan. This feeling was crystallized for me when he came to the end of 'Lapis Lazuli'. He went normally enough, if rather slowly, as far as:

' "*Their eyes mid many wrinkles, their eyes,*
Their ancient, glittering eyes . . ." '

and then fell silent for a full ten seconds. This, as can readily be checked, is a very long time, and since his still rather baleful glare at his audience did not flicker, nor his frame move a hair's breadth, it certainly bore its full value on this occasion. At the end of this period his mouth dropped slowly and widely open, his lips crinkled like a child's who is going to cry, and he said in a tremulous half-whisper:

' "*. . . are gay.*" '

He held it for another ten seconds or so, still staring and immobile, his mouth still open and crinkled. It was magnificent and the silence in the room was absolute, but . . .

Not very long afterwards we were all back in the pub, Griffiths included. With his performance over, Thomas's constraint had disappeared and he was clearly beginning to enjoy himself. Griffiths, however, was monopolizing him more and more and exchanging a kind of cryptic badinage with him that soon became hard to listen to, especially on one's feet. The pub, too, had filled up and was by now so crowded that the large group round Thomas soon lost all cohesion and started to melt away. I was not sorry to go and sit down at the other end of the room when the chance came. It was at this point that my friends and I finally abandoned our scheme of trying to get Thomas up to my house when the pub shut. After a time the girl student who had been with us earlier, and who had stayed with Thomas longer than most, came over and said: 'You know, nobody's talking to him now, except that Griffiths chap.'

'Why don't you stay and talk to him?'

'Too boring. And he wasn't talking to any of us. Still, poor dab, he does look out of it. He was in a real state a little while ago.'

'How do you mean?'

'All sorry for himself. Complaining that everybody'd gone and left him.'

We all felt rather uncomfortable, and rightly. Although I can vividly recall how tedious, and how unsharable, his conversation with Griffiths was, I am ashamed now to think how openly we must have seemed to be dropping Thomas, how plain was our duty not to drop him at all. Our general disappointment goes to explain our behaviour, but does not excuse it. We were unlucky, too, in encountering him when he was off form and accompanied by Griffiths. At the time I thought that if he had wanted to detach himself and talk to the students he would have found some means of doing so: I have since realized that he was far too good-natured ever to contemplate giving anybody the cold shoulder, and I wonder whether a talent for doing that might not have been something that he badly needed. One of us, at any rate, should have found a way of assuring him that he was being regarded that evening, not with a coltish mixture of awe and suspicion, but sympathetically. Then, I think, we should have seen that his attitude was the product of nothing more self-aware or self-regarding than shyness.

1957

Fowler's *Modern English Usage* can still be enjoyed today, but the enjoyment is solely that of seeing a strong, though narrow, intelligence at work, not that of witnessing the fulfilment of a promised task. Contradicting its title, that impressive book gives us not description but prescription: English as she *ought to be* spoke and, more particularly, wrote. Merely catching sight of the present work* is enough to suggest that it follows a similar policy. An actual account of American, as of British or Australian, English would fill many volumes.

Members of that small minority who care about the use of words are likely to be dismayed, or outraged, or infuriated every time they open a newspaper or a periodical, and nearly every time they open a contemporary novel. But they can only go on caring. Honour demands that they continue to set an example. But to prescribe correct usage, however continuously and persuasively, will change nothing, will not hinder, let alone begin to undo, linguistic innovations regarded by the minority as harmful. Such proclamations are heeded only by the minority. The unwitting architects of these innovations – the people in advertising, journalism, television, publicity – are not listening. One might as well hope to check the flood of pop music by going on about its harmonic banality, rhythmic monotony, etc.

Wilson Follett intermittently realizes this. He adopts a rather am-

* *Modern American Usage* by Wilson Follett. Edited and completed by Jacques Barzun and others (Longmans, 1966).

biguous stance whereby new usages he has no particular objection to ('Frankenstein' instead of 'Frankenstein's monster') are accepted as established, while ones he dislikes ('reaction' for 'response' or 'opinion') are stigmatized as absurd or improper. This leads him now and then into what I, from a lofty pinnacle, would call inconsistency of attitude. It seems odd to defend 'recap' (for 'summarize' or 'summary') and attack 'symbology' as not only pompous but also incorrectly formed. The haplographic shortening from 'symbology' is surely justified. Nobody would want to restore 'idololatry'.

But these are minor cavils. The book is a sustained, ferocious and above all witty assault on an enormous range of linguistic barbarity. A few examples must suffice. Follett is effectively caustic about the fearful, would-be-terse dropping of '-ing' in compounds like 'frypan', 'sparkplug'. (He might have added a note on its brother, the fondness for 'stocking' feet and 'bottle' beer.) The 'I do have' construction – 'Have you got a match?' 'Yes, I *do*' – receives its share. So does the comparative novelty that replaces 'old enough to know better' with something like 'old enough so that he ought to know better', now heard everywhere from educated Americans.

All these are Americanisms, not yet upon us, but elsewhere we are far from immune. The article on pronunciation shows, among other things, how closely British changes are linked with American. We, too, are beginning to hear 'ay' for 'ee' in certain words: 'renegue' rhyming with 'vague', 'spontanayity', the 'Dayity'. And the preciosity of 'tissyou' for 'tishoo', 'faw-hed' for 'forrid', has been with us for thirty years at least. This effort to introduce some fancied 'correct' pronunciation, indicated by the spelling, has recently become rampant on British television: 'Chrisst-Ian' belief, 'viz-you-al' effect, and the ubiquitous 'Road-easier' or '-eecier' for 'Ruh-deesher'.

There is more, however, to be got out of this book than appreciation of the accuracy with which its various targets are peppered, an accuracy that, in my view, equals or surpasses Fowler's. It works positively by clearing up some of those intermittent but nagging problems about the meanings of set phrases, 'begging the question', for instance. It pricks our own complacency; I, for one, will not again write 'represents' when I mean 'is'. And, read through rather than dipped into, it reveals its true function, to serve as a lasting reminder of the need for continuous self-criticism on the part of any writer. The price of good style is eternal vigilance. At one point, Follett sums up his theme – in a passage about euphony, but its gist will serve for the whole book:

> *The writer who fills his pages with ugly dissonances and tells himself that they are not worth the trouble of rectifying, because not one reader in fifty will ever test him by voice, is deluding himself. His bad readers may not mind, but his better readers will follow him with pain and inward protest if they are sufficiently interested in his contents, and otherwise not at all.*

Personally, I should have liked to hear more about genteelisms; in particular, those 'phrases that try to conceal accidental associations of ideas, such as "back of" for "behind"'. A few minutes' reflection produces another dozen examples from American usage. 'Rooster' is notorious enough. I have seen 'roach' for 'cockroach'. 'Bag' once meant 'scrotum', so we get 'paper sack' and, for 'handbag', either the inappropriate 'purse' or the wildly inapprofriate 'pocket-book'. Anybody knows what 'stones' can mean; hence 'rocks' where hand-missiles are meant, and 'pits' in fruit.* 'Tidbit', and 'exhibit', where a show of work of art is meant, need no gloss. The thought that produced 'raise' as against 'rise' in wages seems pretty obvious once you think about it, and I strongly suspect that the same thought produced that old enigma, 'elevator' for 'lift', 'Faucet' (with a guess at what 'tap' might once have meant)? 'Putter' about? Possibly.

I wish Follett had occasion to speculate on the mysterious collective decision to outlaw words like 'titbit'. It must have been taken long ago, for the supposedly harmless substitutes are used today by very non-

---

* Admittedly, this general principle is like most others in encouraging the seeing of what is not there. However: colloquially, Americans refer to precious stones too – rather fancifully, when one thinks about it—as 'rocks', and it is odd that such a practical nation should have accepted the cumbersomeness of reckoning such things as people's weights in pounds only, rather than adopt the useful British stone along with virtually all the rest of our weights-and-measures system.

Finally, I must register my wonder and delight at hearing an American friend, and a committed non-puritan at that, refer to what I soon saw was a buoy. He pronounced the word, not 'boy', in the British fashion, but 'booey' – rhyming, appropriately, with 'phooey'.

genteel Americans. Or is some trait in the national character still at work? Quite recently I was ill-advised enough to see a film called *Journey to the Seventh Planet*. Its gripping tedium was only, but much, relieved by the stolid consistency with which the characters referred to 'Urahnus'.

1966

A NEW JAMES BOND

Why do it? What could persuade a writer who has become reasonably successful in his own field – that of the more or less straight novel – to switch to a remote genre, step into a dead man's shoes, undertake to continue – even if only for a single occasion – the saga of the admired and despised James Bond?

An answer to that one must have started forming on plenty of pairs of lips before their owners' eyes had reached the end of the sentence. 'Money', plus grumbles about 'jumping on the bandwagon' and 'selling out'. Well, yes, I do indeed expect to make quite a lot of money out of the venture, and jolly good luck to me. But most people who have done much writing will probably agree on reflection that to write at any length *just* for money (as nearly all of us, including myself, have had to do at some stage) is a uniquely, odiously painful activity: not really worth the money, in fact. And in any case I only listen seriously to talk of bandwagons from those who have turned down the offer of a ride on one of the size we are talking about. Not, I think, a numerous company.

Apart from the money, then, why? What at the outset was an unimportant motive, but has since developed into a major fringe benefit, is the thought of how cross with me the intellectual Left will get. A lot of the persons who will accuse me of having done it for the money will also, such is their nimbleness of mind, accuse me of having done it not for the money, but because I have embraced the *ideology* of Fleming and Bond, as was proved some time back when I declared my support for Allied resistance to Communist aggression in South-East Asia – not really enough, that, to constitute a whole ideology, you might think, but this now seems to be the official Lefty term for anything less than full approval of Russian imperialism.

As far as I know, the first tie-up between James Bond and America's Asian policy was made, not surprisingly, by a writer in *Komsomolskaya Pravda*, the Moscow youth paper. From Ronald Hingley's account of the matter at the time, several years ago now, it appears that the man was not fully aware throughout his article that Bond was not a real human being, and how he (Bond) could have done quite so much to further American aims in Vietnam and elsewhere was never really made plain, but anyway he was mixed up in it all somehow and should be vigorously resisted.

Again as far as I know, and again not surprisingly, the next Bond-Vietnam collocation came in a letter from Graham Greene to the *New Statesman*, and a contributor to the same journal, presumably with the same idea in mind, remarked only a few months ago that: 'Bond . . . is almost uninterruptedly unpleasant; it [sic] fits congenially with the ideology of Kingsley Amis.' It is, of course, true that Bond, like me, is pro-Western, pro-British, even, by and large, pro-American, and this is on first principles anathema to a great many people. The intellectual's spy novelists are Deighton and le Carré, who may be obscure to the point of frequent bafflement and short on action respectively, but in whose work there is at least no nonsense about our side being better than their side.

The 'unpleasantness' of Bond deserves a moment's further notice. The curious momentary suspicion one feels from time to time, that the critics have somehow got hold of a completely different version of the work one has been reading, has never invaded my mind more powerfully than in the case of Fleming and his critics. Bond emerges from their treatment as a frightening snob, a ceaseless fornicator and a brutal scourge of the weak and helpless; these are the principal charges. Although you will probably not believe me when I tell you, none of them has any substance.

Not once, in the twelve novels and eight stories, does Bond or his creator come anywhere near judging a character by his or her social standing. We hear a good deal about high living and the elegant scene at Blades Club, but that is a different matter; at worst, harmless vulgarity. The practice of fornication in itself is not enough, these days, to brand a man as a monster, but then perhaps Bond goes at it too hard, weaves a compensation-fantasy for author and reader, is on a wish-fulfilment deal and all that. I myself could see no harm in this even if it were true, but it is not. One girl per trip, Bond's average, is not excessive for a personable heterosexual bachelor, and his powers of performance would not rate the briefest of footnotes in Kinsey. It is true that all the girls are pretty and put up little resistance to Bond's advances, and this may help to explain his unpopularity with those critics who find it difficult to seduce even very ugly girls.

Again, despite what I have read and heard round the place, actual perusal of the Fleming text establishes that Bond is gentle and considerate to his womenfolk. Nor is he ever wantonly cruel to his enemies, though he does have this habit – no doubt objectionable to some – of fighting back when people are trying to kill him. (There is a possible Vietnam echo here, on the principle that their side can use violence but our side must not.) However, it is vain to expect anybody in Bond's line of work to adopt a dove-like policy when confronted by a charging Korean with hands like clubs or a female K.G.B. operative with poisoned spikes in the toes of her shoes.

Enough of negatives: I consider it an honour to have been selected to follow in the footsteps of Ian Fleming. Right from the beginning, he attained a mastery of action scenes and of description and of the art of interweaving these. His work combined a passionate interest in the externals of the modern world – its machinery and furniture, in the widest senses of both words – with a strong, simple feeling for the romantic and the strange: the gypsy encampment, the coral grove, the villain's castle, the deadly garden, the mysterious island. Fleming technologized the fairy-tale for us, making marvellous things seem familiar, and familiar things marvellous. He was a great popular writer.

This judgement leads me to take a brief swipe at the view, or the parrot-cry, which ascribes the vogue for espionage fiction to the supposed fact that the spy is a key figure in the contemporary consciousness (or unconscious, according to taste), that he enacts the dilemma of modern man, etc. I dare say he is and does, but he would have got nowhere without Bond. To take a parallel case, I doubt if the vogue for detective fiction that started in the closing years of the last century had much to do with the Victorian consciousness or any dilemma-enacting on the part of the sleuth. It happened because Conan Doyle had invented Sherlock Holmes. And, now one comes to think of it, Wells surely did more to get science fiction moving than any amount of key-figure stuff could possibly have done. Where a literary explanation for a literary phenomenon is available, it has a strong claim.

Conan Doyle and Wells are, at any rate, two of the company with whom I would place Fleming, though both of them surpass him in range. Others would be Jules Verne – more in common there than might appear at first blush – and Buchan. Nobody contemporary. Our cultural puritanism does not encourage the writers of thrillers or adventure stories, any of the genres, unless it can be maintained that the genre in question is being used as no more than a vehicle, a metaphor, and that the author is really going on about modern society and the human heart with the best of them. Hence the highbrow taste for le Carré and for Patricia Highsmith, and, contrariwise, the absence of such taste for any of the professional science-fiction writers, who seem, like Fleming, to lack the kind of ambition, or maybe the pretentiousness, to hit the intellectual charts.*

I lament this – I mean I lament what I take to be a trend against the genres. It might well be agreed that the best of serious fiction, so to call it, is better than anything any genre can offer. But this best is horribly rare, and a clumsy dissection of the heart is so much worse than boring as to be painful, and most contemporary novels are like spy novels with no spies or crime novels with no crimes, and John D MacDonald is by any standards a better writer than Saul Bellow, only MacDonald writes thrillers and Bellow is a human-heart chap, so guess who wears the top-grade laurels? And, whatever abject mess he might have made of everything else in the story, no self-respecting television

* No longer true. Mystification, and shock-tactics in style and layout (nothing more, as far as I can see), have recently got writers like J.G. Ballard and Brian W. Aldiss into magazines like *Encounter*, which never printed their earlier and much better, indeed often brilliant, work within the genre. For the moment, at any rate, and notably in England, the trend in science fiction is all trend, i.e. threadbare avant garde. Most of this stuff is only science fiction in the tenuous sense that those who write it used to write science fiction. Much the same sort of thing happened in Jazz – a final parallel between those oddly linked modes.

dramatist would have brought Desdemona momentarily back to life after Othello had smothered her.

Well: I was born too early, or fell among critics too late, or perhaps am just too wonderfully tolerant by nature to see literature in terms of a rigid hierarchy of kinds. The genres, with the ghost story and the horror story added to the ones already mentioned (I have somehow missed the Western), have been fascinating me continuously for over thirty years. I had always vaguely wanted, and for some time had been a little more purposefully intending, to write a thriller. When the Bond thing came up it seemed like a gift from the gods. Here was the shove needed to get me moving on my thriller project, and to be able to imitate an admired writer under licence, so to speak, is a unique way of paying him tribute and at the same time of taking some particle of his genius to oneself.

There are, of course, no gifts from the gods in any literary sphere, only labours imposed by them. The whole task had to be taken with the utmost seriousness in all senses. In the preliminary stages, fears were expressed in some quarters that I might produce a sort of Lucky Jim Bond, rampaging through the back streets of Wigan with a packet of fish and chips in one hand and a broken beer bottle in the other. Not a chance. Quite apart from the responsibility to one's original, no send-up (can we all agree never to use this hideous term again?) is bearable for more than a couple of thousand words or three or four minutes of screen time. Some sort of valid continuation, neither parody nor radical new departure nor mere rechauffage of Fleming ingredients, had to be worked for.

As with other sorts of novel, the precise starting-point of this one proved impossible to recall once the main idea had taken shape. Semi-thoughts drifted through my head over the weeks. Where? Not Jamaica – Bond been there too often. Not the States – too expensive. Not France – too many Frenchmen about. Greece? Yes – Bond never been, I never been, sounds good, islands just right. Also, Eastern Mediterranean a sphere of Russian expansion, British interests there too. (This was in September 1965.) But Russia versus Britain too old-hat. Then Red China versus Britain and also versus Russia. So Bond could team up with Russian agent. Female. Tough, like all Bond's girls. And Red China as villain is both new to Bond and obvious in the right kind of way. And Chinese master-villain would be fun . . .

At what must have been a roughly contemporaneous stage, studying a map of the Home Counties for some forgotten purpose, I noticed the mutual proximity of three key points: Sunningdale, where Bond has often played golf, Windsor Park, where M has his beautiful little Regency manor-house, and London Airport. On this basis, a discussion developed between my wife, one of my sons and myself. I was out of it for some shorter or longer period, to answer the telephone or go to the pub. Anyway, the draft conclusion was: Bond plays golf – Bond visits M – M in enemy hands – fight – Bond escapes – M taken drugged (?) through Immigration at the airport and off to Greece. After that, well . . .

I now had a beginning to the story as well as to the plot, and could get some preliminary work done on both: a visit to Sunningdale, notebook at the ready, and selection of a site for M's house under the suspicious eye of a park warden; repeated and finger-biting self-communion about what the hell could be devised in the way of an assassination or other stroke that would damage Britain and Russia together and to roughly to the same degree, and belated recognition that the Chinese party must inflict painful damage on one adversary and pass this off as the work of the other. As to what and how, well . . .

It had been clear to me all along that I was not by nature or experience the ideal person to take Bond inside the gambling casino, aboard the hydrofoil yacht, down the advanced (in fact down any) ski-run or into many parts of the world Fleming had constructed for him. Yet something not too dissimilar must be offered if the consumer were not to feel, justifiably, that Bond had been resuscitated in name rather than in substance. The opening of the story, obviously the best opportunity for awakening a sense of recognition in the reader, turned out to be, or possibly had been semi-intentionally constructed as, suitable for this purpose.

Golf – a game I hope fervently to go to my grave without once having had to play – was there in the first sentence, larded with technicalities transcribed verbatim from the friend who took me to Sunningdale. Bond's Continental Bentley comes in on page 17, and exits for the duration of the story on page 19. On other early pages I did what I could with more or less bare references (Scott's restaurant in Coventry Street, M's Silver Wraith Rolls) and the presences or names of familiar characters (Bill Tanner, Miss Moneypenny, ex-Chief Petty

Officer Hammond, the last-named of whom, I am afraid, turned out to be expendable when the Chinese action group arrived at M's place).

But this kind of thing, eked out later with Athenian scenes in the bar of the Grande Bretagne and in Dionysos's restaurant overlooking the Acropolis, was obviously not going to be enough on its own. I had got to devise some bits of expertness, or of apparent expertness – there is no difference on the printed page – to recall that expertness of Fleming's which so deeply characterized the existing Bond saga. What had I got, what might be polished up, what could I acquire without a university course, a descent in a bathyscaph, a visit to Russia?

One thing I had was a detailed first-hand knowledge of some of the main infantry weapons in use in the Second World War, easily supplemented by research. It proved simple and cheap, though at times not particularly comfortable, to take a fifty-foot converted fishing-boat from Piraeus across to the islands of Naxos and Ios. It was no trouble at all to establish, by inquiry and experiment, which were the best and most characteristic local foods and drinks, the best olives, the best shellfish, the best of the resinated wines. And anybody who kept his eyes open could take in enough scenery in a day's Aegean journey to furnish most fictional characters with a month's worth of backdrop.

One way or another, then, Amis-style Bond was to find himself attacking the enemy with hand-grenades, being outsailed by an ordinary commercial motor-boat, fortifying himself for the night assault with a picnic supper, closing in on the opposition on his own two feet or, when the going got rough, on hands and knees. No rockets, no hovercraft, no helicopters, and no lumps of caviare doled out between whiles by white-jacketed waiters under tastefully subdued lighting. When, after all is over, Bond takes off the jeans and sweatshirt he has worn through most of the action, and puts back on the outfit gimmicked for him by Q Branch in the early stages (pick-lock and midget transmitter in the heels of the shoes, wafer hacksaw blades in the lapels of the charcoal-green suit), he says in effect: 'I knew I wouldn't need any of that stuff' – he has got by on strength, determination and ingenuity.

This probably makes him sound like a remodelled character, and admittedly he does rather more thinking than his predecessor normally went in for. But the contrast is much, much more with the Bond of the films, that wisecracking dandy with a personal jet-pack or mini-H-bomb constantly within reach, than with the original Bond, the real Bond, Ian Fleming's Bond. The Bond of the books was always a gun and fists man, a Bentley man but not a midget atom-powered-submarine man, an oysters-and-champagne man but also a ham-sandwich-and-gin-and-tonic man. And although he was mostly a fantasy hero, drawing the reader-reaction: 'I wish it were possible for me to be and do all that,' he never lost elements of the realism hero, evoking: 'I just might be able to do that if I were as strong and as fit and as well trained.' My Bond tips the scales a little towards the latter figure. I had to write him in that way. I am tired of gloss and gadgetry, and I think the audience is too.

Like any other writing, it was great fun and a great grind. Now and then there was the bonus of telling oneself that *he* would have approved, would have handled the situation or the sentence just so. But, a little more often, came the realization that *he* would have been so much neater, quicker, more inventive. Beneath all the surface glitter in Fleming, all the dash and flair, there was a formidable amount of ingenuity and sheer brainwork. I am in a unique position to appreciate that.

1968

A NOTE ON THE MAN WITH THE GOLDEN GUN

In most of the Bond books it was the central villain on whom interest in character was fixed – or at least we heard a lot about his impressively repulsive physical characteristics: one thinks of Hugo Drax, Dr No and the Blofeld of *You Only Live Twice*. Scaramanga is just a dandy with a special (and ineffective) gun, a stock of outdated American slang and a third nipple on his left breast. We are told a great deal about him early on in the ten-page dossier M consults, including mentions of possible homosexuality and pistol-fetishism, but none of this is followed up. Why not?

It may be useful to consider here an outstandingly and untypically clumsy turn in the narrative. Bond was always good at ingratiating himself with his enemies when he had the chance, notably with Goldfinger, who took him on as his personal assistant for the Fort Knox project. Goldfinger, however, had fairly plausible reason to be deceived. Scaramanga hires Bond as his security- and trigger-man after a few minutes' conversation in the bar of a brothel. (At this stage he has no idea that there is a British agent within a hundred miles, so he cannot be hiring him to keep him under his eye.) Bond wonders what Scaramanga wants with him: 'it was odd, to say the least of it . . . the strong smell of a trap'. But there is no trap, and this hefty hint of a concealed motive on Scaramanga's part is never followed up. Why not?

I strongly suspect – on deduction alone, let it be said – that these unanswered questions point to the existence of an earlier draft, perhaps never committed to paper, wherein Scaramanga hires Bond because he is sexually interested in him. A supposition of this kind would also take care of other difficulties or deficiencies in the book as it stands, the insubstantiality of the character of Scaramanga, just referred to, and the feeling of suppressed emotion, or at any rate the build-up to and the space for some kind of climax of emotion, in the final confrontation of the two men. But of course Ian Fleming would never have dared to complete the story along these lines. Imagine what the critics would have said!

If I am right, this self-censorship was only the last and the most weakening example of Fleming's unnecessary, if understandable, readiness to take notice of hostile comment. His later books retreated from the level of violence, sex and rich living set in the earlier. However unedifying, these were part of the unique Fleming world, and the de-naturing of that world in this novel and parts of its immediate fore-runners is a loss. Nobody can write at his best with some of his attention on puritanical readers over his shoulder. It made no difference that the puritanism was really political, based on an objection to Bond's and Fleming's unreflecting dislike of Communism, not moral at all.

1965

A NOTE ON LE CARRÉ AND DEIGHTON

An interest in realism turns up when a genre is past its first youth. Stories about daily Martian life and routine came along after decades of alien monsters; Chief Inspector Barlow of 'Z Cars' and 'Softly, Softly' replaces Lord Peter Wimsey (not before time). Messrs John le Carré and Len Deighton start off with some apparent concern to tell the truth about the Secret Service. They agree in their different ways that it's a dirty game, a conclusion which Ian Fleming, on the evidence of his novels, would never have assented to. Dangerous, devious, coarsening, hardening, yes, but it's Her Majesty's Secret Service we're dealing with. *The Spy Who Came in from the Cold*, Mr le Carré's third and best novel so far, not only portrayed the game as unrelievedly dirty but made you wonder if you had ever realized before how dirty dirty games could be.

The inculcation of this view of the game is the decisive factor in Mr le Carré's (and Mr Deighton's) *succès d'estime*. As if drilled beforehand, critics started insisting on the superior maturity, sophistication, truth to fact and artistic value of all this, compared with Fleming's naive, ill-written fantasies. They just meant that they were more comfortable with books that confirmed their prejudices about the wickedness of the West, a more wicked sort of wickedness than that of the East – an old-hat subject anyway – because the West pretends to hypocritical rubbish to do with freedom and so on, while the East makes no bones about its devotion to things like terror.

However: Mr le Carré's first novel, *Call for the Dead,* since re-titled in paperback *The Deadly Affair*, is as glum as anything he has written since, though it shows a considerable flair for mildly non-U dialogue and an informed interest in snobbery. A civil servant who knows he is only very mildly suspected of having been a Communist while at Oxford seems to have committed suicide because of it. If he really did, why did he arrange for an early telephone call on the morning after the revelatory evening? Or perhaps his wife arranged it for herself. But she is an insomniac. An espionage plot begins to emerge, with a violent denouement.

The initial situation about the suicide recalls the whodunit, and it is thence that Mr le Carré's work partly derives. His second novel, *A Murder of Quality* was squarely, and enjoyably, in the line of the traditional detective story. This ancestry perhaps explains his tendency, even now not cured, to overload his story with mystifications. (The real fault of *Call for the Dead*, however, is that the relations between the suicide and his wife are explored far enough for us to need to understand them, and no further.)

The Spy Whom Came in from the Cold remains a thrilling and genuinely chilling book seven years after publication (and in my case after having taught it in a Tennessee university, which is saying quite a lot in one way, though the class were all for it). One only wants to proclaim that it is of course quite as much of a fantasy as the Bond books it is supposed to be so much more realistic than. The more recent le Carré's, *The Looking-Glass War* (1965) and *A Small Town in Germany* (1968) have not sustained that level. This is not surprising, since if ever a book was a farewell to a subject and a genre it was *The Spy Who*. The later novels resort to mystery-making for its own sake; indeed, *The Looking-Glass War* never answers the question which provides it with its whole structure and raison d'être.

Compared with Mr Deighton, though, Mr le Carré is as limpid as *Black Beauty*. I couldn't read *Horse under Water* and had tough sledding with *The Ipcress File*. The endless twists and turns of the plot, the systematic withholding of clues and even of settings in time and place, are made doubly harassing by a style of dialogue, shared by all the characters, whereby the line of argument disappears under allusions, wisecracks, disembodied reflections. At one, evidently crucial point, the hero, who for some inscrutable reason is left nameless, is given the chance of buying a secret file off a colleague. I couldn't make out whether the hero angrily took the deal or angrily turned it down, only that he was angry, and I wasn't too clear about why, either. Less tense, more descriptive passages are full of his chippy knowingness.

The whole thing is supposedly told to the Minister of Defence, who at an early stage makes what I thought was a reasonable request for enlightenment over some detail. The hero answers with his usual humility:

' "It's going to be very difficult for me if I have to answer questions as I go along," I said. "If it's all the same to you, Minister, I'd prefer you to make a note of the questions, and ask me afterwards."

"My dear chap, not another word, I promise."

And throughout the entire explanation he never again interrupted.'

I know why. He was asleep.

1964 and 1970

A FINAL NOTE

The one remains, the many change and pass. The many writers brought into being by the great spy boom have certainly changed in retrospect and have tended to pass without anyone noticing. As regards the one on whom they all battened more or less, Fleming seems booked for the temporary neglect that death is apt to bring the

75

really successful writer, but he will remain in the end. The James Bond of the film-based cult, an almost separable being, has now (with the showing of *On Her Majesty's Secret Service*) been denatured to the point at which the throng will soon swallow him up. And yet I cannot feel that the rest of the story can be safely foretold.

1970

SHE WAS A CHILD AND I WAS A CHILD

Few books published in this country since the King James Bible can have set up more eager expectation than *Lolita*,* nor, on the other hand, can any work have been much better known in advance to its potential audience. The interest of this first British issue, indeed, is likely to be less in what the thing is actually like – you and I had already got hold of it somehow, hadn't we? – than in what 'they' will say about it. 'They' in this case covers a far wider spectrum than usual, all the way from the inevitable big-review-plus-leader-plus-interminable-correspondence in *The Times Literary Supplement* to the stern clashes of personality and taste round the local Boots counter; and somewhere in the middle will come Richard Hoggart, Cassandra, Lord Montgomery, two or three bishops, Dame Edith Sitwell, the chairman of the Bournemouth East Conservative Association, Dr Bronowski, Professor Ayer, John O'London, Mr Bevan and every last one of the couple of hundred thousand people in Britain who have, or can scrounge, access to some public medium. It is encouraging to see all this concern for a book of serious literary pretension, even if some of the concern, while serious enough, is not literary in the way we ordinarily think of it. One would be even more encouraged if the book in question were not so thoroughly bad in both senses: bad as a work of art, that is, and morally bad – though certainly not obscene or pornographic.

* *Lolita* by Vladimir Nabokov (Weidenfeld and Nicolson, 1959).

At that last qualification I suspect I shall lose quite a number of my readers, though I cannot see anything wrong in enjoying the kind of hot book that so many acquirers of *Lolita* will have found to their chagrin that it is not. But I take it as fairly probable that these are the kind of people who kept the book at the top of the American bestseller lists week after week, and who will doubtless do the same or better over here. Perception of this probability, together with an understandable desire to protect serious literature from the assaults of official and unofficial wowsers, has had its share in evoking the wild hosannas of praise for *Lolita* that have been ringing round the civilized world. As things are, it is not enough that such a book should be declared non-obscene in the eyes of any reasonable person; it must be declared great as well if it is to be quite safe. The issue is further complicated by the fact that what really offends the wowsers is not just presumptive obscenity, but this in combination with an insufficiently reverent attitude in sexual matters. Thus in the case of *The Philanderer*, an instructive semi-precedent to that of *Lolita*, what got the thing into the courts was the theme of philandering as such, rather than any corruptive power imaginable as residing in individual passages and expressions. Actually there can have been few books of overtly sexual content written out of stronger moral conviction or in purer terms (or with duller impact). If only the hero had been properly 'in love', his bedroom antics could have been detailed down to the last twitch without anyone taking much notice.

Lolita, accordingly, reaches the British public preceded by a sort of creeping barrage of critical acclaim: I expect great things from the jacket, which I have not yet seen. Meanwhile, I note a nine-page appendix in which thirty-one critics from nine countries fire off their commendatory salvoes. Only a few of these are content to assert the mere inoffensiveness of the work; the majority, from Lord Boothby via Heikki Brotherus in the Finnish *Soumen Kuvalehti* down to Dorothy Parker, go on to extol its high moral seriousness and/or (usually and) its outstanding literary merits: distinguished – beauty – beauty – brilliant – great – major – masterpiece – power – great – beautiful – beautiful – masterpiece. That ought to be enough to roll up both flanks of any local bench or libraries committee of even the highest wowser morale, not to speak of more elevated powers, and this is fine as far as it goes. But it would be a pity if all the 'masterpiece' stuff got treated seriously, especially in view of the critical direction it takes. 'Beauty' and 'beautiful' and their synonyms set the tone here, and there is much talk of 'style'. The long battle against style still hangs in the balance, and a reverse over *Lolita* could be damaging.

Style, a personal style, a distinguished style, usually turns out in practice to mean a high idiosyncratic noise level in the writing, with plenty of rumble and wow from imagery, syntax and diction: Donne, Pater, Virginia Woolf. There is, however, a good deal of nostalgia for style nowadays among people of oldster age group or literary training; it shows in snorting accusations of gracelessness levelled against some younger novelists and merges into the hankering for 'experiment' that still dies hard. Those interested will have noticed a connection here with that yearning for uplift, or rich man's Billy Graham, which masquerades as reasoned antipathy to modern British philosophy. If we have not got Kant or Nietzsche, at least we have Colin Wilson. And if we have not got Ruskin or Carlyle, at least we have Nabokov:

> She adored brilliant water and was a remarkably smart diver. Comfortably robed, I would settle down in the rich post-meridian shade after my own demure dip, and there I would sit, with a dummy book or a bag of bonbons, or both, or nothing but my tingling glands, and watch her gambol, rubber-capped, bepearled, smoothly tanned, as glad as an ad. in her trim-fitted satin pants and shirred bra. Pubescent sweetheart! How smugly would I marvel that she was mine, mine, mine, and revise the recent matitudinal swoon to the moan of the mourning doves, and devise the later afternoon one, and slitting my sun-speared eyes, compare Lolita to whatever other nymphets parsimonious chance collected around her for my anthological delectation and judgement; and today, putting my hand on my ailing heart, I really do not think that any of them ever surpassed her in desirability, or if they did, it was so two or three times at the most, in a certain light, with certain perfumes blended in the air — once in the hopeless case of a pale Spanish child, the daughter of a heavy-jawed nobleman, and another time — mais je divague.

No extract, however, could do justice to the sustained din of pun, allusion, neologism, alliteration, *cynghanedd*, apostrophe, parenthesis, rhetorical question, French, Latin, 'anent', 'perchance', 'would fain', 'for the nonce' – here is style and no mistake. One will be told, of course, that this is the 'whole point', that this is the hero, Humbert Humbert, talking in his own person, not the author, and that what we are getting is 'characterization'. All right; but it seems ill-advised to characterize logomania by making it talk 120,000 words at us, and a glance at Nabokov's last novel, *Pnin*, which is not written in the first person, establishes that this is Nabokov talking (there is non-stylistic evidence too). The development of this émigré's euphuism is a likely consequence of Nabokov's having had to abandon his natural idiom, as he puts it, his 'untrammelled, rich and infinitely docile Russian tongue for a second-rate brand of English, devoid of any of those apparatuses – the baffling mirror, the black velvet backdrop, the implied associations and traditions – which the native illusionist, fractails flying, can magically use to transcend the heritage in his own way'. This, which enacts the problem with characteristic tricksy indirection, also implies its solution as the laborious confection of equivalent apparatuses in the adoptive language: the whole farrago of imagery, archaism, etc., which cannot strike even the most finely tuned foreign ear as it strikes that of the native English-speaker. The end product sadly invokes a Charles Atlas muscle-man of language as opposed to the healthy and useful adult.

We know well enough that every style has a way of infiltrating what is being presented, so that, offered as the vehicle of Humbert's soliloquy, this style is involved with the entire moral tenor of the book. Thus Humbert is not only decadently sophisticated and tortuously imaginative and self-regardingly detached, he is also all of these things as he describes his seduction of the twelve-year-old Lolita and his long history of cohabitation with her. All this is arguably Humbert himself, and so is his account, 'delightfully witty' in implication, of his murder of a rival; but the many totally incidental cruelties – the bloody car wreck by the roadside that brings into view the kind of shoe Lolita covets, the wounding of a squirrel, apparently just for fun – bring the author into consideration as well, and I really don't care which of them is being wonderfully mature and devastating when Lolita's mother (recently Humbert's wife) is run over and killed:

> *I should explain ... that the fellow with the glasses was Frederick Beale, Jr, driver of the Packard; that his 79-year-old father, whom*

the nurse had just watered on the green bank where he lay — a
banked banker so to speak — was not in a dead faint, but was
comfortably and methodically recovering from a mild heart attack
or its possibility; and, finally, that the laprobe on the sidewalk
(where she had so often pointed out to me with disapproval the
crooked green cracks) concealed the mangled remains of Charlotte
Humbert, who had been knocked down and dragged several feet by
the Beale car as she was hurrying across the street ... Three doctors
... presently arrived on the scene and took over. The widower, a
man of exceptional self-control, neither wept nor raved. He stag-
gered a bit, that he did; but he opened his mouth only to impart
such information or issue such directions as were strictly necessary
in connection with the identification, examination and disposal of a
dead woman, the top of her head a porridge of bone, brains, bronze
hair and blood.

That's the boy. Humbert/Nabokov: alliterative to the last.

There comes a point where the atrophy of moral sense, evident
throughout this book, finally leads to dullness, fatuity and unreality.
Humbert's 'love' for Lolita is a matter of the senses, even of the mem-
branes; his moments of remorse are few, brief and unconvincing; it
never really occurs to him to ask himself just what the hell he thinks
he is up to. There is plenty of self-absorption around us, heaven
knows, but not enough on this scale to be worth writing about at
length, just as the mad are much less interesting than the sane. And —
here again the author heaves into view — the human circuit of *Lolita*,
for all its geographical sweep, is suffocatingly narrow: the murderee is
Humbert over again, Humbert's old queer pal is Humbert and unnecessary, Lolita's mother talks like Humbert, writes letters in Humbert's style, so does Lolita's girl-chum — the whole affair is Humbert
gleefully meditating about Lolita, looking up to be ever so European
about some American thing, then gleefully meditating again. There is,
further, an appalling poverty of incident and even of narrative: the
central episode of the book, a long illicit motel-tour round the States,
is related in catalogue, without scenes, as near as possible without the
singling-out of individual occasions; meditation again, an exercise in
the frequentative imperfect tense — there's one you missed, Nab-
okov/Humbert boy.

The only success of the book is the portrait of Lolita herself. I have rarely seen the external ambience of a character so marvellously realized, and yet there is seldom more than the necessary undertone of sensuality. Here she is playing tennis:

> . . . the white wide little-boy shorts, the slender waist, the apricot midriff, the white breast-kerchief whose ribbons went up and encircled her neck to end behind in a dangling knot leaving bare her gaspingly young and adorable apricot shoulder blades with that pubescence and those lovely gentle bones, and the smooth, downward-tapering back. Her cap had a white peak . . . She would wait and relax for a bar or two of white-lined time before going into the act of serving, and often bounced the ball once or twice, or pawed the ground a little, always at ease, always rather vague about the score, always cheerful as she so seldom was in the dark life she led at home.

The pity is that Humbert could not care less about the darkness of her life at home, and although the teenage vulgarity of Lolita's behaviour is caught with an equal precision, he could not care less either about what she was really like. She is a 'portrait' in a very full sense, devotedly watched and listened to but never conversed with, the object of desire but never of curiosity. What else did she do in Humbert's presence but play tennis and eat sundaes and go to bed with him? What did they talk about? What did they actually get up to? Apart from a few sentences of elegant hot-book euphemism – reminding us that the work first saw the light under the imprint of the Olympia Press, Paris – we are not even told that. Do not misunderstand me if I say that one of the troubles with *Lolita* is that, so far from being too pornographic, it is not pornographic enough.

As well as 'moral' and 'beautiful', the book is also held to be 'funny', often 'devastatingly' so, and 'satirical'. As for the 'funny' part, all that registered with me were a few passages where irritation caused Humbert to drop the old style-scrambler for a moment and speak in clear. The 'satirical' thing is a bit better, but it has been rather foisted on to *Lolita* as a result of the eagerness of Americans to hear the worst of themselves. V. S. Pritchett's comparison with *The Loved One* is apt in a different way from that intended: both books score the expected points with great gusto, neither is nearly as devastating as dozens of books by Americans, neither is acceptable as a picture of America. Perhaps only native-born Americans can provide this, which leads one to reflect that Nabokov's tragedy has been his separation from Europe, the source of his natural subject-matter as well as of his natural language. There is nothing in *Lolita* as fine as the seven pages of 'Colette', a story of his dating from 1948 in which the germ of *Lolita* is clearly discernible. Here is the same little monkey with the long-toed bare feet and the bruise on her tender skin, inciting the author to a reminiscence of *Carmen* – in *Lolita* this reappears in the eerie modernized disguise of a pop song. The Biarritz world of pre-1914 is evoked with a tender intensity that none of the Middle West travelogues or Virginia moteliana can match; and here the hero, being like the heroine ten years old, allows his love to slip away from him down a path which Humbert, out of solipsistic brutality, and Nabokov, out of a deficiency of good sense, denied to Lolita:

> She took from her governess and slipped into my brother's hands a farewell present, a box of sugar-coated almonds, meant, I knew, solely for me, and instantly she was off, tap-tapping her glinting hoop through light and shade, around and around a fountain choked with dead leaves, near which I stood. The leaves mingled in my memory with the leather of her shoes and gloves, and there was, I remember, some detail in her attire (perhaps a ribbon on her Scottish cap, or the pattern of her stockings) that reminded me then of the rainbow spiral in a glass marble. I still seem to be holding that wisp of iridescence, not knowing exactly where to fit it in, while she runs with her hoop ever faster around me and finally dissolves among the slender shadows cast on the gravelled path by the interlaced arches of its border.

1959

It is a sad fate to be the child of the urban or suburban middle classes. As a first or a fourth are the only dignified kinds of degree to get, so one's upbringing must be conducted either in several establishments with several bathrooms each or in one with none, if it is to distil any glamour potential. Compared with the upper and lower levels alike – but especially with the lower, to which it has many unlooked-for similarities – the middle stratum is bound to seem drab and glum. Beset by constant anxieties about decorum, it has never devised a traditional way of enjoying itself. Alongside those of the working classes, its fears show up as neurotic, unreal and self-regarding. Among its shrewdest and most cheerful members are the man who still likes to be known by his Home Guard rank, the woman who will refer in every conversation to her shopping days in Town with the wife of the local Member. And its heroes, denied alike a brisk introduction to sex behind the coal-tips and a fructifyingly bad time at Eton, may perhaps be forgiven their occasional outbursts of adolescent peevishness.

The above is, I hope, a legitimate reaction to Mr Richard Hoggart's absorbing and amiable book* on working-class life and culture. Personal experience is at work all the time in his account of mores and mythology among labourers, craftsmen and their families in Leeds and other areas of the industrial North. He draws a detailed picture of a mode of existence that is in itself rich in the concrete and the indi-

* *The Uses of Literacy* (Chatto and Windus, 1957).

vidual. It is the world of corner-shops and fish and chips, whist-drives and bus-outings, pints of mild, packets of ten and boiled ham for tea at the week-end. Some of the female portraits – the wife endlessly working to keep the household warm, properly fed and out of debt, the widow struggling to bring up three or four young children – and the various evocations of Friday-evening shopping or Sunday-morning leisure distil a warmth which cannot fail to engage sympathy, but which might seem more appropriate in autobiography or fiction than in an inquiry avowed to be analytical, even if acknowledged to be amateur and personal. Although Mr Hoggart is at pains to admit how easily romanticism enters such chronicles as his, and despite his periodic correctives, there are perceptible gaps in his story.

Having preludially blackguarded the middle classes, I may possibly be allowed to wonder whether the present work lays enough stress on what appear, to the outsider, as characteristic proletarian vices. I do not refer to the bluntness and coarseness for which Mr Hoggart makes apology: if these qualities are not illusions brought about by variations in class standpoint, they are at any rate below serious notice – 'so love does loathe disdainful nicety'. What I am getting at is the serene intolerant complacency manifested by many working-class people, especially older women; the skin-tight armour against any unfamiliar idea. I remember once explaining to a landlady of mine that the sun didn't really put the fire out (it only looked as if it did) and so she could leave off drawing the blinds on a bright autumn afternoon. She heard me out politely, standing by the hearth, then went and drew the blinds as usual, 'just in case'. I would admit that there can be middle-class versions of that kind of thing. And I must certainly add that it has an obverse side which ought to preclude exasperation: the apathy and bewilderment likely to be shown by working people when they come up against officialdom. Any social worker, children's officer, clinic assistant and so on who reads Mr Hoggart's book (I hope they all will) will find grounds for exercising the utmost kindness and patience in their dealings.

But even on the most unfavourable view there must be ample reason to deplore the spectacle of a way of life, many-sided and involving a delicate system of loyalties, beginning to decay. Welsh Nonconformism, for instance, may enrage or bore unendurably all the way from its emotional barbarities to its attitude to drink and Sunday cinemas, and yet it provided around the chapels a network of personal and social relationships whose loss will be an impoverishment. That loss, together with similar changes in other parts of Great Britain, can be seen as inevitably produced by post-war developments which, since they are accompaniments of assault on poverty, one would not wish to see undone: if a structure is propped up by unemployment, bad housing and an agonizing fear of debt, then we must kick the prop away. But the question which Mr Hoggart deals with in the second half of his book still requires an answer: what is going to replace the way of life we have been busily undermining? If we can answer that one with certainty (which some will take leave to doubt), then there is a supplementary about whether the emergent system is a good one.

With many qualifications and caveats, notably as regards the resilience of the older working-class culture, Mr Hoggart's prognosis is pessimistic. An examination of tendencies in the popular press, in radio entertainment and in cheap paperback fiction suggests to him an eventual triumph of prejudice, incuriosity, shallow conformism, sentimentality and the couldn't-care-less attitude. These are grim predictions. A partial restorative might take in the fact that some of these qualities have been endemic at least since the fall of Athens in 404 B.C., while others (the too-easy tolerance, for example, which Mr Hoggart detects) will make a nice change. One could also point to a number of apparent paradoxes as between certain of the coming attitudes, whereby an enjoyment of group values accompanies an increasing isolation, a self-opinionated quality goes hand in hand with a new loss of certainty. And really it is no use quoting George Eliot in order to establish that popular fiction is of humble literary merit. Nor will it quite do to declare that the latter 'must surely' encourage this bad attitude, are 'certainly likely to' have that undesirable effect. Too little is known about how reading fits into the lives of working people – or of any people, come to that.

But the main trouble with Mr Hoggart's diagnostics is that they are as thin in illustration as his reminiscences are rich. This is partly the result of an absurd decision – on the part of the publishers, I imagine – only to allow invented examples of the less edifying kind of fiction: no such timidity marked Mr Geoffrey Wagner's valuable *Parade of Pleasure*, nor, as far as I know, did any libel actions. However, there is far more to it than that. To talk usefully about anything, from linguistic analysis to rock 'n' roll, it is necessary to see it from the inside, by experience or study. Mr Hoggart was thus well equipped to describe his early background. But he sees his 'mass publications and entertainments' from the outside. He tells us in a note that ballroom dancing is the second largest entertainment industry in the country with its 500-odd ballrooms, but he might never have been in one of them for any sign he gives of understanding the part they play in their patrons' world. His account of modern popular songs is evidently based upon an exiguous, ill-chosen sample and is riddled with precarious intuitions about such imponderables as the kind and degree of self-consciousness displayed. He does not know what television programmes are like or how people behave while they watch them; he does not know that *Astounding Science Fiction* prints some of the best work in its genre despite its name and cover, which are doubtless all he has seen of it; he does not even know that there is more than one kind of comic strip.

One might well, I readily agree, go to one's grave in happy ignorance of all the things I have mentioned; but not if one is going to write a whole book about popular culture. Mr Hoggart says near the end of his that optimism on this subject is likely to visit those who 'do not really know the material'. So is pessimism, as he has proved. And in his case I should judge it not unlikely that the pessimism preceded the investigation and found what it wanted to find, a common sequence of events among amateur investigators. It would be pleasant to say of a book written out of such obvious earnestness and decency of feeling that it represented an achievement, but it is only an attempt.

1957

THE LEGION OF THE LOST

One of the prime indications of the sickness of mankind in the mid-twentieth century is that so much excited attention is paid to books about the sickness of mankind in the mid-twentieth century. The latest of these books* is more readable than most; it is more compilation than original work, and the worst it can do is to make you feel a little overwhelmed at its author's erudition. Here they come – tramp, tramp, tramp – all those characters you thought were discredited, or had never read, or (if you are like me) had never heard of: Barbusse, Sartre, Camus, Kierkegaard, Nietzsche, Hermann Hesse, Hemingway, Van Gogh, Nijinsky, Tolstoy, Dostoievsky, George Fox, Blake, Sri Ramakrishna, George Gurdjieff, T. E. Hulme and a large number of bit-players. The Legion of the Lost, they call us, the Legion of the Lost are we, as the old song has it. Marching on to hell with the drum playing – pick up the step there!

With admirable clarity and unpretentiousness, Mr Colin Wilson shows that all his légionnaires, miscellaneous as they may seem, were animated by the same kind of distress and took up similar attitudes to it. The Outsider – their collective label – is the man who has awakened to the chaos of existence, to the unreality of what the literal-minded take to be reality. He does not accept the conditions of human life, and finds release from its prison only in moments of terror or ecstasy. He tries to solve the problem of his identity, to discover which of his

* *The Outsider* by Colin Wilson (Gollancz, 1956).

many 'I's' is his true 'I', but reason, logic, any kind of thought is no help here, or indeed anywhere. He is anti-humanist ('humanism', Mr Wilson tells us, 'is only another name for spiritual laziness', anyway), but he is not, or preferably not, a man of action. He wants to get out of his predicament, and mysticism of some sort is perhaps his only route; if he is lucky he may end up as a saint.

The most noticeable thing about such an inquiry as this is that it inevitably blurs or overrides distinctions of literary merit. All writers come alike to the ravening trend-hound, whose interest is either in biography or in what is left when artistic qualities have been boiled off. And so we constantly encounter paradoxes whereby men of the stature of Sartre or Camus rub shoulders with the Wells of *Mind at the End of Its Tether*; Blake and Nietzsche serve under the same flag as Nijinsky with his pitiful ravings, Granville-Barker with his pretentious 'idealistic' twaddle, and Arabian Lawrence, who, whatever his claims as a man, was surely a sonorous fake as a writer. Why, one wants to ask, was Mr Charles Morgan's Sparkenbroke not called to the colours? Or the hero of *Gallions Reach*? Or Hitchcock in Mr Ray Bradbury's 'No Particular Night or Morning', who became an Outsider from scratch in a day and a half and jumped out of his spaceship?

There are obviously a great many Outsiders about. There are, I suspect, even more ex-Outsiders. Few people who can read and write could have failed to be wandering outlaws of their own dark minds in their youth's summer, say about the age of sixteen. And it is a persona that many of us revert to in our more shamelessly adolescent moments. Boredom, depression, anxiety, dissatisfaction, even the state of the sexual omnivore in Barbusse's *L'Enfer*, even the feeling of regarding chaos – these are the monopoly of no ideological group. A lot of people get a bit fed up from time to time at not being able to meet in the real world the unsubstantial images their souls so constantly behold. But they do not on this account go round considering themselves as, or behaving like, Stephen Dedalus; at least they try not to, and rightly. At the risk of being written off as a spiritual wakey-wakey man, it is worth asserting that to tear one's fascinated gaze away from the raree-show of one's own dilemmas, to value Mr Pickwick higher than Raskolnikov, to try to be a bit pleasant occasionally, are aims worth making an effort for.

Other characteristics than those listed by Mr Wilson can be added to the portrait of the regular lost légionnaire, the full-time, long-service-engagement Outsider. To begin with, he is always a man. He will have a private income or a patron: the incidence of Outsiderism among builders' foremen or bookies' runners must be low. He is likely to be unmarried and without family ties. He has no strong affections, and his lack of ordinary warmth makes him divide the human race into himself on one side, plus the odd hero-figure or two, and 'the mob' on the other. He tends to amorality, feeling that a spot of murder or child-rape may come in handy as a means of asserting his Will, escaping from the prison of thought, etc., and he is totally devoid of humour. Now it is quite conceivable that chaps like that may really be 'society's spiritual dynamos', but I judge it unlikely. Supposing it is true, then if society isn't sick already it soon will be.

The Outsider's most untenable and annoying claim, which Mr Wilson is ready to make for him if he doesn't make it often enough for himself, is that of possessing a large share, if not a monopoly, of depth and honesty and sensitivity and intensity and acuity and insight and courage and adulthood – especially that. The 'mob' are just mob and no more; they are the *salauds*, in M. Sartre's phrase, who are convinced that their existence is necessary; they are the bourgeois, who never know that they are not free; they include the Victorians, with whom 'we are in the position of adults condemning children'; they none of them ever ask themselves the questions the Outsider formulates. And these, of course, are real questions, the most real questions. Are they? Admittedly, to ask oneself: 'How am I to live?' is to ask something real, though even here it could be argued that the continual taking of moral decisions, a fairly common activity, needs no encrustation of internal catechizing to make it valid. But it would be hard to attach any meaning, except as an expression of lunacy or amnesia, to: 'Who am I?'

'I' is a word that plays a large part in the Outsider's vocabulary. It is significant that his favoured literary vehicle is the journal – the adolescent's confidant, the egotist's outlet, and, incidentally, the lazy novelist's feather-bed. Hypertrophy of self and self-regard is the real sickness of the Outsider; Childe Harold is a miracle of humility beside him. The Romantic who put in a lot of time seeing through shams boggled at taking reality as his pet sham. Curling the lip by numbers is a well established exercise, but it is decent to restrict its target to society and let mankind as a whole get by. Even if this restraint is impossible, there is no need to erect one's boredoms into a system with oneself sitting in the middle. A case could be made out for people shouldering the burdens of their own nastiness, enduring their boredom and depression, without finding it necessary to blame someone or something.

I must say I find Mr Wilson's book a disturbing addition to the prevailing anti-rational mode, feeling as I do that one is better off with too much reason than with none at all. I hate the idea of the kind of people who may already hanker after behaving like Stephen Dedalus being persuaded that there is fashionable authority for doing so, that they were right all along in attributing their folly and apathy to a source outside themselves and their control. And I hope Mr Wilson is right when he says that those who have already volunteered for the Legion of the Lost would welcome demobilization. How this is to be achieved I know no more than he does, and I agree that a course of P.T. and cross-country running, or a good dose of salts, would not quite meet the case. Perhaps there are curative properties in the notion that ordering up another bottle, attending a jam session, or getting introduced to a young lady, while they may solve no problems at all, are yet not necessarily without dignity, and while they may indicate no sensitivity at all, are yet not irreconcilable with it. Right: Legion of the Lost . . . DIS-*MISS*!

1956

POSTSCRIPT 1970

For reasons I have probably made plain enough, I have not looked at *The Outsider* since reviewing it. Nevertheless, I have to admit that Mr Wilson had put his finger on, or near, a genuinely emergent cultural growth. The widespread attention his book aroused did testify partly to that. When I said above that the amoral isolate, the intellectual opter-out, was not to be considered a spiritual dynamo of society, I was being insufficiently imaginative. I got a little nearer the mark when I added that, if Mr Wilson was right after all, society very soon would be sick. He partly was and it partly is: Barbusse and the rest of the *galère* are in no sense the direct progenitors of the hippie, or ideological idler, who would not read even if he could, and I cannot believe

91

in any process of subterranean popularization such as has, I think, conveyed a rather debased form of D. H. Lawrence's teaching to people who have never heard of him and would not want to be told. But the Barbusse gang and the modern drop-out probably share an ancestry, buried undiscoverably deep in the history of Christian belief. I just throw what there is of this off. I should hate to go, or be taken into it.

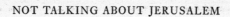

Among many tendencies hostile to good writing, two have recently become prominent: the academic and the journalistic. The academic tendency, exalting style and treatment at the peril of content, is perhaps, despite the continued existence of Henry James, passing its peak. The journalistic tendency seems to be increasing. It ultimately sees a work of literature as an idea or a message boiled up in style, and for preference not too much at that. Thus if the subject-matter of a number of writers can be included in a simple generalization, a group or school can be assumed to exist and can be written about in terms suitable to the popular press: the Angries emerge. This sort of thing is possibly harmless in itself, but what happens if the writers and serious critics take the journalistic view may be more untoward, or at any rate diffuse more boredom.

The journalistic novelist or dramatist starts off with the laudable and necessary feeling that his subject is more important than anybody else's. Unfortunately he then proceeds to behave as if the urgency of what he has to say relieved him from the task of saying it properly – that is, with due attention to matters of style and treatment. He is likely to be hostile to the mere mention of such considerations, which may appear to him as trivial, cold, formalistic, indeed academic. To point out that a novel of protest by a coloured South African, say, is illiterate, stagy and incoherent, will invite journalistic accusations of pedantry (if of nothing more sinister), even

93

a comparison with Rymer's objections to *Othello*. And, in such a case, the critic may well feel, if he is anything of a liberal, that 'life' is more important, that human agony takes precedence over aesthetic distaste, and that his first duty is to decency. But it is not. It is to literature.

This may seem a grandiose prelude to a discussion of Arnold Wesker's plays.* However, the awesomeness of the tributes he has received justifies the reviewer in any amount of soul-searching. So I will go on in confessional mode and admit freely, even with a touch of legitimate pride, that I have never seen any of these works performed.† It is not that I am singling Mr Wesker out for special treatment: the whole of the recent renaissance of the English stage is to me a closed book, closed theatre, rather. For what it may be worth, though, I will confess further that, from what both friend and foe say of it, the revolution I keep hearing about smells rather like a palace revolution. The world of the theatre has an uncanny power of self-perpetuation. I am not of it, which makes me impartial.

If I call Mr Wesker journalistic, it is not in the sense that I find him an accurate reporter of the contemporary scene. I know little of Jewish households in East London and less of rural life in Norfolk and I have never worked in a restaurant kitchen. With the R.A.F. setting of *Chips With Everything* I am on firmer ground. In many ways – the miming, the rituals, the telescoping of action – this is a deliberately unrealistic play. I recognize, too, that the curious *patois* spoken by the officers, however much it weakens any possible claim to serious representational interest, may serve the purpose of indicating how remote and fantastic, or how nightmarish, these Establishment figures are when properly seen into. The character of Pip, however, the upper-class rebel who is corrupted by being persuaded to take part in a bayonet practice, surely evidences some realistic intention. And yet he lurches in and out of cumbersome poeticality, uses the word 'also' like a foreigner, is made to say (of peasants with a grievance): 'They voiced themselves well.'

This air of being hastily translated from some other tongue is endemic to Mr Wesker's dialogue. Here is a short anthology from his

* *Chips With Everything* (1962), *The Kitchen* (1961), *The Wesker Trilogy* (1960) (All published by Jonathan Cape).

† I have since (1966) seen Mr Wesker's *Their Very Own and Golden City*, a piece that seemed to me to fulfil quite thoroughly the promise of its title.

earlier plays, which clearly aim at realism (I have avoided obvious attempts at Jewish immigrant speech and East Anglian dialect):

' "[An industrial society] makes a man stand on his head and then convinces him he is good-looking." (Comment: Mistake for something like "he looks good like that"?)

' "Ada suckles a beautiful baby." (Surely an archaism in speech?)

' "You're not tired, Harry — you're just drowning with heritage, mate!"

' "He stood out here and he looked around . . . and then he stalked off with a 'see you'." (Conceivable in actual speech?)

' ". . . You'll never make the beautiful, rustic estate." (Interpretable as "You'll never build a beautiful life for yourselves in the country." ')

Its not always easy to distinguish this sort of thing from the innumerable phrases that perhaps might be spoken, but only by stupid and/or intolerably self-melodramatizing people, which these are evidently not designed as. (Or are they? Time and time again I had the suspicion that I was reading some fiendishly far-out satirist of sentimental sub-intellectual liberalism. If I'm right, don't throw off the mask, Wesker. They'll assassinate you.) Try these:

' "Don't you want to feel your life? Savour it gently?"

' "You have never cried [? sc. out] against the jungle of an industrial society."

' "I suddenly feel unclean."

' " 'Words and bridges,' he wrote, 'to get from one place to another.' Wait till he's older and he learns about silences — they span worlds."

' "Beatie Bryant could have been a poem — I gave her words — maybe she became one." '

—this last in the mouth of a young man described as talking like a book: surely an insult in most circles, and fully justified here.

'Bookish', however paradoxical it may seem, is indeed the word for much of Mr Wesker's dialogue. Among the books he clearly does not know, however, is Cold Comfort Farm, still required reading for anyone who ventures to portray rusticity. And so we wander from 'That ent too bad just yit — few more weeks and the old mowld'll cling' to 'Roots! The things you come from, the things that feed you. The things that make you proud of yourself — roots!'

Cries from the heart we doubt ever got cried (we hope they didn't, anyway) stud these pages. They foster the action that Mr Wesker's eye and ear for experience are dulled. He cannot even run up a convincing pop lyric, his attempt in *Roots* fatally resembles the folk songs his characters are perpetually singing to one another. His Jewish families constantly fall into the accents of a T V comedy series – less funny than most; his removal men in *I'm Talking About Jerusalem* are like Hancock bit-players – only less funny. In particular, the corporal in *Chips With Everything* is far less funny than many real individuals of the type presumably aimed at – the surly, eccentric, egotistical long-service N.C.O. And we are far now from lamenting a detachable stylistic shortcoming. Mr Wesker denigrates by his practice the interestingness and intelligence of the life he purports to know and care about.

This impression survives a longer view of the events portrayed. I cannot believe, for instance, that the semi-rural existence we are shown in *Roots* need be as thin and uneventful as this, nor that protest (or declamation) about it need be so meagerly motivated and so insubstantial as Beatie's. (At that point, by the way, it is not a speech in a bad book that one is reminded of, but a speech in a bad film: Charlie Chaplin's in *Limelight*.) The bearable interludes in the Services, again, are more bearable than those in parts of *Chips With Everything* – and officers may be agents of corruption, but in concrete and varied ways, not as a row of interchangeable phantoms. And there must have been more to working-class feeling in the 'thirties than fighting Mosley and sitting round the fire singing 'England arise, the long long night is over.'

Let me be clear about why I object to that last part. I am not, I hope, 'afraid of emotion', nor am I just enjoying a sneer at left-wing idealism: it is the sentimentality of its *image* here I find offensive, as I would find offensive a tenor dressed as a general singing 'There'll always be an England.' (I would agree that in that case there would be plenty of other offensive things too.) Still, I'm sure the 'England arise' scene plays well. It's amazing what does.

I cannot apply most of these strictures to *The Kitchen*, in which the factors that make it harder to read than the others – large cast with fairly equally diffused interest, incessant movement – may well make it an original and even interesting piece in actual production. The fact that the characters are mostly foreign tends to conceal any inauthenticity in dialogue. And it is possible that the playwright's claim to be presenting via the kitchen an allegory of life under capitalism survives in performance the many sledgehammer hints that that is what he is up to. But production must be the key, and not only here. As a non-theatregoer who can read, I incline to the widespread view that the presumptive triumphs of the new dramatists rest upon skilful and sympathetic direction – that and the over-fashionable liberalism of audiences prepared to go nine-tenths of the way to meet any public document that seems to be on the right side. That is how messages are got across. It is a pity that this message is so puny. But it is not surprising. Ideas are their treatment.

1962

MEN WITHOUT WOMEN

A British reaction to Dr Leslie A. Fiedler's new volume* can get well under way before a word of the text is read. Its mere physical bulk seems a reproach to the slenderness of the average home product: no half-articulated string of blown-up reviews, clearly, awaits us here. The photograph of the author on the back of the jacket invites as background a row of bottles rather than of Oxford texts: the face and its attachments are beatniked up to a point that reminded an American reviewer of 'the sort of picture you expect to find on an as-told-to book by a junkie'. And there are other indications that the mantle of academicism gives Dr Fiedler an occasional twitch. But, seen from over here, such stuff is a valuable reminder – one which the contents of the book amply bear out – that critics can be people, not disembodied intelligences that have to shut down the moment they leave the study or the lecture-room; nor, incidentally, need they succumb to the polo-sweatered charlatanry that is our own favourite alternative these days. Finally, the front of the jacket carries, between what I take to be an emblem of Oneness or whatever and a kind of Jackson Pollock *chevaux de frise*, a title that promises at any rate a broad scope and a pervading theme. Here, too, we are not disappointed.

Dr Fiedler, indeed, has written a pantograph, a treatise that sets out to explain not only, as avowed, the American novel and its relation to

* *Love and Death in the American Novel* (Secker & Warburg, 1961; re-issued 1967 by Jonathan Cape).

American life, but also American social, moral, sexual, cultural, anthropological and psychological history, in fact the whole of American life, in fact America, in fact everything, or at least everything American – a qualification of, to him, fluctuating importance. Everything and everybody, accordingly, may turn out to be relevant: Conan Doyle, *Beowulf*, the Marquis de Sade (but of course), Gary Cooper, Rabelais, *Frankenstein*, Dylan Thomas. And any source, any method may supply the right answer, a possible answer, significant information, something: *The Allegory of Love*, Marxism either neat or with a *Partisan Review* admixture, Freud and Jung and their commentators, Lawrence's *Studies in Classic American Literature*. My point about this last lot is not so much that it indicates a welcome sense of being at home in the analytical armoury, an eclecticism of the kind that informs some of the best criticism now being written in English, though there is that. Rather I want to direct attention to the fact that Dr Fiedler, so far from attempting to conceal his use of these sources, makes a neat catalogue of them in his preface. Thus casually to lay one's critical kit out for inspection seems very American, or anyway non-British; our own instinct is to assume, even to pretend, that writer and reader have long ago got hold of and absorbed everything that counts, and we all know what counts. Similarly, it takes an American to feel that illumination may come from the least expected quarter, that the relative importances of things are never settled in England, as Mr Malcolm Bradbury wrote recently in a more general context, 'everything has happened before'. (Most of those who have taught American as well as British undergraduates will have felt this difference.) And I connect all this with what I see as the fact that there is something striking – and American – in the mere readiness to attempt a work of this size and scope on such a high level of scholarship and intelligence; one feels that in Britain such an attempt, even if innocent of all polo-sweateredness, would have to be middle-brow, journalistic, popularizing. However: I hope that Dr Fiedler, who has shown some understandable spleen in the past at the cultural complacency of the British will not mind my having taken a moment off to hit them over the head with him.

The title of *Love and Death in the American Novel* perhaps gives no ready clue to its theme. This is roughly that with all those great opportunities, all that 'rich diversity' of subject-matter so eagerly attributed nowadays by bandwagon-conscious Europeans, the whole thing has misfired; in particular, we are confronted by 'the failure of the American fictionist to deal with adult heterosexual love and his consequent obsession with death, incest and innocent homosexuality', and in consequence 'our novels seem not primitive, perhaps, but innocent, unfallen in a disturbing way, almost juvenile'. This malady grips not only, say, *Deerslayer* or *Tom Sawyer*, but the work of contemporaries like Saul Bellow, whom I myself had always taken to be fairly grown-up: thus we are invited to see 'a homo-erotic *Tarzan of the Apes* in *Henderson the Rain King*' and Mr Bellow as 'back on the raft with Mark Twain'. *Huckleberry Finn* is indeed, for Dr Fiedler, one of the two great American novels of platonic homosexuality, the other being that richest mine of analysable and interpretable material since the Bible, *Moby Dick* – this, we are told, is 'perhaps the greatest love-story in our fiction'. And a similar tendency, and/or that of incest, is unearthed in the first of all American novels, *The Power of Sympathy* (1789), in the work of Cooper, whose Natty Bumppo plus Chingachgook correspond to Huck plus Jim and Ishmael plus Queequeg (and, Dr Fiedler might have added, the Lone Ranger plus Tonto), in Hawthorne, in Dreiser, in Hemingway, in Erskine Caldwell, in Truman Capote, while those writers who escape such branding are brought down by a bolas composed of sadism, necrophily and the castration complex: any heroine with unduly long legs, evidently, is likely to render her creator vulnerable to the last-named charge.

To summarize matters in this strain, though perhaps unavoidable and even appropriate from some points of view, does less than justice to Dr Fiedler's tact and seriousness. He is concerned not to shock or titillate but to explain, to demonstrate in concrete terms, the gap between American fiction and American fact. If he often, as he must by now be weary of being told, 'goes too far', he as often goes in a new and illuminating direction. He is at his most convincing when he finds and traces a division in the American novel between the sentimental strain and the Gothic, both of them originally British importations, the first soon degraded into bestellerdom and issuing in books like Herman Wouk's recent *Marjorie Morningstar*; the second, with its variegated trappings of horror and fantasy, available to the sensationalism of a Tennessee Williams, but equally the chosen, or possibly the inevitable, vehicle of a succession of major figures, from

Hawthorne to Faulkner. One might add that the persistence and universality of the Gothic stream in the American imagination are strikingly witnessed by a couple of documents that no doubt turned up too late for Dr Fiedler to fit them in. Alfred Hitchcock's *Psycho*, that incredible salad of demoniacal possession, transvestism, incest and necrophily, with the obligatory miasmic swamp in the background, makes British-made chillers like *Dracula* seem chronicles of harmless eccentricity, and Richard Condon's novel, *The Manchurian Candidate*, opens up a new dimension by making the demon-woman not only the bedmate of her father, and her son, not only the agent of the son's psychological castration, but a Communist spy and all. Perhaps Dr Fiedler 'goes too far' less often than he appears to.

A guarded summing-up – guarded because, for all its length, this is a book of fearful compression, requiring several re-readings and re-thinkings – can lead off with the query whether some of the hard questions may not have been left unanswered. Granted that the American novelist has moved away from the centre of sex (marital, physical) to its periphery (perverted, rarefied), what in him or his environment is responsible? Granted that the bestseller in the United States preceded the serious novel instead of following in its wake, why are the two levels so often inextricably confused to this day, so that, just as in jazz, that essentially American art-form, one is shifted from this moment to that between the authentic and the banal? There are some, especially on this side of the Atlantic, who will feel that, even if fully answered, such questions lie partly, perhaps wholly, outside the brief of the literary critic, as do some of the questions the book has fully answered. To use the American novel as a couch-monologue wherewith to analyse the American psyche is a valid enterprise (and Dr Fiedler's achievement is nowhere near exhausted by being so described), but, again, there is the objection that criticism, rather than tearing aside the surface of a literary work in order to unearth one kind of truth, should concern itself with illuminating that surface ever more truthfully.

A British reader, then, is likely to find matters of style and treatment given something less than their due weight in this book. He will also find insufficient attention paid to British literature, so that, for instance, naivety is held to inhere in a (misquoted) couplet from Marvell, which recalls nothing so much as the local sage who wrote that:

'Alabamans will find some of Mr Anthony Powell's jokes provincial.' But my purpose is not to set the redcoats on to Dr Fiedler, merely to suggest that a survey of fictional relations between white and non-white could usefully be supplemented by a glance at Kipling, or even Rider Haggard, that an account of the child-figure from Poe to *Lolita* might benefit from a recollection of Lewis Carroll, among others. Without this kind of precaution, even the most discriminating critic may go astray, may see as characteristically American what is in fact Anglo-American, or Western, or modern, or human. If Dr Fiedler had extended his search for the novel of mature sex across the Atlantic, his failure to come up with more than a couple or so (in England at least) might have caused him to shorten his line here and there. It does sometimes look as if the novel in English, rather than the American or the Anglo-American novel, is tomorrow's proper study; and for that purpose, as for the one he sets himself, Dr Fiedler's witty, exasperating, energetic, penetrating book will prove indispensable.

1961

Jewish jokes are not funny. They are not even jokes, but potted observations about Jewishness given anecdotal form and a punch line. The response is laughter, though not the sort of laughter that greets the ordinary (usually obscene) male-company story: it is ambiguous, it conceals, or fails to conceal, a ruefulness, a reflectiveness, a sense of resignation. How true that is, we are meant to feel, how wry, how inescapable, how Jewish. Cohen at the travel agency rejects ex-pro-Nazi Italy and Spain, not to speak of Germany and Austria, for his vacation trip; the busy clerk leaves him thoughtfully spinning a globe; when the clerk returns, Cohen says: 'Maybe you got another globe?' That is the basic Jewish joke; hardly a joke at all.

Some of this may go to explain why I did not find Mr Roth's book* funny. Fluent, lively, articulate, vivid, energetic – all that and more,†

---

* *Portnoy's Complaint* (Random House, New York, 1969; Jonathan Cape, London, 1969).

† No, none of that and less, actually, apart from fluent, and this only in the sense that no pauses for breath, except between chapters, are indicated in the narrative. For several, partly inconsistent reasons, a reviewer will be inclined to introduce qualifications into his hostile notices, perhaps, as here, inventing them altogether. He will feel that unrelieved vituperation may suggest personal bias and so be weakened in its effect on the average reader. If he writes books himself, he knows that the really annoying attack is the one diversified with the occasional lordly gesture of magnanimity. And,

but as the stream of Jewish-joke-type incidents and epigrams and soliloquies thickened, I found myself hankering for some variation, something less ambiguously multi-edged, a bit of farce or a comic line at which one was not invited to laugh once and cry twice and gag three times and rage four times – especially that. The book is in essence a heavily orchestrated yell of rage, rage that is nonetheless rage for being presented as often excessive and ridiculous, and rage wears one down.

The hero-narrator, Alex Portnoy, suffers from a psychological complaint described in a fake dictionary-of-neuroses extract included between title page and text – I was always told at school not to manufacture quotes in this sort of way, and my spirits fell a little when I got this far with the present work. However: this complaint is a disorder in which 'strongly-felt ethical and altruistic impulses [I could not find many of these when I came to read about Portnoy] are perpetually warring with extreme sexual longings [I found those all right], often of a perverse nature'. Not a very uncommon complaint, perhaps; but, of course, the title is a pun, and the book is a complaint against this and that much more than an account of a complaint in the psyche or anywhere else.

The this and that referred to is, naturally, being Jewish and what it does to people, or rather to the hero, who is on stage all the time, usually alone, ostensibly talking to the shadowy doctor in charge of his case. We open (how else?) with Momma, in a section called: 'The Most Unforgettable Character I've Met'. This is ironical, of course, but it soon turns out that the hero means it just the same. At this point in the reading, my spirits fell a little further. Even in England, where there are still quite a few Gentile authors about, it is possible to feel that one has had nearly enough of this sort of thing. This Momma, however, is not the usual blend of the exasperating and the wonderful: she is all exasperating, or rather enraging.

The enraging things are well selected and observed: Mrs Portnoy's

---

very much on the other hand, it seems a bit mean to put the boot all the way in at publication time – though I need have had no such compunction in the case of a book that, being so clearly intended to be uproarious, etc., was greeted as uproarious, etc., by all but (I think) three critics, myself included, in the U.S.A. and Great Britain together.

candid and serious view that her biggest fault is that she is too good, her pulling a knife on the six-year-old Alex to get him to eat, her sportsmanship when she loses at Mah-Jongg, all her emotional pressurizing and blackmail, even to the point (I found this believable and terrifying) of half representing a hysterectomy as a cancer operation to drive Alex into line. But these things are not well presented, well written about; they are instant springboards for Alex's rages, for another rash of exclamation marks, italics, and block letters. Mr Roth out-Poes Poe in his recourse to typography.

Before we leave Momma, who crops up at intervals through most of the book, I might just suggest an answer to a question Portnoy never seriously asks – no reason why he should, though we might see her, and her and his environment, more clearly if Mr Roth had implied an answer: if Jewish mothers are so unbearable, what makes them like that? Well: perhaps something to do with the position of women in Jewish society, in particular with how their men behave towards them. And if Portnoy senior in earlier years was anything like Alex in rather later ones (and I suspect he was), then we can forgive Mrs Portnoy a lot. I am not asking for charity, only a little curiosity before the block letters start. Informed rage is deadlier than its blinkered counterpart, and more entertaining too.

As regards Portnoy senior, this character is the best thing in the book: all writers, all men writers anyway, see and portray father better than mother. Poor Mr Portnoy, a constipated insurance salesman, staggers off day after day on his exhausting round, is under his wife's thumb a lot of the time, works for family harmony, pleads for his son's confidence, seems to command our pity; and undoes the whole thing by coming out from under his wife's thumb whenever a chance presents itself to join her in oppressing Alex, by trying to extract gratitude for his admittedly fearsome labours, by emotionalizing all over him. I, the child of Protestant parents who had had a puritanical upbringing, recognize that picture.

Which brings me to the point that all of us, at least most of us over the age of about ten, have had to go through something like this. In Western society, and probably in a lot of other societies, past and present, people constantly try to straightjacket their children to be as they want, use guilt feelings on them, insist on being told everything they do and think, do all they can to make them feel like 'geniuses and brilliant like nobody has ever been brilliant and beautiful before ... sheer perfection on the one hand, and such bumbling, incompetent, thoughtless, helpless, selfish, evil little shits, little *ingrates*, on the other!' Portnoy, or Mr Roth, falls into racial/cultural provincialism by wondering what it is about specifically Jewish parents that makes them go on like this; they are just parents, or, in Portnoy-Roth language, WHAT'S SO DIFFERENT WITH THE GOYIM? WE ALL KNEW ALL OF THAT ALREADY ALREADY!

Another subject of the book is sex, or Jewish sex, or, along the lines of the argument put forward above, just sex after all. This starts off, naturally, with juvenile masturbation, which is gone into at greater length, in more profuse detail, and more honestly than in any book I remember. Portnoy – the grown-up Portnoy talking to his doctor – thinks that his tremendous activity in this sphere stemmed partly from resentment at continuous parental presence in every other. 'My wang was all I really had that I could call my own' – I recognize that too. I only wish Mr Roth had shown us Portnoy senior lecturing his son on the dangers of this dreadful habit; was it insanity or softening of the bones, I wonder, that led the field?

Then Portnoy has girls. What he does with and to them is likewise gone into in depth, as he might say. Some of this is all right, and far from unbelievable. But, since reading is a sort of social experience, in the sense that it is like having somebody talk to you, some of it is embarrassing, and Portnoy's straight-to-audience, tape-recording, person-to-person style of address intensifies the embarrassment. I do not want to be told what I would not myself tell another person without feeling I was showing off – not about my sexual, but my social uninhibitedness, my 'frankness', my feeling of 'what the hell, fellas, these things go on, so let's talk about them, huh?' I particularly do not want to be told it when the speaker's mouth is, as it were, ten inches from my ear. But this is a large subject.

Portnoy's chief girl is called The Monkey, a *shikse*, of course, beautiful and depraved. We hear comparatively little of what they do outside the bedroom, or off the well-worn path to the bedroom, or when not talking about one or the other. Once, for a page or so, she assumes some sort of identity, when she gives him an eloquent denunciation for treating her like a hopeless nincompoop, but at the foot of the next page she is obliging him on a bench in a public park, and on the next, though we do not realize it at the time, she is being quietly dropped from the story. There have been hints earlier that the key to her attraction for Portnoy is that she is so much the wrong kind of girl – sexy, undomesticated, above all non-Jewish – for his parents and for the rabbi (a character we hear all too little of), but, again, these lead nowhere. The Monkey, sadly, never confronts Momma, and in retrospect this bit looks like nothing much more than a perfunctory attempt to impose a little unity on diverse material.

The last sixty pages of the book consist virtually of appendices, though they are not called so – odd scraps that would not go in earlier: accounts of a couple of other *shikses* (both well described), of the moments in Portnoy's childhood when he positively looked forward to becoming an adult Jew, of a trip to Israel plus a sexual fiasco with a female lieutenant in the Jewish army. By this time Mr Roth has abandoned his attempt to persuade us that we are reading anything but a series of sketches whose only real congruity is the fact that the events and people in them could all have fallen within the experience of the same person, or alternatively that they could all, without much implausibility, be incorporated into the Portnoy monologue, neither of which requirements excludes very much.

For most of the book, Mr Roth works quite hard to paper over the cracks between one sketch and another, splitting them up against the run of the chapter headings, holding over material that properly belongs to one sketch and planking it down in the middle of another, and the distinctiveness of Portnoy's tone of voice is a help. But the warning sign is there right at the beginning, on the back of the title page: 'Sections of this book have appeared in slightly different form in ...' several periodicals. The magazine, especially the serious, 'prestigious' magazine, as these are, is the enemy of the novel. I think that we in England are lucky to have no counterparts of our own, no temptations, or arrangements, to send in whatever we are working on as soon as it gets to thirty or forty pages. This must be one of the reasons why the short story, or the disguised short story, has tended to remain the basic fictional form in the United States.

Whatever the relevance of all that, *Portnoy's Complaint* is not a narrative, not simply in that it is incoherent, but in that the commentary swamps, erodes, and drowns out character and incident. As well as being written in the first person, it is written to and for the first

107

person, by, with, and from the first person. (A perennial trap in auto-biographical fiction, as the classic *Way of All Flesh* shows.) Mr Roth's unconcern to narrate is connected with his unconcern to invent – I may be wrong about this; perhaps everything here has been made up out of his own head; but I do not think so. A writer of fiction is doing well if, as often as once in his career, something turns up in his experience which can, without too much alteration, be transcribed in the form of a short story, let alone a novel. But in our time, perhaps with D. H. Lawrence as the first influential example, it has become all right to supplement the deficiencies of one's personal life as source material, not by rearranging it, editing it, extrapolating from it, but merely by coating it with style and tone of voice. Could we have a modest return, or advance, to fiction as fiction?

1969

'It is only in books that one finds the brilliant amateur detective X; real policemen are obstinate and hardheaded, are slow and literal-minded, are frequently mean and nearly always narrow: they have to be. They are part of the administrative machine, a tool of government control . . .'

So reflects Van der Valk, Nicolas Freeling's Amsterdam inspector, on his way to try to stop a beautiful female aristocrat and ex-ski champion from ambushing a Dutch businessman with a hunting rifle on a lonely road in southern France. With this adventure, *The King of the Rainy Country*, Van der Valk confirms his status as one of the most promising arrivals on the post-war crime-fiction scene*. In his account of real policemen he is actually a little hard on himself. Obstinate and slow he may be, but these are only rude names for the Netherlander's inbred conscientiousness. As for literal-minded, he is given to reflecting self-accusingly that he is too much of a northerner, with his veins full of Ibsen, and is able without difficulty to work out the motivation of a suicide by pondering over the poem of Baudelaire's alluded to in the title. Besides all this, he is intelligent, thoughtful and

* An over-euphoric remark, made in the hope the book engendered that Van der Valk had finally broken out of the stolid, concentratedly Dutch environment that in previous novels had seemed to slow him and his exploits down. Alas, he was right back in it in *Strike Out Where Not Applicable*, published the following year (1967).

good-natured – the last of these by no means a standard characteristic of fictional sleuths. (Even Sherlock Holmes has been known to come back at Watson with a quick impatient snarl or so, when the chase is really on.) Van der Valk is an impressive man interestingly rendered. His only shortcoming as a hero, the only thing that robs him of the almost mythical and mystical glamour of a Holmes or a Nero Wolfe, is that he, unlike them, is very much a real policeman.

The point is even clearer with Simenon's celebrated Inspector Maigret. In *My Friend Maigret*, the inspector takes along a Scotland Yard detective called Pyke to investigate a murder on a French island. Pyke – incidentally, an amusing and sympathetic portrayal – is supposed to be studying French police methods. At the end of the book it is suggested that Pyke, apart from having thrown down a good deal of the local wine, has been wasting his time, because there just are no such methods. None, that is, but the universal ones of interrogation of witnesses, suspects, neighbours and the like, thumbing through records and dossiers, consulting London, Ostend, Zurich and the like, and more interrogation. None of those brilliant intuitions, those miraculous leaps in the dark, those questions about what seem to be insanely irrelevant matters, that are so firmly in the middle of the great detective tradition inaugurated by Poe's Auguste Dupin. And Maigret himself, apart from taking an occasional *calvados* too many, has virtually no characteristics beyond those required to solve his cases. We know all too well that he will never in a million years start playing the violin or suddenly insist on cultivating orchids. That sort of thing is the prerogative of the unreal policeman, or rather the unreal nonpoliceman: Van der Valk's brilliant amateur detective X, who exists only in books. All the sleuths we remember and reverence and take into our private pantheon of heroes are figures not of realism but of fantasy, great talkers, great eccentrics, men who use inspiration instead of hard work, men to whom Venetian old masters mean more than police files and a good bottle of Burgundy more than fingerprints. (Scope here for a scholarly footnote on the parallel with spy fiction: James Bond will still be around long after all the spies who came in from the cold, Ipcress-file-mongers and similar 'real' secret agents have been forgotten.)

Half-way between the policeman and the amateur comes the private investigator of whom Dashiel Hammett's Sam Spade and Raymond

Chandler's Philip Marlowe are typical, plus, in a rather different way, Mickey Spillane's Mike Hammer. Theirs is a fantasy world all right, that of the toughie whose sacred objects are the gun, the boot, the bottle of rye and (less so in Chandler than in the others) the male organ. It has often been objected against the tough school that their values are lopsided or non-existent, that in regard to ethics, and pretty well everything else, the police and the D.A.'s men are no better than the crooks or the Commies and the private eye is at least as bad as all the others. This loss of moral focusing is felt to be unedifying, even dangerous. Maybe. My own view is that the immoral or amoral hero of this type is bound to forfeit some of the reader's esteem and, along with it, some of his desire to identify with the hero. The story thus goes rather cold. In crime or spy fantasies the interest is partly a fairy-tale one, good versus bad in a rather basic way; James Bond would not mean so much to us if we were unable to feel that he was on the right side and that his cause was just. The toughies have no decent cause. Self-interest is all.

This would probably matter less than it does if these writers wrote better. Spillane is the best of the three cited – an unpopular view, which I would defend hotly. Legitimate shock and horror at the beast-liness of Hammer's universe should not be allowed to weigh against the technical brilliance with which the whole thing is stage-managed. Few novelists on any level can match Spillane's skill in getting his essential facts across palatably and without interrupting the action, in knowing what to leave out; and the impression received that the nar-rative is just tumbling out of the corner of Hammer's mouth at two hundred words a minute is a tribute to real professional competence. With all this granted, what makes the stories finally stultifying is Hammer's total facelessness, or mindlessness. He is a mere network of gristle connecting mouth, fist, trigger finger and penis. A hero needs more substance than that.

Sam Spade perhaps has a little more. *The Maltese Falcon*, in the period just after its publication (1930), was certainly taken as having opened up an undiscovered area in popular fiction. No doubt the re-moval of conventional ethics caught the taste of a public who, in mid-Depression, must have been more than ready to believe that almost any cynical view of the world was likely to approximate to the way things really were, and did not care to notice the story's manifold improbabilities. Looking back now, it seems hard to understand what the fuss was about. Spade, the blond Satan with the yellow-grey eyes, grinning wolfishly on every other page and making growling animal noises in his throat nearly as often, the most committed cigarette smoker before our friend 007, turns out to be faintly funny. Where Hammett presents Spade's toughness as real and probable, as the way things are did we but know it, the result is unbelievable; where the toughness is offered as exceptionally cool, exceptionally tough, it just seems corny. And both sorts come down much of the time to mere rudeness and bad temper. All of it is ladled out in low-budget-TV-show dialogue. The gloss and the glow, if they were ever there, have been rubbed out by time.

Raymond Chandler was undoubtedly the most ambitious writer of the tough-thriller school, and for some time was, in England at any rate still is, a toast of the intellectuals. W. H. Auden went on record with the view that: 'Chandler's powerful books should be read and judged not as escape literature but as works of art.' This advice strikes me as hazardous in the extreme. The books have undoubtedly worn less badly than Hammett's, having had for one thing less time to do so, since they belong roughly to the period 1930–59. Philip Marlowe is an improvement on Spade. Some of Marlowe's toughness does boil down to meanness, unreticent dislike of the rich and indeed of most other groups and individuals, rudeness to servants and to women. On the other hand, there are some things he will not do, he will protect his clients under great pressure, he can show compunction and even sensitivity. What disfigures him is, again, the way he is presented by his creator. The tough catch phrases – 'don't kid me, son'; 'quit stalling'; 'on your way, brother' – died with, or before, Bogart. There is also a moral pretentiousness whereby Marlowe is now and again made the vehicle for criticizing the sordid lives of Hollywood's denizens: the perverted producers, the writers drowning in bourbon and self-hatred, the chicks who will do absolutely anything to get a part – all that. Most of this comes ill from a private eye, even a comparatively honest one. Bits of stylistic pretentiousness underline the effect. *The Big Sleep* has bubbles rising in a glass of liquor 'like false hopes' and, after an intermission of four words, a girl's breath being 'as delicate as the eyes of a fawn'. Is this our tough Chandler (let alone a work of art), or has some heart-throbbing female dream-purveyor grabbed the pen?

Perry Mason provides a convenient stopover point. There would be a lot to be said for not noticing him at all, if it were not for the hideous frequency of his appearances in print and on television. I am afraid there can be very few people in our culture who would not know that, although Mason is not in the strict sense a detective, is a mere lawyer employing the Drake Detective Agency to do his legwork for him, he does investigate crimes, ending up ten times out of ten by winning one of those objection-overruled – objection-sustained rituals in concert with the D.A. and the judge. The TV films faithfully reflect the Erle Stanley Gardner novels in their portrayal of the inevitable three-stage progress from seeing-the-client through seeing-the-witness to going-to-court, with an expected unexpected revelation at the end. Mason has an impressive claim to being considered the most boring foe of criminality in our time, which is saying something if we make the effort to remember such cobwebbed figures as Inspector French (in the works of Freeman Wills Crofts) or Philo Vance (S. S. Van Dine). The nullity of Mason is nowhere better displayed than in his relations, or lack of any, with his assistant – I cannot bring myself to say girl Friday – Della Street. Della Street, whose name appears in full every time Gardner mentions her, answers the telephone and listens to Mason telling her that the law is not a rat race unless you run with the rats. Oh, and sometimes she worries because Mason looks so tired. Nothing more; whereas the vital role of the assistant in detective fiction is to encourage and provoke the great man to reveal his modern inner nature, as we shall see.

I hope we shall see much more than that. The sleuths put up to question so far have admittedly been treated in a rather carping or, as we British say, 'knocking' spirit. My admiration is reserved for the detective who detects, whose claim to fame is his mind rather than his way with a girl or a jury. Heroes of this type show a strong family resemblance. Such a man will show some physical impressiveness, along the lines of Holmes's tall lean figure and piercing eyes, or Wolfe's vast poundage: 285 of them. If unimpressive, he will be spectacularly unimpressive, small and with an egg-shaped head like Poirot; small, round-faced and bespectacled like Father Brown. He is unmarried, or at least his wife is kept firmly off stage. A crucial point, this. Holmes hit the nail on the head for his group when he declared that he would never marry, lest he biased his judgement. But let Dr Watson spell the point out:

*All emotions, and that one [i.e., love] particularly, were abhorrent
to his cold, precise, but admirably balanced mind. He was, I take it,
the most perfect reasoning and observing machine that the world
has seen . . . He never spoke of the softer passions, save with a gibe
and a sneer . . . For the trained observer to admit such intrusions
into his own delicate and finely adjusted temperament was to introduce a distracting factor which might throw a doubt upon all his
mental results . . .**

And no doubts must be thrown on any of those mental results. Quite
right. But what are we to make of this avoidance of the fair sex, which
in Wolfe's case rises, or sinks, to panic at the mere prospect of being
alone with a woman? Could there be something a bit . . . you know
. . .? Let us take a look at a famous incident in 'The Three Garridebs',
wherein John Garrideb, alias Killer Evans, shoots Watson in the thigh.
Holmes promptly disposes of Evans, and then . . .

'. . . my friend's wiry arms were round me, and he was leading me to
a chair.

' "You're not hurt, Watson? For God's sake, say that you are not
hurt!"

'It was worth a wound – it was worth many wounds – to know the
depth of loyalty and love which lay behind that cold mask. The clear,
hard eyes were dimmed for a moment, and the firm lips were shaking.
For the one and only time I caught a glimpse of a great heart as well as
of a great brain. All my years of humble but single-minded service
culminated in that moment of revelation.

' "It's nothing, Holmes. It's a mere scratch." '

Is it without significance that, whereas the moment of revelation is
dated by Watson in 1902, his account of it was held back from book
publication until the more tolerant days of twenty-five years later?
Answer: Yes. Utterly. Though it might be more fun to believe the
opposite, Holmes is no fag. His lack of interest in women, made a
positive characteristic to aid in the building up of his character, can be
accounted for in at least two innocent ways. Just as the true Western
fans in the moviehouse sigh and groan when Destry stops shooting and
starts loving – and a large part of our feelings about Holmes are on
this sort of level – so we should feel cheated and affronted if the great

* 'A Scandal in Bohemia.'

brain left Watson to get after the Man with the Twisted Lip for a spell and himself started taking Miss Violet de Merville off Baron Adelbert Gruner. Further, although Holmes would not have been difficult to turn into a lover, any adventure featuring him as such could not be a detective story but, as experience of other writers shows, some kind of thriller or pursuit story or psychological melodrama. The magnifying lens and the dozen red roses belong to different worlds.

Holmes is the memorable figure he is because Conan Doyle grasped the essential truth that the deductive solving of crimes cannot in itself throw much light on the character doing the solving, and therefore that that character must be loaded up with quirks, hobbies, eccentricities. It is always these irrelevant qualities that define the figure of the great detective, not his mere powers of reasoning. One thinks of Lord Peter Wimsey's collections of Sèvres vases and early editions of Dante (including the Aldine 8vo of 1502 and the Naples folio of 1477), Poirot's dandified clothes and tiny Russian cigarettes, Dupin's expertise about paving-stones, grasses, astronomy, fungi and probably much more.

In Holmes's opinion, Dupin was 'a very inferior fellow. That trick of his of breaking in on his friends' thoughts with an apropos remark after a quarter of an hour's silence is really very showy and superficial'. I agree. Apart from his irritating mannerisms, all three of Dupin's cases are very shaky. He could never have got ahead of the police in 'The Murders in the Rue Morgue' without their incredible ignorance; his deductions in 'The Mystery of Marie Rogêt' are at least highly dubious at several key points; and in 'The Purloined Letter' he not only again had stupid police to help him out but also a dementedly foolhardy criminal. However, something deeper than professional contempt or jealousy was at work to give Holmes so jaundiced a view of his – rightly or wrongly – famous French predecessor. Holmes was quite intelligent enough to see that Dupin was his predecessor in much more than just the chronological sense.

There are plenty of comparatively minor resemblances between the two detectives: the pipe-smoking, the love of long pedantic monologues (plus, in each case, the presence of a devoted associate who knows just what to break in with or at least stays awake), the hatred of company and intrusions on privacy. Holmes, we are told, 'loathed every form of society with his whole Bohemian soul'; Dupin went so far as to solve the Rogêt case without leaving his armchair, recalling to us a more recent and much fatter detective who makes a point of operating in the same way. More important among Dupin-Holmes resemblances is the possession of vast and variegated learning. Holmes improves on Dupin's astronomy and mycology to the extent of being able to hold forth, in the course of one dinner, about miracle plays, medieval pottery, Stradivarius violins and the Buddhism of Ceylon. As regards the modern world he is frighteningly well informed. It seems that he has always card-indexed the whole of each day's press, 'docketing all paragraphs concerning men and things', a testing task unassisted even for Holmes, 'so that it was difficult to name a subject or a person on which he could not at once furnish information'. Obviously. An occasional pebble from this vast mountain of lore is of course immediately applicable to the case in hand. Just as stuff about grasses and fungi helped Dupin with Marie Rogêt, so Holmes would benefit from the research that went into that unforgettable monograph on the varieties of tobacco ash. But the real point of all this knowledge is much less what you do with it than the simple and memorable fact that you have it.

Knock Dupin as one may, his final and vital legacy to Holmes was what created the detective story as we have known it. However suspect Dupin's chains of inference may be at any particular link, what we are witnessing overall is a convinced demonstration of the power of the human mind to observe and to reason. This is what Holmes is constantly up to. He may, as the story unfolds, deny the reader vital clues and information – or Watson will do it for him, giving him the opportunity, in one of the two stories he narrates himself, to sneer at Watson's habit of contriving 'meretricious finales' by the use of this kind of suppression. A bit hard on poor Watson, this, considering he could only put in as much as Holmes would tell him. Anyway: Holmes may also irk us, or give us the wrong kind of laugh, by overdoing the demonstration, as when he discovers everything that happened at the scene of a fairly complicated crime by working on the footmarks with his lens, or by deducing seventeen separate facts, eleven of them non-physical, about a man by examining his hat, one of the eleven being that his wife has ceased to love him. (Not all that difficult when you know how: the hat had not been brushed for a long time, and its age would have shown the man was too poor to afford a servant.) But many of the imaginative leaps are valid and thrilling: for instance, the moment when Holmes decides why an elderly pawnbroker has been induced to join a league of red-haired men after a glance at the trouser legs of the old boy's assistant. 'Holmes, this is marvellous!' Watson is supposed to cry when this sort of thing happens, though my recollection is that he never quite does. But he would have been right. It is marvellous.

The deductive prodigies are strongly supported by Doyle's gifts for suspense, horror and action writing, all carried forward on an unfailing flow of ingenious ideas. Holmes founded a dynasty. One of its more unexpected recent members is the Martian detective Syalok, a birdlike creature who wears a *tirstokr* hat, smokes a pipe in which the tobacco is cut with permanganate of potash, and in Poul Anderson's story 'The Martian Crown Jewels' recovers the theft of these diadems by a strict application of Holmesian principles – rather stricter, in fact, than the master often used himself. But Holmes has, in one sense, been even further afield than Mars. His exploits have been the subject of fierce controversy in Russia. I am indebted to G. F. McCleary for the information that some years ago the stories were issued there on a large scale, and that the librarians of the Red Army recommended Holmes to the troops as 'the exterminator of crimes and evils, a model of magnificent strength of thought and great culture'. This, McCleary continues, went down badly with a writer in the newspaper *Vechernaya Moskva*, who thought the tales offended socialist ideology by 'poisoning the minds of readers with false morals concerning the strength of the foundations of private property, and diverting attention from the social contradictions of capitalist reality'. Even Holmes himself might not have been able to deduce that much from the facts.

With few but shining exceptions, the heirs of Sherlock Holmes are an undistinguished lot. Lord Peter Wimsey has never quite survived, in my mind at least, the initial impression given by his righty-ho, dear-old-thing, don't-you-know, chin-chin style of dialogue and his mauve dressing-gown, primrose silk pyjamas, monocle and the rest of the outfit. Here I should in fairness make it plain that Wimsey is no more of a fag than Holmes is: he merely looks and sounds like one, as a certain kind of English aristocrat does to virtually all American, and the vast majority of British, eyes and ears. As for Wimsey, one might also plead that the bally-fool persona is, at least in part, put on to fool criminals. But what lies beneath the mask, if it is a mask, is hardly more attractive, and certainly less vivid. Lord Peter is just an old connoisseur and clubman who gets asked along to help out uppercrust families or trips over a stray corpse. In his later career the deductive faculty in him ran thin and he would fall back more on luck. He certainly got it, having once happened, for example, to have deposited a bag at a luggage counter where another bag that happened to be the twin of the first one happened also to have been deposited. The second bag happened to have somebody's head in it. In other adventures he got tied up with a ghastly female egghead, thus establishing to some extent his heterosexual bona fides, but at the same time forgetting about crime and talking to the female egghead instead, clear evidence for my rule that love and detection do not mix. Even in his heyday he often seemed to differ from the other people in the story by being merely slow on the uptake while they were moronic or crazed.

Hercule Poirot, Miss Marple, Ellery Queen, Inspector – later Assistant Commissioner Sir John – Appleby deserve, or at any rate will get, shorter shrift from me. I have never understood the fame of the two Agatha Christie characters, both of whom seem straight out of stock – Poirot the excitable but shrewd little foreigner, Marple the innocent, helpless-looking old lady with the keen blue eyes. And although some of the early Christies (*Why Didn't They Ask Evans?* for instance) had splendidly ingenious plots, the later Poirots and Marples have become thinned down, not surprisingly in a writer who has been hard at work for forty-five years. Queen, who has been around just since 1929, has had his ingenuities, too, but he is too slight a figure to sustain more than a tiny corner of Holmes's mantle, acting mostly as a sounding-board for the other characters, a camera for the story, and a mouthpiece when the author wants to chat things over with the reader. Ellery of the silver-coloured eyes is seldom much more than an extension of the plot.

To label as a similar plot device so distinguished a personage as Michael Innes's Appleby may look a little rough, but here I am doing it, and if Appleby could know, he would do no more than shrug his well-tailored shoulders, murmur a quotation from Donne or Hardy and perhaps reach for another modest measure of that liqueur brandy of his that surpasses anything in the Duke of Horton's cellar. Appleby has become an establishment figure, moving in a world that would be anathema to Holmes's Bohemian soul. The Appleby method of detection is to sit back and wait for the unconscious to come up with a solution, though the sitting back is purely mental: there can be plenty of physical rushing about in pursuit of stolen masterpieces, errant scientists with lethal secrets and such. Appleby is mostly the man to whom it all happens; most of it could happen to anybody, or nobody. The opposite is true of the novels of Edmund Crispin, who yet owes something to Innes. Crispin's detective, Gervase Fen, is an Oxford don, an eccentric after the fashion of Holmes or Wimsey, but funnier and in one sense grander than they, in that he seems to create his own kind of adventure. Nobody but Fen could find himself in a room whose occupant had unconsciously re-created the setting of Poe's 'The Raven', or in a situation to which the only clue depends on an intimate knowledge of Edward Lear's limericks. There is ingenuity here, too, including a non-electronic method of eavesdropping on a conversation out of earshot of the eavesdropper.

So far I have tried to anatomize six American and five British detectives, plus a few doubtful cases emanating from the general northwestern European area. This seems fair treatment of an Anglo-American literary form that has always had connections with France and thereabouts. Despite these connections, which go back at least as far as 1828, when the real-life detective François Eugène Vidocq began publishing his famous *Mémoires*, the detective story has flourished typically in the English language. A. E. Murch suggests in his detailed and fascinating work, *The Development of the Detective Novel*, that the law in France among other places is set up in such a way that the public tends to regard the police with some fear and suspicion, at any rate without the instinctive feelings of support common to Americans and British, who thus find it easy and natural to sympathize with a hero working on the side of the police. Possibly. But then all kinds of genre writing, offshoots from the main stem of literature, are largely confined to English: not just the Western novel, but science fiction, the ghost story, to some extent the cloak-and-dagger thriller. Something vague and basic to do with the language? Decide for yourself.

The three great successors of Sherlock Holmes are G. K. Chesterton's Father Brown, Rex Stout's Nero Wolfe and John Dickson Carr's Doctor Fell. The first is British, the second American, the third British again but written about by an American, and so neatly preserving the balance.

Father Brown is not an eccentric in the superficial, violin-playing or orchid-rearing sense. But he is extraordinary enough, more so today than when Chesterton was writing, for Brown's extraordinariness is founded in his religion. Whether we like it or not, the little man's devotion, total courage, human insight and unshakable belief in reason are at any rate statistically uncommon. Some readers have found too much Roman Catholic propaganda in the stories. I feel that the Christian element, which is sometimes built into the plot, is never narrowly sectarian, and that part of it which overlaps with the advocacy of sheer common sense ought to be acceptable to everybody. It would be truer to say that what propaganda there is gets directed against atheism, complacent rationalism, occultism and superstition, all those shabby growths which the decline of Christian belief has fostered, and many, though perhaps not most, readers will sympathize here, too. My only real complaint is that this bias sometimes reveals the villain too early. We know at once that the prophet of a new sun cult is up to no good, and are not surprised that it is he who allows a blind girl to step to her death in an empty lift shaft.

Like Gervase Fen, though on a more serious level, Brown is made for the situations he encounters and they for him. They embody his love of paradox and of turning things back to front, his gift for seeing what is too obvious for everyone else to notice, his eye for the mentally invisible man. Only Brown could have wandered into a house where the recently dead owner's diamonds lay in full view minus their settings, heaps of snuff were piled on shelves, candles littered the tables, and the name of God had been carefully cut out of the family Bible every single time it occurred. And when the owner is dug up and found to be minus his head, only Brown would have taken this as natural and inevitable, the final clue showing that no crime had been committed after all. (You will have to read 'The Honour of Israel Gow' in *The Innocence of Father Brown* to find the answer.)

Rather too often, Brown runs into impersonations, twin brothers, secret passages, unlikely methods of murder: it would take a lot of good luck to succeed first try in dropping a noose round someone's neck from a dozen feet above him, and again to hit your man on the head with a hammer thrown from a church tower. But the good ideas are many and marvellous. The howling dog that gave away a murderer, the trail to an arch crook that began with somebody (guess who) swapping the contents of the sugar and salt containers in a restaurant, the man who seemed to have got into a garden without using the only entrance and the other man who got out of the same garden partly, but not completely – these are pretty standard occurrences in Father Brown's world. That world is vividly atmospheric, thanks to Chesterton's wonderful gift for depicting the effects of light on landscape, so that the stories glow as well as tease and mystify. They are works of art.

It is a goodish step from here to the old brownstone on West 35th Street where Nero Wolfe and Archie Goodwin chew the fat, eat their heads off, infuriate Inspector Cramer and incidentally catch crooks. The weakness of Stout's hugely readable stories is always the story. The idea of splitting the conventional detective into two – Wolfe to do the thinking, Archie the legwork – cuts both ways. It gives great scope for rounding out Wolfe's character, but it inevitably diminishes Archie in proportion. I find Archie faintly unsympathetic anyhow, a bit too effortlessly attractive to women, a bit too free with his fists, a bit too reminiscent of Sam Spade. Certainly, when he goes ferreting for Wolfe at Cramer's headquarters, or Lon Cohen's *Gazette* office, or wherever the crime may have taken place, the interest slackens. We want to be back with Wolfe. I can seldom be bothered with the details of the investigation, which usually proceeds by revelation and discovery rather than by actual deduction. What counts for most readers, I am sure, is the snappy dialogue, Archie's equally snappy narrative style, his relations with Wolfe (he is always sympathetic here), and finally, massively, triumphantly, Wolfe himself.

Wolfe gets about as far as a human being can, much further than Sherlock Holmes, in his suspicion, fear, almost hatred of humanity. We all have such moods, and Wolfe is there to reassure us that these feelings are quite proper for an intelligent, learned, humane and humorous man. This is perhaps the secret of his attraction, for attractive he abundantly is. Along with this goes a marked formidable quality, such that one would, on meeting Wolfe in the flesh, feel grateful for his approval and daunted by his contempt. All really great detectives inspire this reaction, perhaps by acting as some version of a father figure. Brown does it to us, Dr Fell does; even, granted the shift in general outlook since late-Victorian times, Holmes does. Any kind of real policeman does not, and anybody Mike Hammer took a liking to ought to feel a twinge of alarm.

Another part of Wolfe's appeal is his addiction to views and attitudes that seem both outdated and sensible, reactionary and right, the sort of thing you and I ought to think and feel, and probably would if we had Wolfe's leisure and obstinacy. Who has not wanted to insist on never going out, living to an unshakable routine, distrusting all machines more complicated than a wheelbarrow and having to be heavily pressured each time before getting into a car, allowing hardly anybody to use one's first name, keeping television out and reading all the time, reacting so little in conversation that an eighth-of-an-inch shake of the head becomes a frenzy of negation, using an inflexible formal courtesy such that proven murderers are still referred to as 'Mr' and an eighteenth-century style of speech that throws off stuff like: 'Afraid? I can dodge folly without backing into fear' and: 'Madam, I am neither a thaumaturge nor a dunce'? Wolfe is every man's Tory, a contemporary Dr Johnson. The original Dr Johnson was a moralist before everything else, and so at heart is Wolfe. This, I suppose, makes him even more of an antique.

Lastly, Dr Gideon Fell. I must explain at once that, when writing under his pseudonym of Carter Dickson, John Dickson Carr uses a detective called Sir Henry Merrivale, or H. M., who according to me is an old bore. His adventures, however, are as fascinating as any of Fell's, and I should not want to put anybody off masterpieces like *The White Priory Murders*, *The Reader Is Warned* and *The Ten Teacups*. They are, of course, as are the best Carr novels, minor masterpieces. Perhaps no detective story can attain the pitch of literary excellence. Perhaps it can only offer ingenuity raised to the point of genius. In Carr-cum-Dickson it does, perhaps two dozen times in all, and this author is a first-rate artist. A neglected one, naturally, and likely to remain so while detective fiction remains undervalued, while most of those who should know better remain ignorant of the heights of craftsmanship and virtuosity it can reach. I will offer a small prize to any such person who can read the first chapter of Carr's *The Burning Court* and not in honesty have to go on. Neither Fell nor H. M. nor any great detective features here, only an adequate one. The book is a tour-de-force blending of detection and witchcraft: both ingredients genuine.

To return at length to Dr Fell – it would have been useful in one way to come to him straight after Father Brown. The character of Fell has little to do with that of Brown, but a great deal, especially physically, with Chesterton himself. The huge girth, the bandit's moustache, the box-pleated cape and shovel hat, the enthusiasm for English pubs, beer and roast beef, all these are taken straight from that brilliant and inventive but so often unsatisfactory writer. And more than this, Fell's world is that of Brown made more probable, the wilder flights of fancy brought under control, the holes in the plot conscientiously plastered over and made good. Like Brown, Fell constantly encounters the impossible murder, but Fell shows its possibility more convincingly. Most often, almost always, the victim is discovered in a locked room, last seen in good health, exits and entrances secured or watched or even guarded by responsible and provenly innocent outsiders. Carr boasts that he has devised over eighty different solutions to the locked-room puzzle, and in one of the novels Fell, a monologist with the best of them, delivers a fascinating lecture on the subject. This is *The Three Coffins*, to quote the inexcusable American retitling of the British edition *The Hollow Man*, which perfectly suggests the macabre menace of the story. That man must indeed have been hollow who, watched of course by a responsible and innocent witness, was seen to enter a room without other access in which, later, there is found the corpse of the room's occupant, but of course no hollow man. This is Chestertonian, or Brownian, though its explanation has a Carrian validity; and another novel, *The Crooked Hinge*, takes as the epigraph of its final section a quotation from a Father Brown story that begins: 'There was one thing which Flambeau, with all his dexterity of disguise, could not cover, and that was his singular height.' On finishing the novel one can see that its whole structure grew out of the implications of that sentence. In fact, an ideal reader would be able to solve the murder at that point without further assistance. The explanation is simple and entirely plausible, but you would just not happen to think of it: Chesterton out-Chestertoned.

The light in Gideon Fell's study is burning low. He still works desultorily at his great chronicle of *The Drinking Customs of England from the Earliest Days*, still gives great rumbling sniffs and plies his red bandanna handkerchief. But without conviction. He makes rare and comparatively ineffectual public appearances now. His heyday came to an end somewhere about 1950, and there died with it the classical detective story, in which all the clues were scrupulously put before the reader, the kind of writing of which Fell's creator has been the greatest exponent.

Elsewhere the picture is the same. Recruitment to the ranks of potential great detectives has fallen to nothing. Real policemen are all the rage. Fell always got on well with them, had no hesitation about saving himself trouble by using their findings, but though they were smart and often nearly right, he was smarter and always right. He would view the activities of contemporary real policemen like Van der Valk with tolerance, even appreciation, but he would have little time for the character who has usurped his place in the sun: the secret agent, the international spy. I can hear him muttering under his bandit's moustache about the sad substitution of brawn for brain as the up-to-date hero's essential characteristic, of action for thought and glamour for decency. I would only go part of the way with him there. But I can sympathize.

1966

Horror films have had me by the throat for over thirty-five years, beginning with the Boris Karloff versions of *Frankenstein* and *The Mummy*, and the Fredric March version of *Dr Jekyll and Mr Hyde*. Actually I never got to see more than the trailer of *Jekyll*, because my parents saw it too, and declared the Streatham Astoria out of bounds for the following week. It included an excellent view of what happened to March's face and neck when he had drunk the transforming potion, a much more horrifying and haunting effect than any of Karloff's galvanic awakenings or stumbling pursuits.

The major arts, including prime literary forms like poetry or the novel of society, can perhaps be validly approached out of pure, or mere, intellectual curiosity. The minor genres, such as science fiction, jazz, the Western, and the detective story, can (I think) only be deeply appreciated and properly understood by the addict, the bulk consumer who was drawn to the stuff in late childhood for reasons he could not have explained then and would have a lot of trouble explaining now. It seems widely agreed, for instance, that the essential qualification for any decent film critic is to have spent a disproportionate amount of his early life in cheap cinema seats, swallowing everything he saw in a completely uncritical way.

Such valuable persons rarely say anything about horror films. Never having acquired much of a taste for the effects or the actual contents of these fables, your average commentator will see the behaviour of

Dracula and his chums, not as cavortings both abominable and harm-less, but as symptoms of the sickness of our society and all that. Thus a prominent writer on stage and screen (and friend of the Viet Cong) once explained to me that *The Incredible Shrinking Man*, a Hollywood fantasy of ten years ago with science-fiction as well as horror ele-ments, was 'really about' the American male's terror of not being able to satisfy his wife. I had thought that, with the rather boring, but necessary, difficulties of the four-foot-high hero out of the way, the picture settled down to being 'about' things like the six-inch-high hero's encounter with the household cat, or the one-centimetre-high hero's resourceful and daring battle with the spider in the cellar. But I am a bit of an addict.

It still goes on. Only the other week, Francis Hope discussed horror in the *New Statesman*, concluding, perhaps a tiny bit predictably, that the appetite for it (horror, not the *New Statesman*) was 'diseased' and to do with our society being very violent and very dull, with Vietnam and too much telly. This is an example of – among other things – that historical provincialism whereby so many of even our more literate contemporaries take Hiroshima as the year one. Have a look at this – quoted, with a lot more fascinating material, in E. S. Turner's *Boys Will be Boys*:

> ... *Shriek followed shriek in rapid succession. The bed clothes fell in a heap by the side of the bed – she was dragged by her long silken hair completely on to it again. Her beautiful rounded limbs quivered with the agony of her soul. The glassy horrible eyes of the figure ran over the angelic form with a hideous satisfaction – hor-rible profanation. He drags her head to the bed's edge. He forces it back by the long hair still entwined in his grasp. With a plunge he seizes her neck in his fang-like teeth – a gush of blood and a sucking noise follows. The girl has swooned and the vampire is at his hideous repast!**

The date is about 1850, nearly half a century before Bram Stoker published *Dracula*. Possibly the wars with the Sikhs in 1846–49, and/or too much church and chapel, had bred the taste for *Varney the Vampire* and his innumerable colleagues of that time. Or, more likely, the appetite for horror is a persistent but not very important strand in

* Italics in original.

the cultural weave of the last couple of centuries, no more connected with an appetite for real horror, real blood, than an interest in the Theatre of Cruelty or the bullfight. I think Hope might cheer himself up by reflecting that the modern cinema, which is now the main vehicle of horror in the present sense, takes nearly all its stories and settings from writers of the nineteenth century or just after: Poe, Stoker, Mary Shelley, Le Fanu, Stevenson, M. R. James (whose *Ghost Stories of an Antiquary,* an important influence, appeared in 1904), Gaston Leroux (*The Phantom of the Opera,* 1908).

Anyway, eggheads *out!* – not only out of critical commentating, which leaves unimpaired what we see on the screen, but out of directing and script-writing, which does not quite. The adult Western, like *Bad Day at Black Rock,* demonstrating its intellectual seriousness by short-changing us on action, has not made its mark. The psychological thriller, under Hitchcock, has done better, though it only really clicked when it abandoned the supposedly deep probing of *Spellbound* (the one with the Dali dream sequences) for the fairly straight and very enthusiastic Grand Guignol of *Psycho*: and even here the conscientious clinical lecture at the end was an unreadable footnote.*

Today, horror itself is not safe, when Jonathan Miller can 'adapt' James's splendidly horrific 'Oh, Whistle and I'll come to You, My Lad' for television, knock out the horror along with three words of the title, substitute a revue-level character-sketch portentously photographed, in *Marienbad* style, against an unmeaning background, and earn a whole column – not altogether laudatory, it is true, but still disgracefully respectful – in Hope's *Statesman* article. Next spring, Miller might care to give us an adaptation of *Frankenstein* as the case-history of someone who had been forbidden to play with his little sister's dolls, and whose monster, of course, never does more than twitch occasionally.

But, for a moment, back to James. I was probably exaggerating just now when I called his work importantly influential, and certainly others than Miller have failed to get it satisfactorily on to the screen: the only full-length James film I know of, *The Night of the Demon* (1957; from 'Casting the Runes'), was a pretty mixed affair, with a

---

* I am told that this scene did not occur in Hitchcock's original script and was shot and inserted on the instructions of the 'front office'.

very silly and rickety actual demon lurching down the fatal railway line in the closing moments. Nevertheless, some of the best horror episodes of all – the ventriloquist's-dummy sequence in *Dead of Night* (1945), for example – are very close to James. And it is as if he passed on intact his formula for the creation of these evil beings: they are malignant as well as frightening, physically solid and formidable (no nonsense about mere spiritual hauntings), and, very often, subject to certain rules and limitations.

To define the horror film more closely, even if only to enlighten those who have never been to the cinema, I might attempt an exhaustive list of the permitted varieties of fiend and kobold. In addition to those already mentioned, one would have to include witches, were-wolves, zombies and other members of the voodoo circus, agents called up by black magicians, re-animated corpses of several sorts, and somnambulists – as in what may well still be the best of all these extravaganzas, *The Cabinet of Dr Caligari* (1919). Besides sharing an antique flavour, those catalogued are all *supernatural* beings. They may get switched on by somebody who calls himself a scientist, but it is always taken for granted that the science is not real. Frankenstein's bubbling retorts and arcing terminals are understood as nothing more than a colourful and enjoyable prelude to the main business of the evening, a monster waking up and very soon turning unfriendly. In other cases, the point is underlined by making the scientist a mad scientist. The merely antisocial or bloody rude scientist, as seen in *The Quatermass Experiment* (film version), or 'A for Andromeda' (TV serial), is a hero-figure of science fiction, in which the science, however perfunctory or absurd, is meant and taken to be real.

This distinction is so firm in practice that very few films stand anywhere on the borderline of the two genres. Apart from the adventures of the incredibly shrunken man, I recall chiefly *The Fly* (1958) and its successors. Here, the hastiest of mumbo-jumbo was run through with the palpable design of proceeding to the disagreeable activities and physical appearance of a fly with a chap's head and a chap with a fly's head – especially him. (Even science-fiction science surely ought to have balked at the idea of giving *both* these characters some kind of human intelligence.)

The Man with X-Ray Eyes (1963) is another such that I recall, not only with actual distaste but also with some embarrassment. I was one of the Highly Qualified International Jury that awarded it an award or an honorable mention or something at a great hoolee in Trieste in that year, the first International Exhibition of the Science-Fiction Film.* Now comes my opportunity to clear myself at the bar of world opinion by declaring that the picture won its laurels without the assistance of my vote. (My American colleague thought it was rubbish too, but the French and Italian majority went on about its relation to the contemporary consciousness, I believe it was.)

Well, *The Man* in question led off with 'scientific' mumbo-jumbo, went on with 'comic' stuff about the hero seeing through people's clothes (even those few years ago, what we saw of what he saw fought shy of the region between waist and knee), and fairly got into its stride with him seeing through practically everything, buildings, hills, the earth itself. This promising idea was wrecked by the garishness of the forms and patterns he saw instead, and quite shoved aside by a painful concentration on physical changes in his eyeballs, which went from golden to black to I don't know what. Finally, he encountered an evangelist who told him what to do if his eye offended him, and he did it. Both of them.

This was real horror, without the benefit of a Shakespeare to make such a thing partly tolerable. Effects as extreme as this are very rare indeed in the horror film proper, which relies much more on the expectation than on the actuality of what is dreadful. Nearly every monster, in the course of his wanderings, will at some stage encounter a child – a remarkably unobservant and foolhardy child in most cases. We think every time that he will rend him or her – usually her – limb from limb, but what he typically does is give an anguished moan and shamble off. We enjoy being terrified, not horrified, and, were it not for custom, 'terror film' would be a better label than 'horror film'.

* The best film of this sort showing in Trieste during the festival was *King Kong* (1933), which, dubbed in Italian, just happened to be on in the town that week. It was, of course, ineligible for the prize, which went (without the assistance of my vote) to a piece of avant-garde kitsch, the title of which I will not deign to mention. It consisted entirely of stills. One of the Frenchmen, the one who kept saying we lived in a science-fiction world these days, explained that this severe self-limitation was excitingly experimental. Like having your leg broken before running a mile, I wish I'd thought of saying.

Traditionally, the golden age of horror fell between the two wars, perhaps even in the earlier part of that period. I wonder what we should think of the highlights of Lugosi – Karloff – Chaney cinema if we could see them today: crude, incompetent and slow would be my guess. Horror from Hollywood boomed as the Second World War grew more intense (thank you, Francis Hope), though in quantity rather than quality. The Spencer Tracy version of *Dr Jekyll* was the best of these films that I remember, but some episodes in the British-made *Dead of Night* surpassed it. From 1945 or so until 1957 or so, science fiction reigned almost supreme in the general terror-horror-fantasy area. These years produced such masterpieces as *The War of the Worlds*, *Forbidden Planet*, and *Them!*,* and such non-masterpieces as *The Thing from Another World* (predictable-pretentious) and *The Creature from the Black Lagoon* (straightforward hokum). Then came the great horror revival, still happily in full flood.

The American contribution to this has concentrated to a remarkable degree on Vincent Price, as protagonist, whether receiving or dealing out assorted gory treatments, and on the works of Poe as source material. I have not seen all these efforts, but of those that I have, not much stays with me, apart from a very good nasty moment when the living corpse of Monsieur Valdemar improved on Poe by getting up off its bed and closing with some merely human malefactor. Price, though inclined to jump the gun by acting jittery a long way short of the graveyard gate, is at least adequate to these roles; the trouble lies with Poe, whose individual stories contain too little material for a full-length film and so have to be thickly padded out or, just as bad, combined. More simply, he was a terrible writer.

The British part in the renaissance has been ably headed by Hammer Films, in the first years a largely non-specialist organization, though with, among others, some respectable science-fiction films to

* Not (having seen it again on television recently) what I would now call a masterpiece, though highly respectable for its era (1954), perhaps any era. Science-fiction enthusiasts, while harder than most people on really bad films in the genre, do tend to be a bit soft on anything with a glimmer of merit. It is so exciting to see anything on the screen that even faintly recalls the glories of the written medium, that one tends to respond more to one's own paraphrase of each successive moment than to what actually happens.

their credit: the first two Quatermass stories – the third followed last year – and an oddly underrated chiller, *X – the Unknown*. (Seeing this in a double bill with *The Fiends* took days off my life.) Hammer have come to lean largely on two excellent actors, Peter Cushing, who tends to be Frankenstein, and Christopher Lee, who tends to be Dracula. Cushing conveys to perfection the fanatical devotion to 'science', plus the belated though energetic remorse, that suits a decent-minded re-animator of corpses; Lee, with great physical presence and skill in movement, makes the eccentric Count an accomplished man of the world when off duty, as well as a deadly wielder of the canines.

Cushing and Lee joined, or rather opposed, forces in the *Dracula* of 1957. This was a minor turning-point in cinema history and Hammer's first big commercial success; it pulled and still pulls in audiences in dozens of countries, reportedly outgrossing *My Fair Lady* in the Philippines, which says a lot for Filipino good taste. *Dracula* was an artistic success too, with expertly maintained tension and some fine sudden shocks, like the moment when one of the subordinate vampires gets the prescribed stake through the heart while inactive, and changes in a twinkling from beautiful young girl to horrible, very old woman. At the same (or a similar) juncture, blood spurted up over the executioner's hand. The critics put on a show of moral concern about this detail, I seem to remember, and now would be my chance to chew over the rights and wrongs of horror, whether it is good or bad or indifferent for you, etc., if boredom at the prospect did not utterly deter me. Let it be established, if it ever can, whether violence on the screen in general does harm, before we legislate about a genre so very far removed from the experience and environment of the audience.

To return, thankfully, to *Dracula*: now and again a kind of perverse poetry was attained, as when another young lady, during the period of her conversion, so to speak, by Dracula, awaits his arrival via the balcony, lying on her bed in no state of torpor, rather with erotic eagerness. And by the end, or the virtual end, with Dracula himself reduced to fluff and dust and finally nothing by the early rays of the sun, only his ring left lying on the pavement of the vast hall, achieved a curious desolate dignity. If only we could have had one or two of those splendid strokes from the novel! – the incidents aboard the ship that unknowingly brings Dracula to England in a box of his native earth, even more the sight of him descending the outer wall of his castle *head downwards.* Some danger of a laugh here but a marvellous thing to bring off.

Another time, perhaps.* There always is another time with that robust old Transylvanian blood-sucker. One might have thought him pretty thoroughly worsted at the end of *Dracula, Prince of Darkness* (1965), consigned until further notice to the bottom of an icebound moat. But Hammer are hard at work even now on his resuscitation. Despite the irresistibly funny dogmatic assertiveness of its title, *Dracula Has Risen from the Grave* promises to open sinisterly and even originally enough, with somebody falling through the ice on that moat and taking the trouble to cut his head open in the process, so that after a due interval a revitalizing snack reaches Dracula through the water.

It was on the set of this picture that, a few weeks ago, Sir Henry Floyd, Lord Lieutenant of the County of Buckinghamshire, presented the Queen's Award to Industry for 1968 to Colonel James Carreras, Managing Director of Hammer Films. One cannot help finding something bizarre in the idea of this ceremony. But perhaps one ought to try a bit harder not to. There is nothing very bizarre about an export contribution worth millions of dollars last year, unless its mere rarity makes it so. I cannot share the regret muttered when the announcement was made, at our earning money and renown abroad by purveying buckets of blood. Better that than earn either out of some imaginative reconstruction portraying, let us say, George VI financing Buchenwald out of Crown revenues.

Meanwhile, Hammer are marching on, firmly established enough by now to try a modest innovation or two. Their current offering, *The Devil Rides Out*, is (I think) the first feature film to be devoted exclusively to black magic and the combating thereof. I turned up to see this in more than one frame of mind, having been terrified out of my life at the age of fourteen by the Dennis Wheatley novel on which the film is based, doubtful at the same time whether any team could handle the various evil apparitions both convincingly and without vulgarity. I need not have worried on either count.

* The outstanding Thames Television production of *Dracula* (1968) made great and effective play with the early lunatic-asylum scenes and showed, among other things, how much more there is in the novel than has found its way into the horror-film tradition loosely associated with it.

Unexpectedly enough, the most frightening moment was also that at which technical skill was most apparent: the arrival of the Angel of Death at the edge of the magic circle inside which the anti-devil party is beleaguered. The rearings of the angel's great phosphorescent horse as it tried to cross the supernatural barrier passed out of the realm of horror into a sort of art, pointing forward to new possibilities. A shot of the angel's face jerked the clock back thirty years.

The rest of the picture was similarly up and down. The setting in the 1920s was appropriate and enjoyable, but more could have been found useful in it than a selection of its cars. These, however, looked and moved well, and were cleverly used as weapons in the spiritual battle – the yellow Rolls, headlamps casting deadly light on the forces of darkness, got the goat-devil off his woodland altar in short order. Earlier, the chief bad man had struck at a distance by suddenly fogging up the windscreen of a pursuing adversary. How this was done – what, that is, were the diabolical techniques used – I could not gather. Indeed, altogether too much on both sides was accomplished simply by frowning and glaring hard. Invisible forces, which had taken over the action by the end, are dull on the screen. And – a last niggle – apart from that of Christopher Lee, on the side of the powers of light here for once, the acting was poor, and some of the minor people were oddly unattractive, as if the cast had been made up hastily from the sociology department of one of our new universities.

What is the basis of the appeal of horror and the horror film? Like Mark Twain on a dissimilar occasion, I have an answer to that: I don't know. All the other answers I have come across are, to me, quite unreal, connecting neither with horrific material as I read and see it nor with my feelings as I do so. You may get some light on this – you will certainly get plenty of information and entertainment – from Carlos Clarens's illustrated survey, *Horror Movies* (Secker & Warburg), which saved me a good deal of checking-up time while preparing this article. Or you might care to look up Freud's paper on 'The Uncanny', and ponder on instantaneous wish-fulfilments and the power of the castration complex. And the best of Transylvanian luck to you.

1968

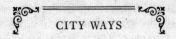

St Hilda's was a place where they had big girls and little girls, but little boys only. All categories appeared to be heavily represented. My bewilderment on the first day, sharpened by the severe bite a boy called John Skelton gave me, went on for a long time. I was a solitary in school hours, coming to life only at teatime, an occasion often delayed by voluntary/compulsory service in the cloakroom, where I was retained in order to tie the laces of those unable or unwilling to secure their own outdoor shoes. Thereafter I would play with the children of my parents' friends, including a Roman Catholic lad who traumatized me by telling me that God was always about and by showing me his set of images. Of my pastoresses and mistresses I remember best Miss Crampton, who taught French among many other things and kept saying: '*Le shat:* the cat' – one of those pictures from the past that seem never to lose their freshness. I fell in love with Miss Barr, whom I see now as a tall, Eton-cropped figure of improbable elegance. She took English, and it is here, perhaps, that we can date my first devotion to the glories of our literature.

It was at Norbury College that I became aware of the vast free entertainment that school life usually represents. Handwork was my only worry: my cardboard bus and plywood cigarette-box never got off the drawing-board, and this humiliated me. In everything else I was fine. From Babington I learnt the chief basic rhymes and enough rude words to hold my end up in conversation. I made Hall cry in a playground fight. Taylor and I discussed the works of Percy F. Westerman and Ian Hay. With Dominy I would go as far as Streatham Astoria to see Richard Barthelmess or Gary Cooper on the screen, the Paramount Tiller Girls or Troise and his Mandoliers (vocalist: Don Carlos) in the stage show. I took forty minutes to make four not out in a pick-up game, played left-back for the Third XI against St Joseph's and was last but one in the 440 Under-Twelve. I fell in love – alas, to no more purpose than before – with the headmaster's daughter, a gay girl who had a fringe and liked Gracie Fields and Henry Hall.

Mr Waller used to read books out when he should have been teaching us English. They were about the war ('I've copped it in the back, sir') or lethal espionage in Eastern Europe ('for God's sake shoot me and have done with it'). He left after a time and Mr Ashley came, bringing with him Alfred Noyes, *The Merchant of Venice* and essays to do with Beauty. Once we all had to write a poem in blank verse about the miracle of St Sophia. Mine was ninety-nine lines long and Mr Ashley said it was the best. I began liking English for its own sake. About that time my first published work of fiction, a 300-word story called 'The Sacred Rhino of Uganda', came out in the school magazine. In it a certain Captain Hartly, evidently less well up in Ugandan *moeurs* than a 'veteran hunter' had any right to be, shot the rhino and was instantly set upon by some 'native worshippers' it had. He got away with his life, I forget how. These events were recounted in taut impressionistic prose: 'He clutches at his side ... pitches forward ... unconscious ...' With this the initial, experimental period of my writing came to an end.

In 1934 I appeared at the City of London School, a large, rather oppressively dignified building on the Victoria Embankment. It had lots of identical passages and a vast agoraphobic playground filled with self-possessed boys in black coats and striped trousers. At this time I was an undersized, law-abiding, timid person. Fear made me vomit on the first few mornings, but I quickly found that this was excessive. Nobody ever used me unkindly, except perhaps King (Science III), who at tuck-shop time every morning would greet me with 'Hallo, Curly' and ruffle my hair, which I currently wore in two brilliantined flaps. His bearing, the tone of his voice and the redness of his own hair made me afraid to punch him. I was soon reconciled, however, and began to be fascinated by the social possibilities of this immense new environment. My fellows, I saw dimly, were drawn from a wide variety of social strata: accents varied from those that discomforted me to those that made me feel superior. But example at once taught me to put such attitudes aside. To be accepted you had only to be amiable; to be liked you needed pre-eminently to be able to raise a laugh occasionally – but here the most vapid clowning served as well as wit.

Efficient mimics of the staff were especially highly regarded. I developed an imitation of the headmaster: 'Get it right, not wrong. Black, not white. Cat, not dog.' This measure had the double advantage of securing esteem and providing a counterpoise to the terrified veneration I felt for my original. As at every school one ever hears about, the masters were imitable eccentrics almost to a man. This can only be put down to the stylizing effects teaching has on demeanour. What is also at work in this situation is the nature of the observer. To the pre-pubertial eye all grown-up behaviour is so fantastic as to defeat discrimination; the youth in his last year or two at school is already taking out naturalization papers for the adult world. It is the boy in his early teens who sees that world with the delighted, faintly hostile astonishment of the tourist, who is entertained to the limits of endurance by its quaint tribal customs, its grotesque ritual dances, its capering, scowling, gesticulating witch-doctors. And if he later becomes a novelist he must strive to recapture, not indeed the undifferentiating vision of childhood, but the adolescent's coldly wondering stare.

However that may be, I shall never forget Mr Marsh sucking the earpiece of his glasses, or Mr Penn accusing us all of having eaten his biscuits, or Mr Carruthers's imperturbability when Rumsey and I dropped the suitcase full of broken glass – long-treasured riot-mechanism – at the back of the room. I remember these things not as facts, but as little mental films with a complete set of sound effects. The most noteworthy figure of all, I realize now, was Mr Copping, who played (one at a time) the flute and the double-bass, who spoke with an Attic Greek accent of the fifth century, who once captivated us all by replying with incomparable, table-turning deftness to a disingenuous question from Rigden about castration: 'I don't know whether any of you have ever been to a horse-fair', the answer led off – I can hear those Periclean tones now. As I do so I marvel at the way the 1938 version of Mr Copping still seems older than the 1958 version of me, a trick of time which will no doubt remain as effective in 1978.

My education, pursued with some obduracy by the masters, was filled out and humanized by the other boys. From Moses I learnt about Fats Waller and Charles Morgan; from Bateman, air-pistols and the dating of girls; from Lightfoot, Borodin and Rimsky-Korsakov; from Williams-Ashman, upper-middle-class life, comprising the possession of actual pictures (not reproductions) by living artists, the voluntary reading of *The Oxford Book of French Verse,* and the notion of foreign travel. But at this distance it is people like Wybrow that I recall with most reverence; Wybrow, that great rampager and heresiarch, loping through the cloisters with one hand ready to dart out in assault, the other clutched inward for defence, his whole being permanently gathered for the delivery of a jeering guffaw, his ravaged face and elbowing, shoving demeanour an advertisement of instinctive revolt. He treated me tolerantly enough and got into the habit of yelling 'Hiya, Sergeant Delius' when I appeared, in allusion to my O.T.C. rank and my imitation of the composer 'three months before the end' – a popular request item at that time. Whenever I remember Wybrow I am saddened at the thought of all that pulsating violence going to waste in commerce or trade, instead of enlivening the culture pages of a Sunday newspaper.

I moved into the sixth form, which meant that I could use the front entrance, go out to lunch at the Lyons' near Blackfriars Bridge, and be harangued slightly by Mr Copping, in his incarnation as my junior housemaster, for hardly ever turning up at the sports ground. I pointed out that this amenity was situated in the far side of London from my home and that attendance there of any but minimal frequency would interfere with my studies. (Inwardly I congratulated myself on the fact that athletic, equally with intellectual, deficiency had no effect on one's schoolfellows' attitude.) In fact I liked having my studies interfered with, but by disruptives of my own choosing: trying to paint in watercolour, reading up on Dadaism, finding out about architecture – three branches of endeavour I pursued not far, but far enough to last me for the rest of my life. I also wrote some poetry; a long thing called 'Prelude' was foisted on the magazine editor. It was a kind of suburbanite's *Waste Land* tizzied up with bits of Wilde. In the same issue or thereabouts there was a story about the war in Spain by the secretary of the school branch of the League of Nations Union. I joined this organization. Meetings were held in concert with the City of London School for Girls.

It was a great surprise when, in the summer of 1939, one or two people suggested to me that there might be going to be a war with Germany. I had not had time to think this over when we were abruptly evacuated to Marlborough. The haversack rations in the train were delicious, far better than those we had got used to on O.T.C. field days. Out of the window everything began to look very countrified and was still looking it as we drew into Marlborough, which turned out to be in Wiltshire. Accommodation was hastily organized: billets in the town for the majority, barns with army-type beds in them for a select band that included me. During the next few days I ate about twenty tins of sweetened condensed milk, the discarded residue of my companions' train rations. My appetite sharpened by the country air, I also ate a good deal in the dining-hall of Marlborough College, an institution few of us had previously had cause to know about. After one such meal, at which the sixth-formers had acted as waiters (in anticipation of Christmas Day in the army), I was standing talking to my friend Richenberg near the front gate of the college. A fifth-former called Horwood, whom we both knew slightly, came over to us.

'You've heard, have you?' Horwood asked. 'He's taken Danzig and bombed Warsaw.'

'Are you sure?'

'Just came over the wireless. I got it off one of the cooks.'

After a moment, Richenberg said: 'Well, anyway, I should say we've got a fair chance of beating him.'

'A fair chance?' I echoed. 'We'll wipe him up.'

They both looked at me. 'They reckon his air force is pretty hot,' Horwood said. 'And his tanks.'

'Well, we've got an air force and tanks, haven't we?'

'Not like he's got, according to what I read.'

'The Polish army isn't mechanized,' Richenberg said.

'But we've been sending them stuff for months now.'

'We haven't got enough stuff for ourselves.'

'Oh, nonsense,' I said.

One of them said: 'We'll see' or something of the kind and the conversation shifted, probably to what school life would henceforward be like. This question, with its attachments of home-sickness and selfish anxiety, interested me more than British military supplies to Poland, though I was to recall Richenberg's line on this when, years later, I happened to see a list of the 'stuff' Chamberlain's Government had actually sent: the largest item was four gun-turrets and mountings for a Polish light cruiser. At the time, the colloquy I have tried to re-create did not have on me the effect it should have had. I did not reflect that Horwood, a boy with no pretensions to being 'well-informed', might be considered to have shown me up as naive and complacent. Nor did I then take occasion to execrate those of my parents' friends who knew people at the office who had got chatting in the train to chaps who had been told confidentially by someone in the know that Germany's economy would not stand a six months' war, or who had been drinking at the golf club with a fellow whose brother-in-law had driven his car into – guess what? – a cardboard tank on a road near Vienna. But, after all, the Poles, not to mention the French, were at the moment still in the field.

With commendable speed, the City of London School tackled the dual task of turning itself into a boarding-school and using the same classrooms, sports facilities, chapel, sanatorium and goodness knows what else as another boarding-school. None of the masters showed signs of the appalling extra burden of work, replete with boredom and irritation, they must have had to shoulder. The boys at any rate were happy as the result of novel surroundings, kind and indulgent treatment from their billet landladies and a whole new world of illegality to explore. They received little comfort or friendliness from the Marl-borough College boys, who remained, apart from some contact be-tween squash champions and the like, entirely aloof. The unlooked-for descent of six or seven hundred London day-boys, many of them noisy and tatterdemalion, was no gift from the gods, but after a time some host-like gestures, in the form of joint debates or even invitations to tea, might reasonably have been expected. None were made to my knowledge in the five terms I was at school in Marlborough. During that period I spent two minutes in conversation with Marlborough boys; they were acquaintances of Richenberg's, now captain of the school. When I look back on that whole situation, it appears to me very surprising, and I would give much to be able to see, in retrospect, the figure of Wybrow ranging contumeliously across the front court of the college, kicking a Marlborough prefect's rolled umbrella out of his hand or jostling an important parent at the gate. But he had left us at the end of that summer.

These reflections, like so many others, did not occur to me at the time. I was busy finding out that organized games, even if approached late in life, were enjoyable and could be fitted plausibly enough into a mode of existence that also included Mozart and Louis Armstrong. I joined the chapel choir, and singing in four-part harmony revealed itself as the apex, still unrivalled in my experience, of non-sensual pleasures. The rural attractions were tremendous, imparting a kind of zest to adolescent melancholy, and to this day my every attempt to visualize a generic country scene calls up some image of Marlborough. The barn where I ate all the condensed milk was soon evacuated; half a dozen of us established ourselves in a cottage on the Bath road. Here there were conversations with Richenberg and Rose that afforded an optimistic preview of the university. It was in this direction that our lives were now bending themselves, and there, in due course, we eventually departed, my two companions going into residence in October, 1940, myself in the following April. I was delayed, I used to plead, by having switched from classics to English, and also by being forced to take Higher Certificate three years running. I passed all three times, naturally, but by a steadily decreasing margin. By 1945 or so I should probably have been failing altogether.

Life at a large day-school in a large city embodies a freedom which I should guess to be unique, a freedom based on heterogeneity. Where there is no orthodoxy there can be no conformity and no intolerance. This was certainly true of the City of London School. I have never in my life known a community where factions of any kind were less in evidence, where differences of class, upbringing, income group and religion counted for so little. In particular, although perhaps fifteen per cent of the boys were Jewish, not a single instance of even the mildest antisemitism came to my attention in the seven years I was a pupil there. The academic teaching was of a standard not easily to be surpassed, but more important still was that lesson about how to regard one's fellows, a lesson not delivered but enacted. Thanks indeed for that.

1958

WHERE TAWE FLOWS

It seemed funny that the first press button ever to become fixed to my lapel should have on it, not 'Press', but 'Y Wasg'. It seemed funny in a different way that I should be here at all, trudging across duckboards, or litter-strewn swamp towards the pavilion of the Royal National Eisteddfod of Wales; I, who five years ago thought of Wales as a rugger ground with Cader Idris on one side and a spoil-heap on the other, populated by pit-dirty miners who only stopped singing 'All Through the Night' to bawl 'Look you to goodness whateffer' at one another, and subjected to continuous rain. About the rain, at any rate, I had not been wholly wrong, and peering now towards the half-obscured sky-line I was able to make out what in all probability actually was a spoil-heap, or 'tip'. I paused to note down this observation.

I arrived among the crowds around the pavilion. This proved to be a large, solid structure of wood and corrugated iron, bearing innumerable small tin notices advertising Izal in Welsh, and holding when full (which it always appeared to be) eight thousand people. I was surprised when I heard that it was nevertheless peripatetic, having done duty last year at Rhyl in North Wales, and doing duty this year at Ystradgynlais, a small mining town at the head of the Swansea Valley and, appropriately enough, a stronghold of the Welsh language and of the 'Parliament for Wales' campaign. I was told later of a proposal to erect somewhere a permanent building for the accommodation of Eisteddfodau. 'Of course,' my informant said thoughtfully, 'We can expect some argument about its location.' Having heard of the four centuries' disagreement on the choice of a Welsh capital, I nodded.

Inside the pavilion, I watched and listened to events from a small stifling wooden box containing no chairs, but with a window giving on to the auditorium. Here, beneath a network of steel bars supporting the roof, were hung baskets of greenery, arc-lamps, the platform for the television cameras, and banners bearing, it slowly dawned on me, the arms of the Welsh counties. And under all this, row upon row of them, were the Welsh, attending to the various items a good deal more keenly, I thought, than is common in England, an impression borne out by their frequent enjoinings of silence upon their neighbours. It occurred to me that, except at football matches, an Englishman can rarely hope to see the Welsh arrayed like this as a people, intent upon some national matter. Seeing on the walls a number of notices saying *Dim Ysmygu*, and thoughtfully glossed in English, I extinguished my cigarette, wondering why these notices seemed so much odder than ones saying *Défense de Fumer* do; no doubt because, to the English, the French are foreigners, the Welsh never – though to conceive one's Welsh friends in some such light occasionally is perhaps essential for fully enjoying them. In full view, perforce, of the audience, I took off, equally perforce, my mac, jacket and tie, and settled down to observe.

From this post, on various occasions during the week, I saw and heard ceremonial awards and greetings, singing of various genres, instrumental playing and orchestral playing, including two adequate performances of the *Rhagarweiniad to Y Ffliwt Hudol*, which sounded just like the *Magic Flute* overture. On Tuesday afternoon, after lunching off pressed-beef sandwiches, gingernuts, chocolate and Guinness, I witnessed the installation of a Welsh Baptist minister as Crown Bard of Wales. This was in recognition of his 350-line poem in free verse entitled *Y Bannau* ('The Beacons'), where he writes, I gather, of the sense of history and philosophy and meditation vouchsafed to the mountain-dweller. Those in need of a sense of economics only were advised to stick to the valleys.

The Crowning, as far as I was aware of it, began with the entry, followed by the TV cameras, of the members of the *Gorsedd*, a kind of bardic council founded by an imaginative eighteenth-century Welshman and incorporated into the proceedings of the *Eisteddfod* in 1819. The *Gorsedd* wore their traditional robes, devised more recently and not by a Welshman, and giving them something of the appearance, as a Welsh friend suggested, of elderly and harmless members of the Ku Klux Klan. 'Most impressive', I heard the TV commentator say from the box next door. When all were settled on the platform, the senior adjudicator of the verse competition delivered a long speech in his native language. Parts of this were interpreted to me by an American from a Pennsylvania steel town who crouched at my side, but on the whole I felt rather like Tarrou in *La Paste* who, it will be remembered, prescribed listening to lectures in an unknown tongue as an aid to being fully aware of the passage of time. I wiped the sweat off my chest. There was the song of the Crowning, a solo feelingly sung to the accompaniment of the green-robed harpist, and the rather pleasing democratic ritual by which the *Gorsedd* send a deputation into the body of the hall to escort the new Bard up to his place. The Crown, made to measure, was laid on his head. And then came the singing of *Hen Wlad fy Nhadau*, the Welsh National Anthem, by the entire assembly, not excluding the American, who accurately rendered the bass part. To me, and perhaps to many others, the singing of this magnificent tune was by far the most moving part of the ceremony.

There were other ceremonies: the Chairing of the Bard (not the same Bard) and the Welcome Home to Welshmen from Overseas, to which Welshmen really had come from all parts of the world. As I approached the pavilion for this occasion, 'Abide with Me' was booming out of the loudspeakers with such fervour that for a moment I supposed the place to be on fire and all exits somehow sealed up. But all was well, and the crowds drifting towards the entrances were absent-mindedly interspersing their talk with snatches of the various parts. I added my baying tenor and nobody looked round. Inside once more, I was a little distracted from the Welcome Home by the soft groanings of a double-bass being tuned up in the Gents immediately beneath my feet, and, pausing only to note that things like 'Men of Harlech' really do get sung at these 'do's', I soon wandered out again into the surrounding field. Here the chatting crowds, having survived with commendable (and typical) cheerfulness the downpour of the previous two days, were enjoying in bright sunshine the social opportunities that form an important aspect of *Eisteddfodau*. There being no free drinks for *Y Wasg*, I bought a cup of tea, available, like everything else here, only in Welsh. I visited the various booths, in particular the

Coal Board's mining exhibition, where I learnt to identify at sight superior consistently-burning domestic fuel, and the exhibition of photographs, where I was struck by a study of a young lady clad only in an academic gown, a proceeding designed, presumably, to underline the traditional Welsh respect for scholarship.

With Welsh song still ringing in my ears, I walked reflectively away and, on showing my press card, was allowed, with flattering reluctance, to leave the *Eisteddfod* area. I thought of the singers I had heard, most of them with fine natural voices, but many showing far too obviously the marks of 'training', and remembered being told that some of the best Welsh performers neglect, for one reason or another, to patronize the *Eisteddfod*. I thought again of the *Gorsedd* with their trouser-legs and shoes showing beneath their bathrobes. What does it all add up to? One item in the account is the fierce argument going on in my bank the other morning between the clerk and a shop-keeper: should or should not a judge of poetry, like a bardic adjudicator, be a poet himself? Not an unfamiliar point, but in my experience an unfamiliar level on which to find it discussed. In Wales, however, it is less surprising. Perhaps the most important part of the *Eisteddfod* is its audience, and people like the miners of the area, who raised over £1,800 towards the expenses by wage-deductions, and were prepared to strike for their right to contribute in this way. I feel I can understand what made Matthew Arnold* write: 'When I see the enthusiasm the *Eisteddfod* can awaken in your whole people, and then think of the tastes, the literature, the amusements of our own lower middle classes, I am filled with admiration for the Welsh.'

1954

* The bloody fool.
I mean by this apparent aspersion only to extend a helping hand to critics, a class never more at sea than when questions of 'seriousness' and 'irony', etc., come up. On re-reading, I feel Arnold was being a little bit starry-eyed about the institution of the *Eisteddfod*, as I in my different way, despite all that clever London stuff, now strike myself as having been too. At the same time, even after having relinquished my adopted Welsh semi-citizenship, I never want to have that institution ridiculed.

'Now, let's see, you must be Mr Ames,'* the manager said, looking at one of the pieces of paper in the large sheaf he held.

'Amis is my name,' I said for perhaps the five thousandth time in my life. Often, of course, I just let it ride, depending on how I feel.

'Right, now this is Mrs Roberts,' he said. A plump smiling lady in an orange hat shook my hand. 'Like you to meet Mr Ames,' he added.

This time I let it ride, especially since somebody was giving me a glass of whisky at that moment.

'Shall we have a look at the forms?' Mrs Roberts said. 'It's quite straightforward. We mark them for General Appearance, Beauty of Face and Teeth, Attractiveness and Beauty of Hair (I'm going to keep my highest marks for the natural blondes, I don't know about you), then Figure (that's where you men come in, isn't it) and Deportment. They do that downstairs.'

---

* The late Evelyn Waugh shared the manager's view of the pronunciation of my surname. An acquaintance told me how he once asked Waugh: 'What do you think of Kingsley Amis?'
'Ames,' said Waugh.
'Amis, actually.'
'You mean Ames.'
'Look, I happen to know him, and he pronounces it Amis.'
'The man's name is Ames,' said Waugh, so firmly that the discussion of my works was broken off at that point.

145

'What sort of marks do we give them?' I asked. 'Supposing we get an absolute smasher, how many – ?'

Mrs Roberts vigorously explained to me what ten out of ten meant, and how it came about that five such sets of marks gave a possible maximum of fifty. I then met the other three judges. By the use of great cunning I wormed out of them what their occupations were, for I had already decided, naturally, that the occasion of the selection and crowning of the Mazda Queen of Light (Swansea Heat) would have to be written up. The trio who confronted me were the editor of a South Wales newspaper, the wife of a police sergeant and the wife of a director of the Casino Ballroom, Mumbles. This last structure was the scene of tonight's competition, and the office of its manager, the small earnest man with rimless glasses who had known at the start what my name was, had been set aside for the judging and the preliminary drinking in which I was now engaged. The room was small and mea-grely furnished, except for a table, five chairs and a great number of bottles.

The manager got us sitting down, drove some of the supers from the room and brought the contestants in to pick their numbers. 'I'll give you a kind of preview, you see,' he told us.

'What do you think of them?' I muttered after a minute to the editor.

'Well, there's nothing to start a riot there, eh?' he said.

It was true. With exceptions, the entrants were such as to arouse mild wonder that they were indeed entrants for a beauty contest. (The same thought struck me last night while I was watching the selection of Miss World on television. None of the six finalists, as far as I could tell, would have looked much out of their element in, let us say, first-year English at the University College of Swansea.) All this lot were blondes, as they had to be to enter at all. This was less rigorous than might appear, since, in the words of the hand-out, 'you could decide to become blonde for the contest or you could have changed to blonde because it suited you', though Condition 6 added rather grimly: 'Competitors must agree to remain blonde for 12 months following the contest.'

This hand-out was informative in other ways, too. Until reading it I had no idea that in 1956 there will have been forty-eight preliminary heats, six regional finals and a Grand Final in this business, with over a thousand pounds in cash prizes. And before 1956 – I cannot do better than recall the author of the hand-out and allow his historical sense and knowledge of the development of ritual to speak for themselves:

'The competition was first held in this country in 1954 when it reintroduced a popular ancient custom after a gap of hundreds of years ... The source and inspiration of the competition was originally provided by the fact that for thousands of years the blonde races of the North chose a "Queen of Light" each year to preside over their feasting on December 21 – the "shortest day and longest night" – when the old year turned its face to the coming spring. As with many other ancient customs, the churches eventually adopted the ceremony and "Queen of Light" celebrations were popular in Merrie England and continued without a break as national custom in Sweden.'

'I'll start bringing them in now,' the manager said. While we waited I first reflected that, in South Wales at any rate, 'now' is going the same way as 'presently' did in the seventeenth century, and then read through the forms on which the girls had entered some personal details. Ages ranged from seventeen to twenty, no further, though crones of up to thirty were admissible under the regulations. Occupations included salesgirl, cashier, secretary, typist, housewife, advertising and consigning clerk, and clerk. Favourite hobbies were the best. There was singing, dancing, swimming, dancing, ballet and ballroom dancing, dancing, swimming, and swimming and dancing. (Honest, now. That is the order I copied down on the ruled feint lines of my Challenge tablet.)

The girls started coming in. All were constrained in manner, and stood awkwardly smiling while the manager put them through a little rigmarole he had devised, first assuring them that they were among friends and then putting a string of questions to which 'Yes' was the almost invariable answer. 'It's really to show off their teeth, you see,' he explained during an interval. I had guessed that several of the girls would have made it a habit to go round beauty contests picking up what prizes they could, and this was confirmed, but their demeanour was notably at variance. 'You wouldn't think that that one was thirty-nine, would you?' Mrs Roberts said at the departure of the girl I had liked best. 'Oh no, sorry, that's her hips.'

There was a pause while the Deportment was being got ready in the ballroom itself. Hastily comparing notes, I found some evidence that

147

the girls at present in the lead were those who came closest to the appearance of models in the women's magazines: neat, refined, underweight, on or over the brink of insipidity, over-elegant as to hair. Sexual attractiveness, what there was of it, was not doing so well. 'That's the trouble when you get a crowd of women on the judges,' the editor murmured when I showed him my findings. 'I knew this would happen.'

For the Deportment the five of us sat at separate little tables spaced round the dance floor while the girls, after an inexplicable delay reminiscent of procedure in the Armed Forces, paraded about us. The girl I had liked best walked briskly round in the manner of someone going to catch a bus. I marked her up for that. All the others produced mild imitations, with varying embarrassment potential, of the film-star wiggle or the mannequin's slow march. I marked them all down for that. This part was accompanied by the band playing 'A Pretty Girl is Like a Melody', oddly enough, and by almost continuous applause, recommended over the loudspeakers by the manager and set going by a man in a maroon jacket who seemed virtually crazed with amiability. Eventually our mark-sheets were collected and handed to the local knight who, with his wife, had turned up to perform the actual coronation.

This ceremony I did not see, being unforewarned and in the bar at the time, but the editor was able to assure me that immediately afterwards the crown had fallen off the queenly head and bent itself slightly. This did not much recompense me for my chagrin at seeing the three leading women's magazine incarnations – none of them with a Swansea address and one from as far away as Barry – receiving their prizes of ten pounds, five pounds and three pounds and being marshalled for their photographs. The editor and I shook our heads in sad unison. 'Always the same when you get a crowd of women on the judges,' he said.

Back in the manager's office, where my wife and six friends were having a drink or two while they waited, I worked out from the mark-sheets that the girl I had liked best had come bottom and the girl I had liked next best had come next to bottom. This made me feel guilty and humiliated in some way. I looked up to see a man, doubtless one of the Mazda representatives, looking round the room with the expression of one about to ask just who the hell all these people were. Instead of that he said: 'Now has everybody got a drink they fancy?' In case they had not he pulled a fresh bottle of whisky out of a fuse-box.

Rather later I was summoned on to the balcony of the ballroom to have my photograph taken congratulating the new Queen of Light. 'Don't look at her, Mr Ames, look at me,' the manager said. 'Then it'll look as if you're looking at her, you see.'

'Let's have it a bit more informal,' the photographer said, pushing the queen's stole down off her shoulders. 'That's more like it. Now stand a bit closer to her, would you? Put your arm round her waist. No, I don't think we need you quite as close as that.'

With the Queen standing as if carved out of dough, with myself grinning mindlessly at the manager, and to the accompaniment of hundreds of feet thundering in the veleta and the crashing of chairs being piled, the photograph was taken. 'Where will it appear?' I asked diffidently.

'Oh, nowhere,' somebody said. 'It's just for records, that's all.' This was untrue. A few days later the photograph appeared on the front page of the *Swansea Voice*. It shows the Queen as quite a sweet girl and myself as a broken-down comedian in the grip of satyriasis – looking, moreover, quite unmistakably at something out of the frame. But perhaps that is just as well.

If any blonde clerk or typist of eighteen with a passion for swimming and dancing is reading this, I can put her in the way of an easy ten pounds. As I write there are still quite a few heats to run. And there's always next year.

1956

POSTSCRIPT 1970

The interested will find a version of this incident in the poem 'Maunders' (cf. 'Mumbles'), in my verse collection *A Look Round the Estate* (Cape, 1967). The various dissimilarities between the two accounts, plus the nine-year gap between the dates of composition, afford a useful lesson on the relations of life and art.

Public lecturing in America is the perfect vehicle for that rich compound of vanity and greed which makes up the literary character. I say 'in America' not because Americans are particularly devoted to the two qualities mentioned, but because in Britain, at least, neither of them will get much of an outing at this form of sport: 'I'm sorry so few people have turned up', one is likely to be told, 'but our Mr Snodgrass is also lecturing tonight – on French cathedrals – with lantern slides,' and again: 'I'm sorry the fee is so tiny, but we find if we charge admission nobody turns up at all.'

In America, under I know not what system of inducement or threat, enough people will turn up to tickle even a writer's vanity, and greed is abundantly satisfied. Instead of having to wait a couple of months for five pounds, the common fate in England, one will probably be given the cheque before the audience has finished assembling, and if by any chance payment should be deferred until afterwards a good reason will be forthcoming: in Washington, I seemed to gather, a compatriot of mine got his little envelope after the preludial dinner and was never seen again.

Conscious of having had either one martini too few or one too many (a finer literary judgement is needed here than most of us possess) the lecturer makes his way to the podium and does his stuff, imperturbable and trying to sound improvisatory with his dog-eared script, uneasily alert for any face in the audience that even slightly recalls anybody who may have heard him deliver the identical talk last week in a different part of the town. This phobia is perhaps an integral part of the academic neurosis, likely to afflict all who have had to go through the motions, year after year, of sounding sprightly about *The Mill on the Floss* or *Martin Chuzzlewit* in front of undergraduate audiences; this year's lot look and behave so much like last year's lot that you can never quite convince yourself they are not the same lot. You need all your reasoning power for the reflection that nobody who has had to take two runs at the first-year English novel course is in danger of recognizing a supposed epigram however often it might be repeated.

But to abandon thoughts of home: our literary lecturer in America will meet, if he has been at all conscientious in preparing his remarks, a polite and attentive reception. The only man who ever made faces at me while I was holding forth turned out to be an official of Her Majesty's Government, which I was mildly denouncing at the time; they were mild faces too. Even that potentially dreadful aftermath, the question period, will generally slip harmlessly by without intervention from the aggressively well-informed or even the plain madman. Those well-tested life-belts – asking for a 250-word question to be repeated, answering it with a monosyllable, breaking into uncontrollable laughter, etc. – can be left unused.

My one major error (the only one I know of, anyway) was committed when I gave an address at a well-known university in Philadelphia. Exhausted by the ceaseless search for wit, I had decided to abandon trying to tell jokes and deliver instead what was conceived as a hideously sophisticated joke in action: a long, humourless, pseudo-academic diatribe on the comic spirit recited absolutely deadpan by a supposed comic writer. As I recall – and one does not recall these things well, being concerned only to maintain continuity and aplomb, for all the world like somebody who has had too much to drink – as I recall it went down rather badly, except for a reference to vomiting which laid a single undergraduate in the aisle. But retribution was swift: during the postludial party at the fraternity house somebody stole my script, which naturally, having a living to earn, I had been intending to run off elsewhere a few weeks later. I see now, of course, that the right way to interpret the felony was as (a) a blow against authority, to be welcomed as such, and (b) a second joke in action, a good deal more pointed and economical than my own. But I thought differently then.

It must have been vanity rather than greed which induced me to appear on a kind of public panel in a playhouse in New York: the topic *Is There a Beat Generation?* My colleagues were Mr James Wechsler, the editor of the *New York Post*, Mr Ashley Montagu, the anthropologist, and Mr Jack Kerouac, who as they say needs no introduction. At the preludial dinner it was explained that Mr Kerouac was very nice, perfectly charming in fact, provided he was convinced that those present were on his side, felt sympathetic to him, in short *liked him*. I said I saw what was meant. Over in the theatre we encountered Mr Kerouac, conservatively attired in giant's-chessboard shirt, black jeans and pigskin ankle-boots. With hand on hip he piped to me: 'Hallo, my dear' (I did need a haircut at the time, admittedly) and said to Mr Montagu: 'I saw you on the Jack Paar show. You didn't have anything new to say.'

Having thus variously put the pair of us at our ease, he crossed to the back-stage piano without giving us the chance to tell him how much we liked him. Then, seating himself at the instrument, he began a version of the dear old Warsaw Concerto, but broke off every now and then to appear before the photographers. When he did this he weaved and bobbed rather as if about to start what we squares used to call jitterbugging. The Warsaw Concerto gave place at one stage to a boogie-woogie left hand, but was resumed after an interval when no boogie-woogie right hand was forthcoming.

Though Mr Wechsler had still not arrived, some sort of gesture towards getting started was obviously called for. We trooped on to the stage and huge high-pitched enthusiasm arose from certain sections of the audience, a salute intended not for Mr Montagu or me, I recognized sadly, but for Mr Kerouac, who responded with more weaves, bobs, and a chimpanzee shuffle or two. After some determinedly sedate remarks from the chair, Mr Kerouac arose for what we all thought was understood to be a ten-minute stint. During it, a stocky figure with overcoat thrown open entered at the back of the hall and made its way on to the stage; no beatnik anarch, as I had begun to fear, but Mr Wechsler, in pretty good shape after a three-day editorial crisis and soon disabused of the idea that I was Mr Montagu. Mr Kerouac was talking about a swinging group of new American boys intent on life, forecasting the appointment of a beat Secretary of State, and saluting Humphrey Bogart, Laurel and Hardy and Popeye as ancestral beats. Half an hour or so later he said he would read his poem on Harpo

152

Marx. The texture of his discourse did not change. Throughout it seemed to illustrate the theme of the symposium rather than actually expound it.

Next there was me. Then there was Mr Wechsler, who formed the considerable feat of advocating political commitment in terms that were both rational and free of cliché. Right at the start of it Mr Kerouac muttered: 'I can't stand this activist crap,' and, wearing Mr Wechsler's hat, began a somnambulistic pacing of the stage, occasionally breaking off to wave balletically at the photographers in the wings. He went on doing this while Mr Montagu's ironies flew above the beat sections of the audience.

Finally there was 'discussion'. Mr Kerouac accused Mr Wechsler, very inaccurately, of having said a lot about what he didn't believe in and nothing about what he did believe in. Mr Wechsler gamely responded with a capsule version of positive views. Mr Kerouac leaned on the podium and said: 'Admit it, Wechsler, you came here tonight determined to hate me.' It was clear that none of us had managed to convince him that we liked him.

Disengaging myself from a 250-pound brunette who had leapt on to the stage to assure me that, contrary to my apparent belief, there was a beat generation, I followed the others out, reflecting that Mr Kerouac's performance had acted as a useful supplement to his novels in demonstrating how little spontaneity has to do with talking off the top of the head. I also wondered, and still do, just what it is that people anywhere in the world get out of attending discussions or lectures by literary persons. For the majority, I imagine, one might as well speak in Choctaw; the visual appeal is what counts. For all his evident casualness, Mr Kerouac was shrewd enough to have grasped that.

1959

POSTSCRIPT 1970

I think I make this sort of thing sound more fun to do than it actually is, but then this probably applies to written descriptions of all activities whatever. Realizing, a few years ago, that I was not going to have to do any more of it for the foreseeable future was hardly less wonderful than ceasing to teach. In one way it was better still, for even the most uninspired academic lecture includes a hard minimum of necessary fact, and ministers however inadequately to a genuine educational end. Lecturing to lay audiences is really a waste of time. The whole conception is impure, in that what is supposed to count is the content of the address, while what if anything really counts is how the lecturer's name and subject look on the programme and in the archives, together with what I have called visual appeal. This creates an uncomfortable gap between the amount of work necessary to devise any sort of new talk – about an hour at the desk per three minutes at the lectern, in my experience – and the amount of any but the briefest narcissistic satisfaction to be derived from performing. Many people who run series of such lectures are unaware of this consideration, and may be surprised and hurt at being told one has something better to do with one's time. (Memorandum to such: if you want an established author to come and deliver a proper talk on a subject you have had a hand in choosing – neither, that is to say, a read-through of his standard script nor an improvisation around notes scribbled in the train – you should properly pay him five hundred pounds. If you or he can arrange subsequent publication, he may – I do not say he should – agree to less.)

On re-reading the above paragraph I would concede that I have made this sort of thing sound less fun to do than it actually is, but that is what is called a salutary corrective.

I think I was a bit urbane in my description of the late Jack Kerouac's activities. This was complacent and unimaginative of me. I did not give him sufficient credit as a pioneer of the movement, now in full career, to reduce argument to animal bawling and culture to egoistic tomfoolery.

The sociologizing generalization, that characteristic art-form of the mid-twentieth century, swells in volume and variety as we near the end of the 1950s. (All we have actually got to the end of is the years that start off 195–, as 'Stickler for Accuracy' must surely have pointed out in a letter to, say, the *Budleigh Salterton Advertiser*; but the modern trend-hound takes no heed of that kind of pedantry.) There can be little harm in adding one more wafer to the hundredweights of labels loading down what I will agree to call the past decade, especially perhaps if its distinguishing mark is seen as that very urge to label, to unearth a new trend and hound it to death, to generalize. It is no accident, for example, that this period saw the emergence of the teenage group as a self-conscious entity: after all, every other group was doing the same thing. Human spontaneity may well appear to have been worse damaged by the labellers than by any of the spectres they have so clamorously and repetitively labelled – mass culture, herd values, conspicuous consumption, status-seeking, success ethics – and the multiplication of diagnosis itself is coming to the point where it obstructs cure.

I myself am not yet conscious of being positively impeded in my social round by the antics of generalizers; I have only reached the stage of firmly opting for any straight hour's worth of mass culture in preference to again being told about it. But I am disconcerted by the smallness of the remaining area in which I can behave without having,

155

without already having had, my behaviour described and explained to me, evaluated, categorized. I can hardly catch sight of an American car without what I used to think was my natural curiosity being drowned out by a string of anti-commercials about male symbols and built-in obsolescence and keeping up with the Rockefellers. At the cinema I have a phantom Dwight Macdonald breathing down my neck with stuff about expensiveness and reassuringness and anonymity and kitsch. And almost any television programme turns out to be a duet between what the producers imagined they were up to and what Mr Richard Hoggart, either in my mind's ear or – increasingly these days – right there on the screen in front of me, explains they are really up to.

It is a commonplace that the presence of an observer will affect that which he observes, and that while in some fields – astronomy, for instance – this perturbation can safely be ignored, the social or socio-logical areas are more sensitive. This is particularly so if the observer is as tirelessly vocal as he is today, when no book page or literary section of TV discussion is complete without its review or article or expert testimony carrying cultural diagnostics a step further down. I say 'down' partly in recognition of the almost equally commonplace fact that to have oneself diagnosed to oneself is becoming a major popular sport among the diagnosable masses, as witness almost any day's TV programmes, and sales figures of the Riesmans and Packards and Whytes and their (duller) British equivalents, the Bermuda-shorted, blue-rinsed, small-town New Jersey housewife whom I re-cently overheard exclaiming passionately to a replica of herself: 'Did you read this wonderful book *The Lonely Crowd*?' A couple of decades ago it would have been *Gone with the Wind* – better for everyone.

I gladly admit the appeal of social diagnostics, especially those in the anecdotal American vein, and I except from my strictures serious academic sociology such as that practised by the Institute of Community Studies associated with Bethnal Green and Greenleigh. But, these matters apart, I should like to see the trend-hound actively dis-couraged for an experimental period of a millennium or so. I view with misgiving the possibility that, by a grotesque irony, those seemingly responsible only for having named group-thinking will turn out to have helped it into power; just as Marx invented as much as discovered economic man, Freud instituted neurosis as a social fact in the course of exploring it as a clinical one. I do not want to contemplate a culture

156

in which every other man is an upper-white-collar coronary-prone left-of-centre tradition-directed mass-valued pyknic infantile-anal togetherness-seeking Kinsey-group-B calcium-deficient mesomorph, *and knows it.* That notion outdoes, in both horror and plausibility, the right-wing Jeremiah's prophecy of a huge delinquent majority maintained in prison and mental hospital by a tiny band of normals, and even its science-fiction equivalent, a society divided into behavers and observers, seems to me preferable to the extinction of unselfconsciousness.

That the past ten years have been the worst, falsest, most cynical, most apathetic, most commercialized, most Americanized, richest in cultural decline of any in Britain's history is the theme pounded out by a double mixed orchestrally accompanied chorus of lone voices. And it would be merely perverse to deny that some of the tumult has been justified, or at least that some of the right persons have been annoyed thereby. But I have little of my own to add, am content to leave in other hands the agitation against the lack of ice in boat-train dining-cars, the H-bomb, the new Jacobethan store in central Swansea, the emergent Britain that (except as regards politeness and efficiency) bases itself on *New Yorker* travel ads, *Dotto,* the Royal Family – here perhaps, having a few months ago denounced Princess Margaret to the man who turned out very soon afterwards to be going to marry her, I might be thought to have special qualifications, yet even these I resign. It ill becomes one who feels that many of the drubbers deserve the most lavish drubbing to drub much himself.

Since I am writing an informal pique-piece, however, I will permit myself one minor drub. Advertising. All those lone voices no doubt agreed at some stage or other (they always do) that advertising was a bad thing before – with that characteristic restlessness Orwell noted in the British intellectual – passing on to horror-comics or what they thought was the latest Dulles gaffe. More recent developments, accordingly, have been rather less generally heeded. I start from the fact that, with some shining exceptions in the book trade and elsewhere, the majority of advertisers are as dishonest as they can get away with being, and the related fact that the talk they go in for about keeping the public informed and the standard up is vicious hot air – vicious because they believe it themselves and are trying hard and successfully to get other people to believe it too. Meanwhile they bash on with their fake consumer surveys, their pseudo-science, their publicity palmed off as fact, above all their high-grade imbecile notions of what is glamorous and exciting.

I was about to continue incautiously with the observation that commercial television is the greatest single vulgarizing influence in our national life, but pulled myself up just in time. Apart from being inadmissibly over-obvious, that sort of thing is lone-voice talk. I mean that it is a protest made on behalf of others who are deemed too comatose or inarticulate to make it for themselves. There are some – children, lunatics, old-age pensioners, illiterates, unemployables, not to speak of the animal kingdom – who cannot fight their own battles, but they are fewer than is often supposed. What a splendid change it would make to find a trend-hound whose gaze was not exclusively directed outwards, an imbiber of Hoggart-wash (as an anonymous friend of mine has called it) who confessed to liking skiffle better than all those rotten old music-hall songs, an honorary watchdog of status-seeking who consciously set himself to see a bit of the stuff on his own account. Lone voices would sound much nicer, and loner, if their song were based on actual experience rather than on the putative corruption of some inadequately visualized pools-telly-and-fish-and-chips Everyman.

With this said, I should do my best to admit only a personal vexation, not to any part of the concern-disquiet-misgiving system that breeds so much altruistic insomnia, were I ever to state in detail my own modest objections to what advertising has been getting up to. Somewhere among these would come the idea that too many young people of demonstrable literacy were being attracted in that direction when choosing their career. They might in time come to raise the grade of imbecility obtaining there, but the thing is doing quite well enough already without mind, and where they are really needed is in teaching. Nobody who has not seen it in all its majesty – I speak as a university lecturer – can imagine the pit of ignorance and incapacity into which British education has sunk since the war. It is a pretty good pit not only in depth but laterally, for it takes in everyone from the kindergarten to the House of Lords, assuming these as opposite poles. Here at last I feel I have come up with a really man-sized 'fifties trend, one which justifies the utmost dis – oops: one which disquiets and vexes me.

158

The trouble is not just illiteracy, even understanding this as including unsteady grasp of the fundamentals of a subject as well as unsteadiness with hard words like 'goes' and 'its'. But for the moment I want to drum the fact of that illiteracy into those who are playing what I have heard called the university numbers racket, those quantitative thinkers who believe that Britain is 'falling behind America and Russia by not producing as many university graduates per head, and that she must 'catch up' by building 'more colleges which will turn out 'more' graduates and so give us 'more' technologists (especially them) and 'more' schoolteachers. I wish I could have a little tape-and-loudspeaker arrangement sewn into the binding of this magazine, to be triggered off by the light reflected from the reader's eyes on to this part of the page, and set to bawl out at several bels: MORE WILL MEAN WORSE.

I do not know whether it is better to have three really bad schoolteachers where formerly there were two mediocre ones, and I have no information about what can be expected to happen to technologists, but I am quite sure that a university admissions policy demanding even less than it now demands – for that is what a larger intake means – will wreck academic standards beyond repair. Already a girl who has literally never heard of metre (I found this out last week) can come to a university to study English literature; what will her successors never have heard of if the doors are opened wider – rhyme, poem, sentence? Not only will examining standards have to be lowered to enable worse and worse people to graduate – you cannot let them all in and then not allow most of them to pass – but the good people will be less good than they used to be: this has been steadily happening ever since I started watching in 1949. Please do not think that I am resenting the prospect of being tugged into the hurly-burly and away from the little circle of devotees with whom I am currently exploring the niceties of Pope's use of the caesura. What I explore with the chaps already tends to be far more the niceties of who Pope was.

My personal stake in this is twofold. I do not fancy teaching in something that is called a university but is really a rather less glamorous and authentic training college. And I do not fancy living in a society which has abandoned the notion of the university as a centre of learning. Powerful forces, both inside and outside its walls, are bringing this notion under ever more intense attack. The mere acceptance of expansion (we are promised a fifty per cent increase in students by 1970) is itself, I have argued, equivalent to such attack. Further, influential opinion takes the necessity of a de-naturing change as virtually beyond dispute. In the May 11th debate on education in the House of Lords, many of whose members must have attended a university some time in this century, we find Lord Beveridge saying: 'The most important purpose of the university [is] to spread knowledge rather than add to it.' Viscount Esher said (I quote from *The Times* of May 12th) that

> *he would like everyone who felt the desire to be able to go to a university without an entrance examination and without cost. This would bring change and give variety to the pattern of university life. At present only boys and girls capable of getting a first or second had a chance of getting in. The pattern was stereotyped. Places must be found for the free-lance, the adventurers, young people of enterprise ...*

Lord Esher is very far from being alone in his view that desire, rather than any archaic nonsense about capacity, should be an adequate entrance qualification, and the same holds true for his feeling that at present the university will take only the academically minded (in the contemptuous sense), whereas in fact it is already taking almost everyone who can read and write. I wish he would tell me where all his unfairly deprived adventurous enterprising free-lances are to be found. We could do with them.

More will mean worse. The delusion that there are thousands of young people about who are capable of benefiting from university training, but somehow failed to find their way to it, is of course a necessary component of the expansionist case. It means that one can confidently mention a thing called 'quality' and say it will be 'maintained'. University graduates, however, are like poems or bottles of hock, and unlike cars or tins of salmon, in that you cannot *decide* to have more good ones. All you can decide to have is more. And MORE WILL MEAN WORSE. Let me assure Lord Esher finally, and all whose prejudices run his way, that many university teachers work hard at *not* stereotyping their students. If many of these enter the great world in fuddled and temporary possession of tutorial opinions this is because, after the most dedicated probing, they have shown no sign of forming any of their own.

The demand for expansion is frequently coupled with the demand for more science, and therefore less arts, in the university. We live in a scientific age, you see. It might be thought that this is just when you want more arts, but no. We are to have more 'general courses' of mixed, i.e. diluted, science and arts, more science for the arts students – oh, and arts for the scientists, too, naturally. If any policy-making educational body should ever turn away for a moment from its corps of nodding vice-chancellors and go so far as to consult someone actually engaged in teaching, they will be told (unless indeed they pick, as they will tend to and be encouraged to, one of the growing body of numbers-racketeers) that it is already hard enough to turn out an arts graduate who knows something about arts, without eating into his time at the university, and at school, in order to provide him with a smattering of biology or physics. What they will almost certainly not be told is that the humanities are in danger and must be defended. That case, to the permanent shame of those engaged in the humanities, is going by default. Last March I wrote to the *Observer* to attack some vulgar TV boost for technology, and inquired whether there was anybody who was prepared to 'refute the phantom dichotomy of "the two cultures", repudiate the ever-more-widely accepted view of the humanities as behind the times, vague, decorative, marginal contemplative, postponable, while science (which in this context usually means technology) is seen as up with the times, precise, essential, central, active, urgent'. I had answer enough. There was nobody. Why are there no voices, lone or otherwise, in our arts faculties?

I am sorry to have been so thin on trends, and for a time I contemplated pushing the score up a notch by naming, as the cultural disappointment of the decade or something like that, the revealed inadequacy of the *Scrutiny* school of criticism – its inability to praise anything Dr Leavis has not praised first, to do so otherwise than in his prose style, and to deal with contemporary literature otherwise than by denigration, thus abdicating from the essential critical task (if there be such a thing) of trying to range modern writers in order. Everyone has been too occupied, I would have gone on to say, in saluting the institution of D. H. Lawrence as 'a great English writer', to use the *ipsissima verba*, on which my comments would have been two: first, Lawerence's arrival as a great Sinhalese or Ghanaian writer would have been more remarkable, and secondly, thank God he neither is, nor has arrived as, a great anything writer. From there I might have proceeded to trace to Lawrence a large part of the decline in sexual morality during the decade, noting the infective properties of his belief in selfish will, of his faith in the validity of mood and whim, and of that Calvinistic psychotheology whereby some are born to sweet delight, but very few apart from you and me, and those who dispute the arrangement are born to an endless night of the dirty little secret.

To get it all said properly, however, would have meant trying to read through some of Lawrence's books. And I am not even sure that there has been a decline in sexual morality. The trouble is – and hither I trace in part my failure with the trends – that the past decade is really the first I have noticed as such. I was only eight in 1930, and the 1940s were too unusual and, for me, too replete with incident to allow of much trend-truffling. Until 1945 or so I was mostly occupied either with thinking about having to join the army or, what is evidently much rarer among those of a literary bent, actually being in it. And then there I was back at Oxford, working, getting a degree, getting married, getting children, getting a job, getting settled here in Swansea. I kept telling myself, I remember, that I simply must look out of the window one of these days and notice how the 'forties were doing, but something else kept coming up and stopping me. It was an unreflecting time.

I seem to myself now to be at a great distance from that cottage outside Oxford where I tried to write a book on Graham Greene, write a novel, prepare for a research degree and help to look after the baby. (The Greene opus got as far as the Argentinian university which for some unfathomable reason had commissioned it, but no further; the novel, which was about a young man rather like myself, only nastier, got finished but not published; the research degree was not granted. The baby, however, will soon be as tall as I am.) When I look back on the 'fifties I can see, despite the quarts of adrenalin they made me release at times, small cause for complaint in matters affecting me personally. The world of letters, into which I finally contrived to infiltrate, proved benign, not at all in the grip of that 'London literary racket' I had heard so much about before I got there. It contains, to be sure, some persons of more influence than ability, but however 'disquieting' their existence may be, they have never done me any harm that I know of. And, starting off as a non-affluent non-Etonian without acquaintances in that world, I found it a surprisingly easy one to move about in.

162

Even that business about the Angry Young Men, which is going to look so wonderful if anyone remembers it in a few years' time, had its appealing side. It is difficult to sound sincere in repudiating free publicity, so I was lucky in never having to. In any case, the simplifications and distortions inevitable in gossipy booksy journalism fell short of tempting me irresistibly to break the writer's first rule and start explaining what I 'really meant' by my books. And if it was boring at times to be asked by new acquaintances what I was so angry about, I was amply repaid on other occasions by seeing people wondering whether I was going to set about breaking up their furniture straight away or would wait till I was drunk. Sometimes I would meditate on how nice it would be if one's novels were read as novels instead of sociological tracts, but then one morning the whole shooting-match just softly and silently vanished away, and there we all were, reduced to being judged on our merits again. Which ought to be all right, if the merits hold up.

If they do, then some of us will have the chance of becoming lone voices in the only way that really matters: by writing well. The less appealing side of the Angry Young Man business was that it embodied and encouraged a Philistine, paraphrasing, digest-compiling attitude to literature, one which was favoured not only outside the phantom 'movement' (on the dailies' book pages) but inside it as well (in the works of Colin Wilson and others). The taking of such a view is a constant temptation to everybody, not only where literature is concerned — I wonder how much of the vilification modern British philosophy encounters comes from its tendency to resist the act of paraphrase, to remain obdurately philosophical in the face of attempts to boil off its 'technique' and reduce it to a series of assertions constituting a 'world view'. But that is not my battle. Literature is, and the situation there is more serious, for this, as no other, is a field in which any fool can have an opinion. Nearly any fool, plus many non-fools in their weaker, more fatigued, less attentive moments, would rather read a book as a purée of trends and attitudes than as a work of art having its own unique, unparaphrasable qualities. And here comes my chance to do justice to *Scrutiny* by observing that at any rate it fought hard against this kind of Philistinism, and that it represented the only important body of opinion on that side of the fight.

Any decent writer sees his first concern as the rendering of what he

163

takes to be permanent in human nature, and this holds true no matter how 'contemporary' his material. Now and again he may feel – we should perhaps think less of him if he did not ever feel – that there are some political causes too vast or urgent to be subordinated to mere literature, and will allow one or other such to determine the shape of what he writes. But by doing so he will have been guilty of betrayal. He will have accelerated the arrival of the day on which it is generally agreed that a novel or a poem or a play is no more than a system of generalizations orchestrated in terms of plot and diction and situation and the rest; the day, in other words, on which the novel, the poem and the play cease to exist, and that is the worst prospect of all.

1960

POSTSCRIPT 1970

Most of this still strikes me as fair enough. I was wrong about the 1950s not finishing until the end of 1960; it was only the sixth decade of the twentieth century that lasted until then. However, I shall certainly be greeting the new century on 1 January 2001, not 2000, assuming that, at the age of seventy-eight, I retain my interest in such finer points.

The trend-spotting thing has moved both upwards and downwards, or at any rate outwards, since I wrote. Ten years ago, observed or fancied trends were taken to be bad; nowadays they are usually thought of as good, if not potentially profitable. Fashion, in styles of dress and related spheres, must be taken to be both enjoyable to its pursuers and generally harmless, unless one is prepared to set up as knowing better than other people how they ought to spend their time and money. But, in the arts, to follow the trend is not quite necessarily the way to excellence, and to be tacitly (or vocally) encouraged to do so is harmful to all but the most stoutly independent spirits. To be sure, fashion has always played an unacknowledged, unapproved and far from sinister minor role among the mass of influences on virtually all works of art; but when that role becomes acknowledged and approved it ceases to be minor and becomes sinister. Swinging poetry is the enemy of good poetry, and the critic who fastens just on anything that is new – not original, only new in the sense in which a new washing-powder is new: different on the outside but really just the

164

same as all the countless others up in the forefront – well, I was going to say that such a critic should back down into the glossy magazines where he belongs, but nowadays he gives himself critical airs even there. Swinging ones, of course.

Something comparable has happened to mass culture, though here a polarization – good God! I mean a split – has taken place along clear political lines. A consensus of the 'sixties – an intellectual consensus, that is, not a real one – has been that whatever is revolutionary (or destructive) is good, and you know what you can do with anything indifferent or inimical to that spirit. So, with mass culture of yesterday or the day before, folk or folkish songs of the Left ('How the money rolls in') are the spontaneous expression of popular feeling, whereas those of a less liberal tendency ('Up your pipe, King Farouk') are impositions by a fascist-minded officer class or something.

The picture is wider, though at least as clear, when it comes to today's stuff. Technique imported into 'art' from advertisements, comics and the like are deemed not only to have mysteriously shed the guilt attachable to their capitalist origins, but to impart a 'much-needed' dose of 'vitality' into our tottering culture. At least, this applies in politically acceptable cases, as when Lord Kitchener, say, is portrayed as a dough-faced moron. A cartoon of Mao Tse-tung trampling on Chinese peasants, on the other hand, would be found to be without artistic merit, a typically mindless and dehumanizing product of the mass media. This has to be an imaginary example, because nobody could be found to draw or publish such an enormity. A pair of real examples is provided by – what else? – the *Observer*, now no more than wetly trendy in such matters, to be sure, and so preferable to the active and sometimes vicious Leftist propagandizing of the *Sunday Times*.

Like other papers, the *Observer* provides its readers with a summary of the day's television programmes and snippets of comment on them, though, unlike its contemporaries, it smuggles opinion in here disguised as information. Recently, within a few weeks of each other, two old movies received very different treatment in this column. One, concerned with the rounding-up of a Communist spy-ring in Hawaii, was described as 'an unpleasant reminder of Hollywood's brief Red-baiting phase' and also as 'unpleasant' – the man (or girl) who wrote the couple of dozen words of comment clearly felt that this was no time for literary nicety: after all, the thing had the notoriously unpleasant John Wayne in it. The other film, *Man Hunt*, was enthusiastically commended as 'Fritz Lang's anti-Nazi thriller' – what more need be said?

It happened that I watched both pieces, hoping, like most people, for nothing more than to be entertained. The Wayne film was, so to speak, exceptionally average, treating its Communist bad men as no more than bad men who were Communists because they had to be something, and certainly not 'unpleasant' to any way of thinking bar that which finds the very notion of a Communist bad man intolerable. The 'anti-Nazi' thriller was a leaden travesty of the Geoffrey Household masterpiece – *Rogue Male* – on which it pretended to be based, rising to mediocrity only at the rare moments when it faintly recalled the book, and featuring for most of its length an excruciating portrayal by poor Joan Bennett of a Cockney trollop. I dislike Nazis myself, but, it seems, not *enough*.

A good rough rule is that, to be certain of being accounted *aesthetically* 'exciting' or 'challenging' or whatever you please, any new bit of mass/popular culture/entertainment has got to take an unfavourable view of the status quo, to celebrate protest as the paramount of underlying heroic quality, to exalt a Peter Sellers (that innocent millionaire) into a martyr to the pressures of our society. I pass (gladly) over the point that current stage drama need only affront most people's moral, not political, susceptibilities in order to achieve artistic success, and can round off this part of my re-appraisal by remarking that, for the moment at any rate, serious fiction remains a form in which political tendency is less than an infallible guide to merit, always provided that the novelist concerned has won sufficient respectable – and here I mean truly respectable – critical support. Thus Anthony Powell has not as yet been found artistically disreputable on the grounds of undue attachment to bourgeois values, even though Elizabeth Taylor, Elizabeth Jane Howard and others have been seen to lack literary value out of devoting attention to 'unrepresentative' and 'irrelevant' social groups. But this takes me some distance from the topic of mass culture.

Advertising. I was wrong about commercial television being very vulgar and all that, or perhaps I only mean that I now find myself watching that channel nine-tenths of the time I spend in front of the set, much to my non-edification whenever I glance at a TV critic's column. And I have much less fault than formerly to find with the commercials. Either they have grown funnier or I prize any relief from the din of impartial, fact-finding, anti-democratic reports on today. Trend-men, too, seem to have decided that advertising in general has stopped being bad and has become good, now that so many of them and their friends have got into it. Possibly they are not the same trend-men as those who were denouncing the whole thing back in the 1950s.

Education. Oh dear. All I will do for the moment is protest against the way my trenchant slogan about the consequences of a violently and artificially increased university intake, 'more will mean worse', has been so regularly misquoted as 'more means worse'. As I have several times unavailingly argued in letters to the press intended to rectify the misquotation, the two versions are not interchangeable. What I wrote, even taken out of its context, implies a particular situation, a fore-seeable future, an argument about priorities and material. What so many usually hawk-eyed commentators go on as if they thought I wrote implies some sort of immutable principle, perhaps extensible beyond the point at issue. If I feel increasingly, in my darker moments, that there is something to be said for that principle, I did not invoke it in what I wrote in 1960. I feel too that any hawk-eyed commentator who has proved himself so clearly unacquainted with what I wrote about the relation between more and worse must also have failed to acquaint himself with the reasons I adduced for my version of it. And, if I may say so, with much else besides.

Mr Henry Fairlie has taxed me, in conversation, with having unat-tractively, and perhaps self-pityingly, gone to the lengths of 'writing about' my early struggles in the closing page or so of the above piece, pointing out that all of us have had to endure something like, or worse than, that. I think now that he was right, though the observations I add immediately afterwards still strike me as engagingly genial and tolerant.

My remarks about Dr Leavis and Scrutiny seem to me, ten years later, rather less than fair. My present view is that he and it have, on balance, done more harm than good to literature and its study.

KIPLING GOOD

Lord David Cecil once remarked that when we say a man looks like a poet we don't mean he looks like Chaucer and we don't mean he looks like Dryden and we don't mean he looks like Shakespeare. I forget exactly who he said we did mean he looked like: Shelley, perhaps, or Dylan Thomas. Anyhow, Lord David might well agree that when we – that is, persons living in the middle of the twentieth century – say a poet we don't mean he looks like Chaucer and we don't mean he looks like Yevgeny Yevtushenko.

On my experience the other week in Cambridge, Yevtushenko's looks were the most striking thing about him. His clothes reflected perfectly his elegant and casual demeanour: light-grey silk suit with variations in tone that did not quite constitute a pattern, navy-blue brass-button shirt with a vertical chequer-board strip running up and over the right shoulder. His hands looked strong and deft, like a precision mechanic's. But his face held the attention. With its clear blue eyes, thin upper lip above delicate teeth, and generally flattish planes, it was both grim and gay, seeming to hold both these qualities at once when in repose and lending itself to swift alternation between the one mood and the other. I have found that kind of emotional agility to be uncommon among non-English-speaking intellectuals, and rare still among those of any nation who present themselves as poets.

No photograph of Yevtushenko could do justice to any of this, to the directness of his gaze or to his personal magnetism, a quality I had

168

hardly cared to believe in before I met him. The prospect of several hours' conversation through interpreters with a literary Russian had not thrilled me much, but when I arrived at the lunch and was introduced to him, all but one of my reservations vanished. The remnant was slight disquiet at the notion of being cross-examined about Russian and other foreign literature. This foreboding was justified: I ended the day feeling ignorant, which I imagine does one no harm occasionally.

We began well. Through one or other of the interpreters, who were both British, Yevtushenko complimented me on my novel *Lucky Jim*, which he said had been well received in Moscow. I said truthfully that I was pleased to hear it.

'Since the appearance of *Lucky Jim*, some people have found they've had to take up a new position,' one of the interpreters said.

'People in Russia? Good God. Tell him –'

'Er, not quite,' the other interpreter said. 'What Mr Yevtushenko wanted to know was whether, since the appearance of *Lucky Jim*, you've found you've had to take up a new position.'

'Oh. Well . . . not really.'

'But you've come to Cambridge. Won't that make you change your line? Do you like it here?'

'Oh yes. It's not too bad.'

'It's bourgeois, though, isn't it?'

'Yes, I suppose it is. But the people are quite pleasant.'

When this reached him Yevtushenko looked disappointed: I had become corrupted, perhaps, or else had just clammed up on him. He switched the talk to politics.

'In many countries,' he evidently said, 'there is a conflict between the bureaucrats, the Philistines (that's as near as I can get, it's got a broader meaning in Russian), and the people who want to live ordinary private lives.'

'Between the power men and the sensualists?'

'Possibly. There are really two international nations in existence, each with its own interests in common, and these override national interests.'

He developed this neo-Marxist thesis for a time, but always in general terms. In an attempt to give things some sort of concrete turn, I mentioned the power man's supposed indifference or hostility to bodily enjoyment, and instanced the tale that Hitler abominated smoking, feeling myself on safe ground here with one so clearly committed to the cigarette.

'Hitler's cigarettes were the chimneys of the extermination camps,' was the reply. There were more such *sententiae* later, all as hard to answer as this one.

'What do you think of *Dr Zhivago?*' I was asked.

'I haven't read it. I don't know Russian.'

'It has been translated.'

'I know.' I thought of doing my piece about an interest in the paraphrasable content of literature being an anti-literary interest, but refrained. It felt too boring in anticipation.

After lunch we went across to King's chapel. Yevtushenko's height and youth and foreign look gave him an authority which had nothing to do with arrogance. In the way he looked about him I thought I detected the courteous interest, the concern to see but not to make comparisons, of a man looking at something impressive that the Other Side had done.

'You atheist?' he asked me in English.

'Well yes, but it's more that I hate him.'

I felt he understood me very fully. He gave his delightful grin. There was in it a superiority impossible to resent. (It might be real.) 'Me,' he said, pointing to himself, then gesturing more vaguely towards the roof, the other people there, the Rubens, but also seeming to include the being I had just mentioned; 'me . . . means nothing.'

Outside again, we walked towards the river. 'You like Kipling?' he asked. 'Kipling . . . good.'

'Isn't he an imperialist?'

He gave a brief shout of laughter. 'Oh yes. But . . . good. Russian translator Shakespeare . . . good. Translator Shakespeare translator Kipling. Good.' Then he declaimed something I can only represent as:

'*Boots, boots, boots, boots, koussevitsky*
   borodin,
Boots, boots, boots, boots, dostoievsky
   gospodin . . .'

and so on for another two or three couplets.

'It sounds good,' I said.

On the way up in the car we noticed some uniformly clad figures flitting about beyond the trees. Yevtushenko turned round animatedly. 'Football,' he said.

'Cricket, I think.'

'Football.'

We stopped the car to prove it to him. He turned round again. 'You like football?'

'Well, not soccer so much. I prefer Rugby.'

'*Roogbi*,' the interpreter said. 'What else can I say?'

Yevtushenko did his disappointed look.

When we stopped finally he leaned over and grasped my wrist in the way he had – I forget what led up to this – and spoke with great earnestness. 'I am only a writer by coincidence. My readers would write exactly as I do if they wanted to write. They created me, I didn't create them.'

We got out. I indicated my house. 'Bourgeois?'

He gave another shout of laughter. It had no edge to it.

The press boys were waiting. Yevtushenko refused brandy, said unavailingly: 'No photo,' and went and sat down on the lawn. A sort of interview developed. I found it natural to look at the interpreter when I was talking and also when he was talking. Yevtushenko, however, looked at me more or less throughout, so that he could put his points with maximum conviction and then, while these were being translated, be on the alert for each fresh access of bafflement or horror as it dawned on my face. He always did this, I was told later. It disconcerted me a little at the time.

He was rather severe, for him, when I expressed indifference to the work of Henry Moore and said lamely that I preferred something I could make a bit of head or tail of. 'There is an old Russian proverb' – I gazed unbelievingly at the interpreter – 'which says that some kinds of simplicity are worse than theft.'

'Yes. Would you ask him who are the readers he writes for?'

'Russian writers have always written for the people. Some of my poems are for the workers and soldiers, others for the intelligentsia.'

'Doesn't he find it hard to be two men at the same time?'

'There's no difficulty. The bonfire is the same even though the flames fly out in different directions.'

'Does he feel his primary responsibility is to literature or to the Russian reading public?'

'To both.'

Hereabouts the interpreter explained to me that time was getting short; Yevtushenko was booked for his reading at the Union in about an hour, after an undergraduate tea and a game of ping-pong – he had to have that before he read.

When he had said: 'Some poems are like some children: the ugliest are the best,' we wrapped things up. A little of the damp from the lawn had transferred itself to the seat of the poet's trousers. He cured this himself, politely taking an electric iron off my eight-year-old daughter and vanishing into the play-room. It was all over before the photographers could do anything. 'That's the shot of the year gone,' they said morosely.

Rather as earlier, the thought of a poetry recital in an unfamiliar language had not greatly excited me. The reality was for long periods absorbing and at no time dull. Yevtushenko's voice, leaning hard on vowels not at the beginning of a syllable but an instant later, ranged from sad quietude to sonorous declamation in a way that perhaps suggested a good Russian actor reciting Shakespeare. The renderings were evidently word-perfect* and under complete control. Everybody listened hard.

Each poem was preceded by an admirably un-'poetical' prose translation. The evidence of these would have convinced me, had I needed to be, that the man before us was not a charlatan. But I wondered, trying to allow for my ignorance, whether I was right in detecting a lack of the power of statement. The 'They' whose presence, expressed or unexpressed, can be felt in Soviet verse seem hostile to the very quality of that verse by pushing it into dealing with pluralities and abstractions. Is it a bourgeois or other prejudice to feel that poetry had better deal with the particular, with the concrete, with the present indicative and the preterite rather than the durative present and the imperfect? And similarly, that if poetry is pushed too far away from statement in one of two opposite directions – towards fiction or towards symbol – it may be weakened? Anyway, if there really is a lack of statement in Soviet verse, I would back Yevtushenko as the man to put it there. 'One day,' as he said, 'it will be normal, not courageous, to write the truth.'

* I was told later that at one point Yevtushenko got a line wrong and instantly improvised a following line that both rhymed and made sense – a convincing example of the professionalism that marked his whole performance.

The reading was a great and genuine success. Afterwards we took our leave in what seemed to be the Russian rather than the English manner. That was all right with me. Yevtushenko went off waving his joined fists in the boxer's gesture. He is the first completely good reason I have met with for liking the U.S.S.R.

1962

POSTSCRIPT 1970

In the autumn of 1968, it will (perhaps, I suppose, just about) be remembered that Yevtushenko's name was put forward for the then vacant Chair of Poetry at Oxford University. Retaining affectionate memories of our meeting in Cambridge more than six years earlier, and not having specially noticed what he might have been up to in the meantime, I felt an initial surge of interest and expectation. Yevgeny in Oxford? Quite an idea ...

I had forgotten the odious but inescapable fact that there are some nationalities whose members are not just members of those national-ities, that whereas an Australian, say, is just an Australian, and a Dane just a man from Denmark, a Russian is more than just a Russian, at any rate outside Russia: if he comes to England and goes away without defecting he is somebody working in the service of his horrible govern-ment, not by any means necessarily an 'agent' in a full sense, but somebody trusted to uphold and advance the interests of that govern-ment – it cannot, sadly, be otherwise. And Yevtushenko, unac-companied, had been, not only to England, but to Cuba, Italy, the United States, Spain, Australia, Senegal, France, Denmark, Mexico and Portugal.

Despite this, despite his having put a recognizable Soviet line across on these trips (or missions), despite the endorsement of his candidacy by the Russian Embassy in London, despite his proven failure to have signed any of the dozens of protest documents that had reached the West from the U.S.S.R. over the previous few years, the word in our liberal press and among Oxford students was that Yevtushenko was a rebel, an anti-Establishment figure, an opponent of all orthodoxy and so (never mind his ignorance of English) just the chap for the Oxford Poetry Chair. Bernard Levin and I, independently at first, opposed him in the public print.

The response was immediate, widespread and extraordinarily virulent. It was clear that Levin and I had wandered into the middle of a concerted campaign to win the post for Yevtushenko. The Thomson press, with three *Times* diary boosts and five *Sunday Times* articles, led the chorus. The editor of the *New Statesman* said more impartially that Levin and I might be right on this issue, but added that we had supported American action in Vietnam, so where did that leave us? A correspondent in *Tribune* said there was no problem, because Yevtushenko was against capitalism and I was for it. So it went on.

One disturbing – and bloody annoying – feature of the affair was the difficulty those on the anti-Yevtushenko side encountered in getting that view of the case into print. The editor of the *New Statesman* at first refused to publish Levin's and my answer to attacks on us (these had included at least one flat lie) and then found room for half of it three issues after the original attacks. The editor of the *Sunday Times* refused to publish in full our retort to two Yevtushenko boosts, invoking some newly minted rule whereby we must confine ourselves to the length of *one* of the boosts, and explaining that he needed space for another article on the subject – which turned out to be another Yevtushenko boost. The editor finally printed a third of our letter alongside yet another Yevtushenko boost, and closed the correspondence the same moment that it opened. The editor of the *Spectator*, much more surprisingly, closed his correspondence, re-opened it to slip in a further Yevtushenko boost, and instantly closed it again. And people complain that our press has a Rightist bias!

Long before the dust had finally settled, Yevtushenko lost the Oxford election by a substantial but not overwhelming margin. I still wonder what were the motives of those who supported so tenaciously a man who had gone out of his way – this, I think, was finally established beyond doubt – to denounce colleagues of his who really are courageous fighters against, or victims of, tyranny. Some, I am sure, and have shown I understand, must have been won over by Yevtushenko's personal qualities. Others, like the accredited translators of his work into English, had a legitimate professional stake in the matter as well. Others again were the dupes or the conscious agents of a Moscow-inspired attempt to plant a trusted Soviet publicist right in the middle of the British cultural scene.

Three closing observations occur to me. I may, I think, have overestimated in 1968 the degree to which Yevtushenko reflects or reflected the *central* Soviet line, that of the top leadership; he may rather have been a representative of a more 'liberal', or less inflexibly anti-liberal, faction some distance from the top, as his previous association with Khrushchev would indicate, and as his mysterious 'telegram' to Brezhnev about the invasion of Czechoslovakia, never to my mind satisfactorily established, might also suggest. Nevertheless, 'liberalism' of such a kind is, or ought to be, quite illiberal enough for most Western tastes, and (second point) a couple of Yevtushenko's more recent poems, about the Sino-Soviet border disputes and the Pinkville massacre respectively, seem to testify to a dismaying readiness to turn out versified propaganda of the most orthodox possible sort.

Thirdly, it is important, in considering matters such as this, not to succumb to the keen temptation to lament the destructive effect of governments and politics and what-not on what should be a free, supra-national community of poets and scholars. Not the existence of governments, but of Communist governments, not politics but totalitarian politics, divide and impair that community. It will always be the same, until Russians become nothing more than Russians.

My first visit to Cambridge was, perhaps by way of omen, to fail a scholarship. I find it ominous too that, although I can still visualize fairly sharply the environs of the digs I stayed in for that couple of days in 1940, I was never able to locate them in the Cambridge I saw in 1961–3. Similarly, I suppose I must have sat the examination somewhere in St Catherine's, but renewed inspection of that college brought no twinge, not even of remembered apprehension. I might have known that Cambridge would never come to hold what Oxford still holds for me, the affectionate, dimly melancholic appeal of a place one has done some growing-up in. That appeal is untransferable.

To have set off with a personal note or two is appropriate. Although I consider myself better off outside Cambridge than in it, I am not going to offer a supposedly objective account of its defects as an institution or of those in our higher education system at large. Both Cambridge and system, indeed, seem to me very much worth defending, especially against the kind of encroachment recommended in the Robbins Report. But one of the more grateful rewards of ceasing to teach is that of being able to lay down one's arms in this all but lost battle – hardly a battle, really, more like a campaign with the two armies for the most part out of range of each other, and thus doubly exhausting. In any event, my withdrawal from the academic scene means that, when (or if) in due course people start noticing that we have more university graduates than we know what to do with and that their standard is low, I shall be able to enjoy saying 'I told you so' at a comfortable distance from the *débâcle*.

At Oxford – to continue with reminiscence – my relations with the dons were never close. My tutorial experiences as an undergraduate, and later as a graduate student, plus some attempts to drink port and crack walnuts as a Senior Common Room guest, made me think there were two sorts of dons. There were old dons, port-and-walnuts men who were courteous and had once written a book, but who said little about literature except that Chaucer was a perpetual fountain of good sense and Milton had organ music. And there were young dons, brusquer figures who were, or had been, often absent in places like the Ministry of Information and who knew a tremendous lot which they did not ordinarily divulge.

My tutor in 1941, the late Gavin Bone, partook of both types. On my first visit, my eye was caught by a set of handsome blue-bound tomes on his bookshelves. Their general title, *The Works of Chaucer* or words to that effect, led me to believe that here was a set of the works of Chaucer. I drew attention to it. 'That's a nice set of Chaucer you've got there,' I said.

'That? Oh, that's not an edition,' Bone said. 'It's a list of the variant readings in the different manuscripts. Have a look if you like.' He brought one of the volumes over. 'Photographed typescript,' he explained. 'No printer could set up this sort of stuff. The Americans did it.'

I suppose I made some reply. The incident impressed me. That was Oxford scholarship: there was no knowledge but they knew it, or anyway could get at it by stretching out a hand. At the same time they were very upper class (like so many of their pupils). A few provincials might have got in because of the vulgar recency of their subjects, or as egalitarian window-dressing, but the main outline fitted in with my early picture – which I have since had to modify only in detail – of British culture as the property of some sort of exclusive club. I never liked this, but when in 1961 a job at Cambridge came up, I told myself that things like the passage of time and a couple of Labour governments would have put paid to the class business and also seen off the old dons. Cambridge, moreover, was not Oxford: to my contemporaries it had always seemed mysteriously more 'go-ahead' than the other place. And the presence there of Dr Leavis guaranteed that, if nothing else, nobody could get away with talking about fountains of good sense and organ music.*

My expectations of Cambridge, then, were naive. They had somehow survived the general drubbing which a dozen years of teaching in the provinces had given my ideals. They were also predominantly intellectual, in the sense that I felt I was in for an experience primarily concerned with the things of the mind, the study of English literature in particular. That hero-figure of my youth, the don who whether old or young was devoted to serious, disinterested inquiry, was about to be made flesh. I found quite early that not only was he not going to emerge from the mists of illusion, but that the experience I was in for was primarily not academic but social. Like many an undergraduate, and to no better effect than many, I found much of my energy leaking away in a struggle to replace the one by the other.

With the possible exception of the subscription dance (in aid of the local youth club or whatever), no more powerful instrument of social unhappiness exists than the dinner party. I differentiate this from the often rewarding habit of having a few drinks and something to eat in the company of friends and their friends, and I contrast it very unfavourably with the cocktail party – so often vilified by its keenest attendants – and the pub session. Unlike either of these, the dinner party prohibits late or casually attired arrival, early or manifestly drunken departure, total non-appearance without grave illness or domestic tragedy as an excuse. Worse, the characteristic form demands that the sufferer spend a good two hours immovably trying to talk and listen to people he has never seen before.

The Feast, or similar college function, goes several better than this in its enforcement of active boredom. It starts by habitually excluding women – the sole excuse (and a poor one) for dressing up in those ridiculous and uncomfortable clothes. It prolongs matters by Latin toasts and loving-cup ceremonies and by multiplying the number of courses – by a horrible irony, these last are almost always delicious and accompanied by marvellous wines, so that the experience of eating and drinking them in strange company is rather like listening to Mozart, say, while suffering from toothache. (Mozart at just less than comfortable volume, too: there is never enough wine.) The hall is

* But you could get clean away with talking about normative significance, achieved actuality and the transcendent genius of Đ. H. Lawrence.

unheated. Hours of nicotine-starvation elapse. And, just in case your man might have struck a congenial neighbour, at dessert next door he is placed with a completely fresh set of people, drinking first-class after-dinner drinks which he must remember to keep passing leftwards or cannot get at because someone else has forgotten this duty.

The above may sound peevish, or obvious. My dislike of being compelled to converse with strangers is perhaps excessive. Although guest-nights in other colleges might involve some port-passing protocol, or even a lecturette from the Master on the provenance of the Combination Room panelling, dining ordinarily in one's own college, among colleagues, not strangers, is pleasant enough. No penalty is awarded for non-attendance at Feasts, and the city's restaurants, pubs and private houses are always available. Nevertheless the Feast is Cambridge at its most Cantabrigian, and to have ceremonially burnt my dinner-jacket in King's Parade was the valedictory gesture which attracted me most, ahead of tearing up my notes on Jane Austen or dropping *Biographia Literaria* into the Cam. I am objecting not to an exhibition of snobbery, but to a mode of social behaviour which narrows and formalizes and stiffens ordinary intercourse, which colours to some extent all other collegiate modes and which the new-comer will either conform to or retreat from into a sulky leather-jacketism.

I should point out here, and in general, that truth as well as piety leads me to salute Peterhouse as an oasis of good nature and common sense. Possibly its smallness helped. I never saw there any of the 'college politics' which, together with port-quaffing, form the total of donnish activities in the popular mind. I suspect anyway that such 'politics' are not a besetting sin in Cambridge at large, and that warring factions are actually to be found in a couple of other fields. Dispute abounds between the colleges on the one hand and the University on the other: the main issue here is the right, or non-right, of the colleges to appoint Fellows freely, according to their needs and preferences, rather than under dictation from the University. Elsewhere the scene of conflict is within (no doubt occasionally between) individual Faculties. I saw little of this, having no lecturing post in the English Faculty, though at the one general meeting I was invited to I witnessed a first-rate clash of opposing juntas, perhaps staged expressly for my benefit.

My contact with my fellow academics, then, was not often directly professional. Very good. I sat back for a dose of original and well-grounded talk about English literature. I did not get it. (I am sure I did not give it, either.) To my dismay, what I got was talk about intra-Faculty discord and personal quarrels, syllabus changes, the proportion of firsts to other classes, the attendance at old Joe Soap's lectures, etc. – necessary topics, no doubt, but discussed in my presence far more exclusively than I remember from my provincial days, when a remark about Donne would come up now and then. In general – I encountered three shining exceptions to all this, two of whom have now gone elsewhere – in general, were they so pleased to be at Cambridge that they thought less about anything else? Certainly, I thought Cambridge meant too much to Cambridge. A history don in another college told me of how, after a year at Yale, he came back quite eager to discuss with his colleagues what he had learnt there. They listened for a time and then asked him if he thought Snooks had the weight for this new Readership. 'You go south of Royston,' my informant ended gloomily, 'and you're in the outer darkness.'

On the other hand, one expectation of mine was realized, at any rate in part. At the donnish level, the class thing did seem to have faded away. The commonly held view that the selection of candidates for college entrance has a class bias is misinformed. On the contrary, many colleges lean over backwards to admit grammar-school boys, so much so that once, at a scholarship meeting, I found myself arguing that a boy's having been to a well-known public school should not be held against him. What keeps the class thing going at the *undergraduate* level, what sees to it that only nine per cent of entrants come from working-class homes, is the clear general superiority of public-school education. The way to bring it about that the highest I.Q.s get to Cambridge, or Oxford (if this is thought desirable), is not to lecture selection boards on their sensitivity to accents, but to reform the school system, which is a good idea anyway.*

However understandable it might be that undergraduate Cambridge is still the resort of the upper classes, the results of this depressed me.

* By 'reform' I meant 'improve' – by raising teachers' salaries to attract more able people into the profession, increasing expenditure on buildings and equipment, etc. – not 'reform in accordance with progressive educationists' theories'.

To hear all those young chaps – a small minority, no doubt, but how vocal – braying and baying to one another across the street or the interiors of pubs distracted me from thoughts of Donne. At times I became a one-man resistance movement, broadcasting baleful glares, trying to force them to thank me when I stood aside for them in shop doorways, stopping them from hijacking taxis. No good. They were too firmly seated. Early one lunchtime I was enjoying a quiet beer and minding my own business in Miller's Wine Parlour when a voice suddenly bawled:

'Well of course I know that style of acting's been pretty much left behind these days but I must say that a fellow like Gielgud does seem to *me* to have a certain *presence* and *authority* and at least one does get the feeling that the man's read a *book* occasionally and can come on to the stage without *throwing himself about* like a . . .'

There was more. What arrested me was not the content of this discourse but its volume. I looked about me in amazement. Nobody else was taking the least notice; even Stanley behind the bar went on calmly polishing glasses. If I had been the father of the orator – he sat surrounded by parents and relatives – I should have laid my finger to my lips or, if that failed, my hand across his mouth. But then, I reflected, I am a child of the lower middle classes, whose members keep their voices down in public lest others may hear and condemn. And I had not had time to get used to Cambridge.

All these dissatisfactions may be thought to have their root in a sense of injured merit. Perhaps I felt I got less than what I felt was my due as a man of letters. Perhaps. But what I expected was far less a D. Litt. *honoris causa* than a going-over or two, an occasional outbreak of threats and abuse. Even these were denied me. (A writer in *Delta* did complain that he had not found a novel of mine so much as funny, but Cambridge is the least damaging place in England in which not to be found funny.) However, it was conveyed to me repeatedly and authentically that an eminent figure in the English Faculty, on being told that Peterhouse had such-and-such a view of such-and-such a problem, had retorted: 'Peterhouse can't expect to be taken seriously about anything now that it's given a Fellowship to a *pornographer*.'

This was taken to refer to me, rather than to any of the recently appointed Research Fellows in branches of the sciences. The imputation surprised me at first. I have always thought my work very chaste, somewhat concerned with sex, admittedly, but so sparing of physical descriptions as almost to incur the opposite – and to me far graver – charge of discreditable reticence. But it is not for me to determine, or to know, what other people may find sexually stimulating. Only the other day I was reading about a man who got a kick out of winding pyjama cords round himself and kissing pieces of paper. Should somebody feel impelled to use my books for this sort of purpose, I can have no valid objection.

I was even more surprised to hear from many sources that I was widely regarded in Cambridge as a homosexual. It is not for me to quote evidence against this idea, but if there is any of that in me it must operate at a level inaccessible to introspection. Anyway, after being disconcerted for a time, I thought I had found the reason for such a view of me. I was sometimes to be seen round the pubs drinking with my pupils, who were perforce young men. In the provinces this would hardly be noticed – in some Swansea pubs, for instance, the absence of such circles would be unusual – but at Cambridge it seems to be rare, at any rate in the humanities. I am not going to pretend that, on the occasions mentioned, literature was seriously discussed very often. But it was sometimes, and I think this can be very valuable. It is not that pubs have any mystical virtue; it is just that in their ambience teacher and pupil can talk on something much nearer equal terms than is possible during the supervision period or tutorial hour, when, inevitably and rightly, a degree of formality prevails. There is an important general point here.

At some stage in talking to every other undergraduate I would ask him what he most felt the lack of in Cambridge life. All of them without exception, however much they differed in other ways, said they wished they had more contact with senior members of their college and of the University. The first time I heard this was after the meeting of a literary club I had been giving a talk to. I pointed out that many a well-disposed don was probably nervous of anything more intimate than the official sherry party. There were too few even of these, they said. I argued that an uncommonly fine tact was needed on the don's side if he were not to appear either merely dutiful or excessively chummy. 'Yes,' a dozen young men seemed to say in unison, 'but he could try.' Any complaint so universally and warmly voiced, at any rate in Cambridge (and Oxford too? – but the provinces less?), needs urgent attention. The undergraduate deserves to feel one of the same group as his pastors and masters: the etymology of the word 'university', in fact, proclaims the unity of teachers and taught. The confusion and apathy of many students, the lack of sense of direction – not to speak of more painful troubles – so often commented upon, all derive in part, I suggest, from failure to bridge the gap. One notices that undergraduate isolation seems more acute at Cambridge and Oxford, where the dons are less accessible, than in the provinces, where, I have said, relations tend to be closer.

The (Cambridge) tutorial system and the (Oxford) moral tutor system are inadequate solutions. With the best will in the world – and the will is very often of the best – a don who is busy with administration as well as with his own work cannot be expected to become more than acquainted with the dozens of young men under his care. He will be resorted to, if ever, only when trouble has become acute. Far more radical measures are needed. A change of heart among dons in general would help, a decision that the company of one's pupils, however distasteful, must be cultivated. And why should it be distasteful? The don to whom the society of the young is not positively congenial has little reason to be where he is. I saw few of his kind at Swansea.

Changes of heart, however, are unreliable. Nothing less will do than a planned return to the days when dons (being forbidden to marry) made the college their home, and when, consequently, the college community had a chance of being a real one. Nowadays most dons are family men; major interests take them out of college, which becomes a place where they teach and eat some of their meals. I am not advocating anything so drastic as a reimposition of celibacy. The married dons and their families must be moved bodily into college or – to use a term more appropriate to what I envisage – on to campus. (Churchill College has made a start on this.) Such is the only arrangement I can think of whereby don and undergraduate could achieve the kind of casual neighbourliness from which both would benefit. The accommodation problems would be immense, let alone the mental readjustment. But if the colleges want to defend their autonomy, and I think they are right to do so, they must show that there is a college life which is worth defending.

Nothing I have said so far has much bearing on my decision to leave

Cambridge. However formidable its social barriers, my wife and I managed to keep on circumventing them. As time went on I found myself increasingly drawn to certain scientists, people who were not going to tell or ask me anything about the English Moralists paper in Part II of the English Tripos and who, with their love of music and interest in contemporary writing, seemed to unite the two cultures, or rather to demonstrate the unity and breadth of the one, in a way hardly possible to the humanities man. They and their wives lit up a rather shadowed picture, a town whose most characteristic images – King's chapel, say, at dusk in a thin mist – seemed cold and lonely, a setting more appropriate to an unhappy love affair than to the bustling exchange of ideas that is supposed to go on: inhospitable despite the ceaseless ceremonial parade of hospitality. Arrival at that curious railway station, with its endless single platform like something out of Kafka or Chirico, ought to tip off the sensitive. But I should not have wanted to write this part if Peterhouse and its gardens and its occupants (not least its kitchen staff) could have been put on rollers and shifted to somewhere in the Cotswolds or upstate New York.

What really drove me out was paradoxically what made me most reluctant to leave: teaching. Nobody who has not experienced it can fully imagine the peculiar drain which this activity makes on one's energy, nor its unique rewards. Ten or twelve hours a week, old boy? the businessman or journalist (or educationist) asks incredulously: you don't call that a job of work do you? I do. Leaving out preparation – and I had plenty of that, it never having occurred to me before that the works of Racine or Strindberg were necessary parts of an English course – I found myself fit for nothing much more exacting than playing the gramophone after three supervisions a day. I count this kind of teaching as about one-third as tiring as appearing on television. Try visualizing yourself getting home and carrying on with your novel after an hour in front of the cameras. Perhaps you could do it; I couldn't. And I am one of those who begin to feel uneasy after more than two or three days away from the typewriter. It seemed to me I had little choice.

The main point of teaching, in my view, is not simply that it affords an irreplaceable contact with youthful intelligences, though there is that. What distinguishes it is, in a sense, its social aspect. Serious, detailed and exhaustive discussion of literature is impracticable in any other context. The swapping of arguments over a glass of beer can be. I have suggested, a most valuable supplement to formal teaching, but it is no substitute for it. And to reach for the text during a chat among friends ('it just so happens that I have my *Paradise Lost* with me. Now if you'll glance at the passages I've marked near the beginning of the Sixth Book . . .') is something we are right not to do or to tolerate in others, unless in effect we are agreeing to teach or be taught. But reaching for the text, and at an early stage, is what we must do if discussion is not to peter out or shift its ground. The solitary student is thus under a handicap, and here is one half of the reason why teaching and research must go together. It is not just that the teacher can try out his ideas on the pupil, as on the dog. Teaching his ideas teaches him what these ideas are.

I miss my pupils not only as instruments of my own education, but as people. They were an amiable and tolerant lot. One of them was always hunting and shooting and fishing when he should have been telling me about *Middlemarch*; another brought me forty pages on *King Lear*; a third did not know what satire was. (That was back in '61.) But I survived this. I forgive them all for forcing me to read *Volpone* and *The Anatomy of Melancholy* and *Bleak House* (especially THAT) and *Heart of Darkness*. Can I say more?

1964

POSTSCRIPT 1970

When I re-read this I was mildly staggered by the remark near the beginning about 'British' culture (these days I should write 'our' culture) seeming to be the property of some sort of exclusive club. How things have changed in six or seven years! I thought – or how inattentive I had perhaps been to changes then already in progress. On further reflection, however, I feel the description may stand. It is true that classical music, with the doubtful exception of opera, is not open to all, and that jazz and its derivatives always have been. But poetry, the theatre and what used to be called the fine arts (to name three fields in which there might be supposed to have been considerable broadening of appeal and audience) remain in essence exclusive. The larger public obtain a simulacrum of aesthetic experience – if that – from what is usually a simulacrum of art – if that. This in itself may or may not be deplorable. Possibly a simulacrum of such experience is better than nothing, and probably simulacra of art have no adverse effects on art. But I cannot see the exclusivity of the latter ever being much alleviated. Indeed, as education (not a *sine qua non* for the attaining of aesthetic experience, but, in our society at least, a major route to it) becomes harder and harder to come by, one might expect some further narrowing of the genuine artistic public.

Life at High Table, my own college apart, was a good deal crappier than I overtly stated in my article. To put it journalistically, the moment when I finally decided it was not for me came when I was dining out at — never mind. Throughout the first course and most of the second, the talk at my end had turned exclusively upon the paintings, drawings, engravings and whatnot my neighbours had been buying. Noticing, presumably, that I had nothing whatever to contribute to this discussion, another guest asked me: 'And what is *your* particular, er, line of, er, country in this, er?' With truly operatic humility of tone and gesture, I said: 'I'm afraid I don't sort of go in for any of that kind of thing.' The other man said: 'H'm' – not a vocable in actual common use, but he used it. Then he said: 'I think that's a dreadful thing to say.' I went on keeping quiet for some time after that, wishing, for perhaps the hundredth time since arriving at Cambridge, that I were Jim Dixon.

My remarks about student difficulties carry today a rather attractive period flavour. As the reader will have noticed, I did not foresee the speed and thoroughness with which passive discontent would become active. I was wrong in supposing that, because of the closer connections between students and faculty I had found outside Oxford and Cambridge, youthful malaise was likely to be more acute at those two places. I had not thought of the harm which could be dealt the intellectually innocent, and the intellectually depraved, by too-close connections with a member of the faculty near to them in age and tastes and full of revolutionary afflatus. But I was right in taking the relationship of teacher and taught as the place to look when students are unhappy or disaffected. In the U.S.A., by a sort of irony, dissatisfaction with the admittedly imperfect state of that relationship has led in effect to its destruction. In this country, such unanimity as remains, or ever was, in the student 'movement' has concentrated on trying more or less peaceably to remove the distinction between teacher and taught, rather than the one simply assaulting the other head-on.

There are, of course, anterior factors. Reckless expansion of the student intake has brought to the university a large and increasing proportion of young people – some of them teachers – who, by intellect and/or temperament, are unfitted for the academic life and are painfully bewildered by what it requires of them. It is natural that they should start questioning a system that makes them feel like that.

My father stood five foot eight or nine: average height or a little over for one born at the end of the 1880s, rather short compared with his grandchildren's generation. With a stocky frame and some breadth of shoulder, he had a good build for games-playing. This was a passion of his life, and he kept it up longer than most men, playing vigorous tennis well into middle age and actively skippering the local cricket side in his sixties. His eye outlasted his wind; to the end he remained a stylish batsman, with a late cut I have rarely seen surpassed. His glance was direct, appraising, humorous and warm, yet also, at times troubled and petulant. He had a decent big nose that caused him, so he said, to be occasionally mistaken for a Jew by Jews; our name, with its closeness to Amos, may have contributed to this. He would tell anecdotes about it – embroideries, I imagine now, on a couple of ambiguous interchanges – with a typical mixture of amusement and unemphatic irritation.

In fact he was Nonconformist English from, ultimately, East Anglia, and if, much more ultimately, the Amises had come from France, there was no trace whatever of any of that by the time they produced my father, the most English human being I have ever known. This was one of the things I had against him in my teens. Nobody in the novels I was reading then was without his Russian grandmother, Italian aunt, Austrian step-sister, and even my school friends all seemed to have their bits of Scotch and Irish. The best I could do was a couple of American cousins, my father's sister's children – hopelessly unexotic.

Not only were my environment and upbringing insular almost to a fault – I went abroad for the first time, and then not voluntarily, in 1944 – it was also fiercely non-crazy: another let-down after the novels. My father's father had done a lot to set the tone. It is true that, beyond admitting to Norfolk origins, he would never say where or what he had come from, but I realized quite early that this reticence must spring from nothing more romantic than snobbery. He was a glass merchant in a fair way of business until Woolworth's came along and undersold him. There was one good story about the time, demonstrating to a potential customer, he broke an unbreakable tumbler, but, again, that was an accident. Habitual glass-smashing is not typical of chapel people.

It was, I believe, literally at chapel that my father first met my mother. Like his, her parents were Baptists of the Denmark Hill community. Her father, a self-taught musician, played the organ on Sundays. A lot of the rest of the time, when he was not serving in a local outfitter's, he played the piano or, according to my mother, had his nose in a book. The book was likely to be one of the standard English poets that filled his shelves. I should have liked to know what he thought about these, but he died when I was a child.

Chapel, as such, was a thing of the past by the time I was old enough to care about such matters. Reacting against his upbringing – boldly as it might have seemed then, mildly enough by present standards – my father had turned his back on any form of worship and, I suspect, on the Christian faith as well. I only suspect this, because he was not one for that sort of discussion, but I doubt if he would have needed to add much to the stray remark he let fall once or twice about there having to be some meaning to life, or a similar post-Protestant shred of belief. Anyway, he never put the slightest pressure on me to have anything to do with religion, explaining that he knew far too well what it felt like to be forced to attend chapel. The most he would do was to rebuke me for using the name of Christ as a swear word, and even this, superstition rather than piety, he dropped when I was grown up.

At the same time, of course, it was totally characteristic that, when plunged into unusually deep despair about my shortcomings, he was likely to put them down to my complete lack of religion. And I should not be truly his son if I had never felt that he had something there. But that was as far as doctrine went, no distance at all compared with the tremendous inroads of the morality associated with that doctrine. Matthew Arnold would have worried less about the survival of Christian ethics in an age without literal faith if he could have had a couple of chats with my father.

For parts of the training I received I can only be heartily grateful. I cannot claim to be more honest and responsible and thrifty and industrious than most people, but I am pretty sure I would be less distinguished in these fields if I had been brought up quite outside the shadow of the chapel. On the other hand, as I came to sense the image in which my father was trying to mould my character and future I began to resist him, and we quarrelled violently at least every week or two for years. It was not, I think, that I was unusually intractable by nature, nor that he took less kindly than most men to having his deeply felt wishes flouted, or at least contested, by somebody he had power over. Certainly, he had embarked on parenthood comparatively late, so that by the time I started noticing that he could be wrong about things he was already in his middle forties and, perhaps, less resilient than earlier. He had not, moreover, re-embarked on parenthood, and this had the common effect of sharply personalizing our conflict.

An only child is short not so much of allies, of supporters, as of means of dilution and diversion, another body to share the weight of parental care. This isolation may make him over-ready to defend his interests. For my own part, I had acquired from somewhere a very liberal helping of adolescent intellectual's arrogance, while inheriting in full measure my father's obstinacy. The last factor alone was enough to launch us regularly on one or another conversational collision course, immediately recognized as such by both, indeed by all, parties, but not to be deviated from at any price.

We were divided on the issue of sex to fully the expected degree, my father a card-carrying anti-self-abuser-cum-anti-fornicationist, myself opposed to neither. There was once a very big scene over the first of these, full of warnings about thinning of the blood and eventual hopeless insanity. I had the remarkable good sense not merely not to believe this, but to keep my disbelief to myself. Thereafter I went my own sexual way under a pact of silence and dissimulation. This suited my father, who was normally as reticent about this as about other basics. Apart from the fact of my own existence, no sort of detail of his sexual life ever reached me. I have often been tempted to think that it was never a very active one, but experience teaches that nothing is likely to fall more wildly astray than this sort of judgement, even as regards contemporaries whom one knows intimately.

What might roughly be called art was much more productive of overt friction between us. Art, not a word or a concept my father had much truck with, consisted for him of Gilbert and Sullivan, the Edwardian ballads (almost none of which ever came my way again) he and my mother and their friends sang at the piano, West End stage successes in which musical comedies of the Leslie Henson/Fred Emney type came to predominate, and detective stories by such as R. Austin Freeman, Francis Grierson and John Rhode. This list, admittedly not exhaustive, seemed and seems to me woefully short, especially for somebody by nature neither stupid nor incurious. Anyway, I had my own ideas of what art consisted of.

The art that most reliably provided a domestic *casus belli* was music. This was partly because it was the one for which my father, in his way, a way I had no time for at all at that stage, really cared. He wanted me to like Gilbert and Sullivan and took me to *The Pirates of Penzance* and *The Yeoman of the Guard*; I meanly exaggerated my boredom. He tried to get me interested in the ballads; I disparaged their lyrics and wanted to know why there was no Schubert or Wolf under the lid of the piano stool. I would go on to accuse him of not really liking music, to which he would retort, with annoying relevance, that that would come better from someone who, like him, could play some of the stuff. But a more important irritant was the nature of music itself. If I chose to waste a fine afternoon in an art gallery or to ruin my eyes over a book when I could have been out in the fresh air, then that – at any rate in my father's more tolerant moods – was up to me. Music kicked up a row, and I really could not expect to have the damned wireless or gramophone blaring through the house all the hours there were and upsetting my mother. Especially that sort of music . . .

Actually it was most sorts. My father's catholic distaste ranged from Dvořàk to Troise and his Mandoliers, from Benny Goodman to Haydn. He was not content with just registering objection in each case: he would deliver a critical verdict, often in the form of an analogy. There was a piece of Duke Ellington's, for instance, I think

191

from the *Black, Brown and Beige* suite – anyway, something about as far from primitivism as jazz had then got – which put my father in mind, or so he said, of a lot of savages dancing round a pot of human remains. 'The Swan of Tuonela', on the other hand, called up successive images of a small animal in pain and a large animal in pain. Perhaps it was the element of horrible truth in this which prevented me from seeing how funny it was and made me come up, as I surely must have done, with one of my blanket charges of dislike of all music.

These and related problems could have been easily solved in a different kind of household and house. We lived until 1940 in a short series of post-1918 suburban villas in which a kitchen, bathroom and box-room were added to the two-up-two-down formula. The partition walls were not specially thick, and most sounds went through them. And the room where one was in the evenings was naturally the one with the wireless in it.

Those who have grown up with the B.B.C. Third Programme and Music Programme might find it difficult to imagine how little music was broadcast in the 'thirties. One would go months without a chance to hear individual works in even the standard repertoire. So I would very much want to listen to Brahms's Second Symphony any time it was available, and my father, after a day at the office and getting on for an hour's journey home, would very much not. And there we were.

The smallness of 14, Buckingham Gardens, S.W.16 and of its successors was made mildly claustrophobic at times by my father's constant concern to prevent my getting away from him, in several senses of the phrase. He and my mother could not have restricted my choice of friends, and my chances of seeing them, more assiduously if there had been a long family history of male prostitution or juvenile dipsomania. When I was at home, as when not at school I usually was, I kept finding that reading in public was deemed rude, while reading in private was anti-social. There was a thing called joining in the family circle that has left me with a life-long non-enjoyment of sitting over the remains of a meal. This pattern persisted. Whenever, after my marriage, my family and I visited my parents or they came to stay, everything had to be done with everybody present: no recipe for getting the best out of people.

As if we had not had enough on our plates already, my father and I came to differ about politics. But I need spend no time on that: he was an ex-Liberal of the Lloyd George denomination who went Tory after the first war and for years was active in his constituency and in the local Ratepayers' Association. After what I have said about other disagreements, my reaction here is rather depressingly easy to imagine. In this field as in others, my father inevitably failed to turn me into the sort of person he wanted me to be.

That sort of person was, of course, a version of himself; a more successful version, for he got no further than a senior clerk's responsibilities and pay in the mustard firm he worked for, and considered himself a failure. He was never bitter about this, but meant to see to it that I had a better chance than he. Here he succeeded at considerable financial cost: scholarships notwithstanding, he had to go on supporting me and being deprived of a youth's earning capacity. Although he never had much idea of what I was about, he was delighted when I began to make my way as a writer – while not forgetting to deliver the expected warning that I must not make the mistake of thinking I could actually support myself in this fashion. All the time, I think, he would really rather I had gone into commerce, a word I can still not hear without starting to feel drowsy.

Boredom, I am sorry to say, came to be my chief reaction to my father's company, though I did not want to feel like this and grew better at hiding it – I hope. As ageing people (among others) will, he would recount and reminisce without relevance: cricket, the City, friends he had made since I left home, a chap in the pub, a chap in the train. I am sure he on his side was not much entertained when, on request, I would tell him of my doings in a world as alien to him as commerce was to me. There was not a lot to be done about this, given the burning sincerity of all boredom. It is depressing to think how persistently dull and egotistical we can be to those we most value, and how restless and peevish we get when they do it back to us.

But this would be the wrong note to end on. The era of the quarrels was also, not surprisingly, the time of greatest intimacy. In those years my father would exploit a talent for physical clowning and mimicry that made him, on his day, one of the funniest men I have known. Every story called for the full deployment of facial, vocal and bodily resources, and was conscientiously acted out. My mother used the same techniques, so that at one stage I thought they were standard in anecdote-telling, and to this day find something lacking when they are not used. It is in mid-story that I see my father most clearly, quite a dapper figure in one of his grey or light-brown business suits (though he never could tie a tie properly), hobbling across the room in the style of some decrepit director of the firm, or forcing his face into lines of disquietingly silly uncouthness as he became the man next door.

1967

IN MEMORIAM W.R.A.   *(ob. 18th April, 1963)

> A *Cricket Match*, between
> The *Gentlemen of Cambridge*
> And the *Hanover Club*, to be played
> By the *Antient Laws* of the *Game* . . .
> [Two stumps, no boundaries, lobs,
> Single wicket, no pads – all that]
> In *Antient Costume*
> For a *Good Cause*.
>
> Leading the Gentlemen,
> I won the toss and batted.
> With a bat like an overgrown spoon
> And a racquets ball, runs came fast;
> But as, in my ruffles and tights,
> I marched to the crease, I was sad
> To see you nowhere
> About the field.
>
> You would have got the point:
> 'No boundaries' meant running
> Literally each bloody run.
> When I 'threw my wicket away'
> And, puffing, limped back to my seat,
> I wanted to catch your eye
> Half-shut with laughter
> (And pride and love).
>
> Afterwards, over pints,
> Part of a chatting circle,
> You would have said I was right

194

To declare about when I did;
Though the other chaps went for the runs
And got them with plenty in hand,
     What does it matter?
     The game's the thing.

     Later: the two of us:
     'That time—do you remember?—
We watched Wally Hammond at Lord's,
And you said you wished you were him,
And I fixed up a coach, but you said
You were working too hard for exams?
     Oh well. A pity
     You never tried.'

     I know. And I foresee
     (As if this were not fancy)
The on-and-on of your talk,
My gradually formal response
That I could never defend
But never would soften enough,
     Leading to silence,
     And separate ways.

     Forgive me if I have
     To see it as it happened:
Even your pride and your love
Have taken this time to become
Clear, to arouse my love.
I'm sorry you had to die
     To make me sorry
     You're not here now.

                                                    1967

* Reprinted from my collection *A Look Round the Estate*.

In 1956, while laying down the law about Socialism to a Fabian Society summer school, I let it be known that I had always voted Labour and, 'unless something very surprising or very nasty happened', always would. In 1964 I voted Labour for the last time, chickened out the following year by voting for the Anti-Common Market character who put up in my constituency and voted Conservative for the first time at the G.L.C. elections this spring.

But – unless you place George Brown's appointment as Foreign Secretary in one category or the other – nothing very surprising or very nasty had happened. So why had I crossed the floor? – a question worth answering on general grounds, considering how many writers and such since Wordsworth have made a similar rightward journey, and one that offers me the chance of explaining that to have repudiated the Left does not set one shoulder to shoulder with Colin Jordan.

A more important event of 1956 was Russia's war of intervention in Hungary. This put paid for ever to my hopes that Communism might not be as bad as more and more voluminous and unignorable evidence kept suggesting to me it was – hopes that had flickered up momentarily at and after the death of Stalin. I shall never forget the surge of excitement I felt on hearing the four little words, unemphatic but so startlingly unexpected from such a source, in which the new leaders pronounced on the defunct administration: 'Mistakes have been made.' It saddens me to recall that now.

196

To return: a curious feature of the Hungary episode, in its effect on British opinion at least, is the speed and thoroughness with which its memory has been revised or effaced. What at the time was almost everywhere taken as a mortal blow to the far Left, has mellowed here, if not elsewhere, into an unfortunate error that would certainly not be made today, an interesting contemporary accompaniment to the real major crime of Suez, or even a civil war, as Ben Whitaker, erecting a milestone in the history of euphemism, tried to get away with calling it in a recent letter to the press. (I prevented him; but he did try it.) Whereas to that fabulously uninquisitive congeries, the young Left, Hungary is at most something that happened to middle-aged people.

Over the years after Hungary I noticed cultural signs of that accelerating swing to the Left among our intelligentsia which has only just now, perhaps, begun to go into reverse. My response to these – the marches, the Chelsea poems attacking South African apartheid, the first twangings of the protest song industry, *Dr Strangelove* and its reception – was inactive annoyance.

It still seemed to me logical to support the Labour party that Bevin, Attlee and Gaitskell had shaped and led, or at any rate to oppose the Conservatism of Eden and Macmillan. The latter lot, I said to myself, had failed to devise measures which would give the country a sense of purpose and propel it into the 1960s, though how I would have recognized such measures I hardly know. Anyway, it would all be different when Labour came back to power.

It has not been, of course, except as regards the speeding-up of trends I had already noted with disquiet during the years of Tory rule. To me, the most important of these concerned education, which I had already started getting reactionary about in the mid-'fifties: see, if you can be bothered, *Lucky Jim*, chapter 17. It is never very difficult, as a colleague remarked, to be modern-minded and forward-looking in approaching questions of which one knows nothing. Here, as elsewhere, experience is a Tory. Mine, at that time, told me that bull-at-a-gate expansion of our universities would lead to a lowering of standards.

I think I was right. Not that one had to be specially observant to be right. My prediction was based on the simple fact, well known to any teacher and available to all at the cost of a little reflection, that if you pack your class with thicks you will either have to ignore them and teach only the bright people, or, if like most teachers you feel re-

197

sponsible for all levels of pupil, you will compromise, i.e. lower your standard.

Unlike most educational problems, this one is a straightforward matter of quantity. You will use up less of your allotted time, and thus enable yourself to cover that much more ground, if you can say 'As Eliot wrote', instead of 'As Eliot wrote ... What's the trouble? Oh, sorry. As T. S. Eliot – ee ell eye oh tee – the poet, dramatist, playwright that is, and critic wrote ...' While the thicks get what they need, the bright people doodle.

This, obviously, is just as true at school. Labour's educational policy at this level seems almost consciously destructive. As if moved by a fear that, despite every obstacle, a few tough customers may still emerge from the university knowing something, the Crosland illiteracy commandos get to work on the schools, chucking aside the principle of streaming which alone made the comprehensive system intelligible, and in particular undermining the traditional sixth-form method which saw to it that freshmen came up knowing at least the fundamentals of their subject – a deadly blow at standards, this, as the Vice-Chancellor of Liverpool University and others pointed out recently.

What could be the point of this policy? I thought nobody believed any longer that a country could survive, let alone do better, without some kind of educated elite. But perhaps those responsible just don't care. After all, the structure will last their time, they have benefited from the existing system, and can still buy their children real education.

That is my main quarrel with Socialist home policy. I am no economist and, if I strain myself, can nearly imagine that the unchecked rise in the cost of living is part of some frightfully subtle plan to send it rocketing down again. I would say more, if I knew more and had thought more, about those governmental decisions which reflect, if they are not actually designed to promote, the increasing power of the State over the individual – the 10:2 jury rule, the railroading of the decimal currency scheme and (as I write) the airport at Stansted.

Even a year ago I would have dismissed as Tory mythology the idea that the Labour Party would like to see us less free and means to do something about it. In a sense I still do dismiss it, having too little reason to believe that the Conservatives would treat us much different.

This gives me the chance to say where I stand. I am not a Tory, nor pro-Tory (who could be pro *this* Tory Party?), nor Right-wing, nor of the Right, but of the Centre, equally opposed to all forms of authoritarianism. What I am particularly not is a Fascist, though I have been called one quite a lot recently by correspondents of varying degrees of literacy, with Yankee Crawler and Tory Lickspittler thrown in here and there. However, I quite understand their use of the term. They sense, accurately, that I am anti-Left, and 'Fascist' is useful, straightforward and soundly-precedented shorthand for 'opposed to the policies and interests of the Russian Government; pro-American; pro-British' and other shabby heresies.

Anti-Left entails, in the present situation, anti-Labour. I might think differently if Mr Wilson had done what he ought to do and what, after gaining his increased majority last year (1966), I fairly fully expected him to do: crack down on that perishing Left wing of his, boot half-a-dozen of the Communist M.P.s out of the Labour Party and threaten the rest with expulsion unless they step into line. And *say why*.

Well, why? For a set of reasons odiously familiar to both sides in this matter: because a Communist's loyalties lie, not with his own country, but with a foreign Power, one that is, both externally and internally, hostile to democracy, and therefore our enemy. To some of us, enemies of our country are worth opposing; others find something positively attractive about them. It is having at last become fully aware of this that has led me finally to break off my lingering love-hate affair with the Left, and it is here that I can perhaps contribute a useful diagnosis of the Left-wing mind and heart, because I was like that myself once.

My concern here is not with the professional Communist or open fellow traveller who just wants his side to win and makes no bones about, for instance, campaigning for the Viet Cong. I mean the kind of person who, over that conflict, professes neutralism while reciting Hanoi's line; who says the East European satellites are really swinging places that have stopped bothering with politics; who used – when it was more newsy – to go on about Ian Smith's Fascist regime; who thinks student freedom is impaired when a college applies its statutes; who buys unexamined the abortion-divorce-homosexuality-censorship-racialism-marijuana package; in a word, the Lefty.

The Lefty starts from an unfocused dissatisfaction with the way

199

things are. One need not drag Freud into the argument in order to suggest that 'the way things are', the social system, will strike the young or the youngish as a product of authority, of parents and schoolmasters and vicars and employers, the people who seem to limit freedom for the sake of doing so.

Stage two prolongs this: the frustrations of trying to get on in a competitive society where most people, by definition, cannot get on very far. Then, like the fire from heaven, the hint of an explanation and an ideology: the reason we are failing to get on, or simply not having a good enough time, is not because we are lazy and stupid, but because of the system. So now we oppose the system.

The reason why prominent Lefties go on opposing the system long after having got on pretty well by most standards is perhaps threefold: political habit dies hard (as in my own case), success is always relative (the controversial poet gets bad reviews from the pundits, the popular actress finds an extra and even more appreciative audience at rallies), or an increasing bitterness develops as the system, having been repeatedly shouted at to pull itself together, chugs on much as before.

Here, I think, we are near the crunch. The system exists, so to hell with the system. Damn you, England! Damn you for not listening to me! But, of course, plenty of people are listening, the rank-and-file Lefties with no rhetorical skills, no individual viewpoint, only a readiness to demonstrate and march against the system, to grasp at that wonderful and unique and paradoxical satisfaction which the Left offers: of swimming with and against the stream at the same time, of being both rebel and conformist, of joining in the massed choir of half a million voices crying in the wilderness. On either or any level, emotion is calling the tune. Some pretty powerful set of emotions, clearly, is at work when, after being revealed as unworthy of even the most cynical kind of support, Nasser and the Arab/Russian cause go on being supported, as vociferously as ever and without even a decent delay, in our correspondence columns.

The other and sufficient example is the disgracefully cordial reception here of Premier Kosygin, that morose, unlovable figure, Stalin's tool (as his mere survival proves), at one time a member of the Government that signed the Nazi-Soviet Pact, now the head of a State that imprisons its writers on unconstitutional charges. Bulganin and Khruschev, far more amiable old things, had a rougher trip; but Leftyism was not trendy in their day. And they, the Pact, Stalin, Sinyavski and Daniel are all non-facts in the Lefty consciousness.

Or rather – to take a step nearer the crunch – fact and non-fact at once. We are dealing with a conflict of feeling and intelligence, a form of wilful self-deception whereby a part of the mind knows full well that its overall belief is false or wicked, but the emotional need to believe is so strong that that knowledge remains, as it were, encysted, isolated, powerless to influence word and deed.

Again, I confess I speak from experience. I once assented to Lenin's epigram, 'Liberty is indeed a precious commodity – so precious that it must be rationed', although I knew it was evil sophistry. 'In Russia', somebody who claimed to have been there said, 'they're amazed when you ask why people can't vote against Stalin. "But who would ever want to?" they say.' I thought that was awfully good; but I knew it was wrong. What I did not then know – I must not be too hard on myself – was just how many people were to have died for having wanted to vote that way, or for having looked vaguely as if they might want to. This is known now all right, or rather not known. So are more recent facts, or non-facts.

Any Lefty who can read, or ask questions, *knows* that there is nothing to be said for a system which, economically, has taken fifty years to do what capitalism could have done in less than twenty and, politically, has in some respects not yet caught up with the Tsars, far less with the Provisional Government of 1917. He *knows* that East Germany and Poland are full of misery and corruption. He *knows*, above all, however hard he tells himself 'things are getting better there', that things could get much better there and still be bloody awful, still be what at his Leftiest he could never wish for himself and his family. He knows, but the knowledge is unreachable, unusable.

It is, if you like, easy for me. I have done all right (but, forgive me, so have plenty of others). Growing older, I have lost the need to be political, which means in this country, the need to be Left. I am driven into grudging toleration of the Conservative Party because it is the party of non-politics, of resistance to politics. I have seen how many of the evils of life – failure, loneliness, fear, boredom, inability to communicate – are ineradicable by political means, and that attempts so to eradicate them are disastrous.

The ideal of the brotherhood of man, the building of the Just City, is

201

one that cannot be discarded without lifelong feelings of disappointment and loss. But if we are to live in the real world, discard it we must. Its very nobility makes the results of its breakdown doubly horrifying, and it breaks down, as it always will, not by some external agency, but because it cannot work.

You cannot *decide* to have brotherhood; if you start trying to enforce it, you will before long find yourself enforcing something very different, and much worse than mere absence of brotherhood. All you can reasonably work for is keeping things going, plus as much improvement as they will stand: an injustice righted here, an opportunity extended there. This is not a very romantic-sounding programme. In fact it is not a programme at all. I like that.

1967

POSTSCRIPT 1970

One has had to grow used to the howls of pain and rage which, in the Western democracies, greet even the mildest anti-Left pronouncement, and the above provoked these in plenty; but there were also whinnies of sincere puzzlement. How could a chap like me, an intellectual with an interest in jazz and science fiction to protect me from total fuddy-duddyism, *possibly* not be on the Left? I must be posing, doing it for the publicity, taking means – whatever I might say, in the article or later – to safeguard my enormous personal fortune.*
Nothing in the merits of the situation, it was felt, could have induced me so to fly in the face of nature.

At work here (as elsewhere) was and is an unexamined conviction that the outlook of the Left is an objective view of the world without the intervention of 'bourgeois ideology', a faithful reflection of reality. Any non-Left standpoint is thus by definition perverse at best, and to express it is to distort the truth, or else just to bumble eccentrically. For instance, a by no means unsympathetic critic of mine, D.A.N. Jones, recently reprehended me for 'partisan gaucherie [droiterie, surely] when attempting nonfiction', and connected this with my having written a ghost story. On a lower level, a fine expression of this attitude turned up today as ever was, in the *Sun*. A B.B.C. news com-

* It is, of course, all right for people on the Left to have one of these, especially if they have not had to work for it.

mentator had said that, bad as American atrocities in Vietnam were, the Viet Cong had killed many more innocent people. 'I don't know if this is true', said the writer (providing a text-book example of the not-knowing-of-established-facts syndrome I mentioned in my article), but its having come from a commentator made it 'biased' and 'propaganda' and 'rather sinister' – it would have come better from an official American spokesman, presumably because everybody would have known straight away that such a man must be lying. The writer ended: 'So pack it up B.B.C. [sic]. I want news, not views.' No he doesn't. He wants his own views presented in and with and through and as the news.

The Leftist orthodoxy is so much an orthodoxy that it is accepted unquestioningly even by intellectuals who are not really politically minded at all. I asked one such to give an example of a totally independent, uncommitted, coldly impartial journalist. The answer was James Cameron. And even non-intellectuals will often not dream of *calling* themselves anything but Left. 'What sort of Left?' I asked one such: 'How do you stand on Vietnam, and on the student business?' She said firmly: 'Escalate the war, and cut off the troublemakers' grants and send them to gaol if they get violent.'

Well: in the intervening two or three years, the Lefty has revealed parts of himself more plainly. 'Damn you, England!' is not just a cry, but a statement of policy (not that John Osborne, who coined the cry, would care for the policy). Anybody, anybody at all who talks or acts against British interests is good. Nasser is good, even though he keeps his Communists locked up; Catholics are good in Ulster while Catholic countries remain bad, except of course for Spain over the Gibraltar issue; Welsh nationalism is very good; the Argentine shows a lonely streak of goodness when the Falkland Islands come up. Conversely, any historical figures that minister to our national pride are bad: Churchill, Nelson, Drake, Wellington, Fighter Command in 1940, Queen Victoria . . . I wish somebody would undertake an analysis of the Lefty psyche, with special attention to its horror of father- or family-figures. Somewhere in it, room should be found for the anecdote about the successful manager of pop singers who, on being asked at an interview what was the first thing he looked for when auditioning new youngsters, replied: 'A face the kids' parents will hate the sight of.'

The other revelation is the hypocrisy of the claim that the Lefty hates oppression, injustice, etc. He likes them, or at best ignores them, will not write about or discuss them, when they are wielded by a Left-wing government or fighting force. He only hates what such governments or forces are opposed to. Most of my vestigial respect for his sincerity and common sense (not that I ever had much of the latter) went when I read that, on famed 27 October 1968, seven people in London demonstrated against the Russian invasion of Czechoslovakia while fifty thousand, at the lowest count, were demonstrating against U.S. 'imperialism' in Vietnam. The rest of that respect went when I read about the total lack of interest in the appearance of an East German soccer team in Cardiff during the run-up to the Springbok protests. (I am against *apartheid* myself, but *non tali auxilio*, thank you.) Will there ever be any evidence to damage the view that, via who knows what network of deceit, charlatanry, credulity, ignorance, wilful blindness and herd-instinct, Moscow's enemies to this day reappear unrevised – in the same rough order, with no additions or cuts – as the enemies of the Western Left?

Not all the dissatisfaction with my piece was voiced by the Left. In a characteristically entertaining and sharply expressed tirade in the *Spectator*, Colin Welch laid a stern duty on the shoulders of those who, like me, have become refugees from Leftism – actually I was a long time in transit before making landfall on the shores of reason. We are to erect a whole new structure of political belief of a complexity comparable with the one we have abandoned – actually my old structure was never very complex. The carrying-out of this task, it is foreseen, would benefit the resident Righty as well as the recently arrived ex-Lefty. But it will not be easily accomplished:

... *Convicted indeed that socialism is silly or worse, they* [the refugees] *still view conservatism as an evil, if perhaps a necessary one* faute de mieux *and the lesser perhaps of the two. The idea that conservatism is in any positive sense materially, socially or morally defensible often remains alien and unpalatable to them. They are accordingly reluctant to learn its language, to study and accept its premises and its conclusions.*

To find at the age, say, of forty or more that most of one's intellectual possessions, so painfully acquired, are in fact just trash to be thrown away must be in itself a discouraging experience. Who can

blame those daunted by the prospect of grimly acquiring, mastering
and thoroughly developing a whole new philosophy of life? Yet this
is what we ask of our immigrants, for their good as well as our own.
They will never be happy, fruitful or at home, till it is done.

Probably not. And well urged. The situation of my kind of ideological 'immigrant' is not very pitiable, but I have never seen it described anywhere else, and gladly accept the proffered sympathy.
Nevertheless, what is this language I must learn, where can I find set
out that whole philosophy of life I am to acquire, master and
thoroughly develop?

Perhaps the language comes by use, like speech itself; the philosophy, the premises and conclusions are more difficult of access.
Gibbon, yes; Dr Johnson, yes; others, no doubt, but Tory-style observations in the 'Old and True' category are mere ammunition, useful for
backing an assertion or putting down an opponent, not much good in
any systematic way. I want something pitched between ancestral ver-
ities and the next Conservative Party policy statement. Shall I ever get
it, either ceremoniously handed to me bound in vellum or knocked
together after prolonged argument and revision, a tattered typescript
with emendations in many hands, including perhaps my own?

The second alternative sounds just possible, even an attractive project for somebody else to set in train. And yet I am hardly alone in
thinking that this 'philosophy' resists formulation by its very nature,
being nothing more, and nothing less, than a mass of instincts and the
unarguable beliefs stemming from these. Probably, in an age in which
everything else seems to have been formulated, Conservatives have a
special duty to keep their beliefs below or above the level of formulation. Certainly, a lot of them go on as if they had. And this is not, or
not simply, a sneer. So far, to formulate in the contemporary context
has been to formulate for the contemporary context, to argue with
Socialism in Socialism's terms and so, inevitably, to outline a point-by-
point alternative to it. I feel, I sense, I dimly apprehend (I dare not say 'I
think') that this is not what Conservatism can ever be about.

To return finally to our metaphor: I must not be thought the kind of
immigrant who goes round in an uncritical daze of satisfaction with all
he sees. On the contrary, many of the faces and voices and attitudes I
find round me are horribly like what I was used to on the other side of
the water.

ON CHRIST'S NATURE

I might as well begin by indicating where I stand in matters of religion. My parents evidently underwent a fairly gruelling nonconformist nurture in and around a Baptist chapel in south-east London. By the time I came along they had moved a certain distance away from this environment. The training they gave me was strong in morality, rudimentary and quite uninsistent in questions of doctrine apart from a conventional taboo or two. It took some months in the army, for example, to enable me to blaspheme quite placidly, and even today the use of obscenity and the name of Jesus Christ in the same phrase is not really second nature with me.

My parents took me to a few services at Easter and Christmas and on Armistice Day, and when I was ten or eleven a religious contemporary took me to some ordinary ones. At school there were the customary daily prayers and once-weekly Scripture lessons. I got a credit in this subject in School Certificate, but this was the result of having woken up at 6 a.m. on the morning of the examination and found close to hand my Matthew, my Epistle of James and my notes (the only ones in this field I had ever taken) on the authorship of that epistle. That question happened to come up, and I remember being fairly grateful at the coincidence.

However: I have never attended, voluntarily or alone, any act of worship as such. When my school was evacuated from London in 1939 I joined its newly formed chapel choir voluntarily, but that was because I liked music and enjoyed singing. When, later, the army took to marching me to church, I suppose I could have stood about outside during the service, but it was a point of honour with my generation never to opt for the slightest inconvenience on conscientious grounds of this kind. We let the army have its way and put 'C E' on our identity discs, and were rather sophisticated with the occasional militant who insisted on 'A G N[ostic]' or 'N(o) R(eligion)'. There seemed to be enough fuss about most things already, and to make any sort of 'gesture' in the direction of agnosticism, let alone atheism, implied agreeing with the godly that their notions were important enough to be accounted worthy of public opposition.

In the same way, it has never occurred to me to pick up the Bible, or any other religious writing, in the hope of spiritual comfort or ethical guidance. However, I am in no danger of forgetting that, in Western society, ignorance of the Bible is likely to be accompanied by barbarous incuriosity about fundamentals. And it would take a very stupid unbeliever to deny the Bible's function as a stimulus to the examination of the self and of the conditions by which human beings live and die. There are some, perhaps, for whom no such stimulus is necessary beyond merely observing the order of things.

Such is my approach to my subject, the nature and image of Jesus Christ as we see them in the Gospels. I confine myself to the received text, which I read as it stands, as the mass of supposedly educated laymen read it; I cannot offer myself as a scriptural commentator. Hence I am not to be refuted at any given point by evidence of mistranslation from the Greek or by any kind of specialized canonical interpretation.

I start from the obvious and general. The habitual, undetailed, unanalysing view of Jesus taken by most people, whatever their attitude towards Christianity or the Church, is unlikely to fall below an admiring respect. Seen as the human manifestation of a mysterious or (it may be) impossibly remote Godhead, he appears by contrast accessible to personal sympathy, even affection. One so often portrayed as a baby – virtually the only aspect in which he cannot fail to reach the popular mind, once a year at least – will have a claim on our tenderness, whether or not we concern ourselves with the manner of his conception.

His policy of choosing as his associates men of no particular distinction, his preference for the company of ordinary sinful folk over that of the conventionally virtuous, the simplicity of his teaching: these and other attributes can be very dimly visualized and still serve to humanize him further, to make him identifiable, however vulgarly and erroneously, as a good chap not impossibly unlike other good chaps, i.e. oneself. He plays, I suppose, an equally congenial though more elevated and dramatic role in a vaguely political context, as a revolutionary leader triumphing in death over an oppressive authority. This authority is identifiable with almost any group or force, political and other, which the average individual may find hateful in his own life.

It must be on grounds of this kind that Jesus can appeal as a heroic figure to those who remain unconvinced by his larger claims. He has established himself as such in spite of having thrown away at the outset the strongest – one might have thought, the indispensable – card in the hand of the contender for heroic status: devotion to violence. I find it very significant that the non-violent Jesus of the Evangelists remains undimmed by the violent behaviour of the Church that bears his name. It is only quite recently, after all, that this Church was deprived of the power to continue persecuting and making war and had to fall back on sanctioning any violence deemed necessary or desirable by civil and military authorities, all this being accompanied by explanations that Jesus actually was violent on the whole and had nothing against the killing of human beings provided the right people were doing it. The Gospel hero's ability to survive this situation quite unsmirched testifies to a remarkable depth and durability in him, though I am not denying that he might have become even more eminent if the Church's version of him were correct. (I am not a pacifist or non-resister myself, by the way; I only feel that no Christian who can read has any excuse for not being such.)

Descending now to the particular, and trying to re-create the experience of reading the Gospels for the first time since leaving school, I find the image of the Christ hero standing up well to scrutiny. I encounter, however, one grave initial difficulty. Even if we retain in memory quite large sections of the text – I was surprised at the amount I recognized, and recognized with some intimacy – the selective powers of memory are such that we can half-consciously edit out the less acceptable portions. If Jesus should happen to wander into my

208

casual thoughts, I for my part would be able to edit out his claim to be the Son of God. When I turn to the printed page I notice this claim being made with inescapable persistence.

My difficulty is not simply that I am unable to accept such a surprising suggestion and, recognizing how hard it is to be honest in these matters, think I can say I have always been unable – I may well have had a few moments of doubt around the age of eleven. Indeed, I can bypass this difficulty altogether by deciding to read the phrase 'Son of God' as analogous with 'son of the soil', 'son of Ben' and, for the matter of that, 'son of Man' (or 'bride of Christ') – as denoting, that is, a relation so intimate that the filial (or marital) tie is a natural metaphor for it. It may well be that this notion is common ground among humanists, rationalists and such, but I have never had any inclination to attend to these.

Further venturing for a moment the risk of spelling out a platitude, I notice that this metaphoric interpretation is supported by a possible reading of the Jesus presented by St John. (Here I feel I have to do some spelling out, since so few people, especially among the young and even among the reputedly literate, appear to know their Bible half as well as I do.) The personage referred to is much given to declaring that he and his heavenly father are in some way transposable or identical: 'I and *my* Father are one . . . I *am* in the Father, and the Father in me.' Less conspicuous than these, but quantitatively very much more prevalent, are utterances entailing the ordinary dualizing concept of Jesus and God as discrete – albeit specially associated – entities: '. . . the word which ye hear is not mine, but the Father's which sent me . . . As the Father hath loved me, so have I loved you . . .'

Theologians will tell us that these two accounts of the status of Jesus are not contradictory. I will not argue with them. No doubt I am not the first to have heard, in Jesus' assertions of his oneness with God, the voice of somebody trying without very great success to communicate a state of heightened spiritual awareness, a sense of that closeness to the divine which we commonly call mystical. Jesus was without question a remarkably articulate man, but it might be that the language he spoke, while clearly fitted for theological disputation, was imperfectly equipped with the means of defining and conveying so intractable a notion as the one which may have possessed him. To see him in some such way as this does not trouble me.

What does trouble me – and I return now to the grave difficulty I mentioned earlier – is the association of a man who has many claims on my respect and sympathy with a God who has none on either. 'Son of God' I can accept; 'Son of God' I cannot. I am one of that company (large and rapidly growing, I hope) which says: 'I think the traditional God of Christianity very wicked.' – I quote Professor Empson, whose total position I do not necessarily share, but whose insight in reaching this main conclusion while still at school I greatly admire, having taken much longer to get there myself. However, this is perhaps a large subject, one which takes me outside my brief. I therefore drop it, offering only the observation that to have devoted a major part of his discourses to apologizing for God's iniquities is the least that might have been required of a personal representative of that deity.

I will try to proceed similarly with the related problem set by those sayings in the Gospels which might be figuratively described as proceeding directly from the Almighty, rather than from the much finer and more humane sensibility of Jesus. I refer to the many passages which echo or parallel Matthew xiii 49 ff.: 'So shall it be at the end of the world: the angels shall come forth, and sever the wicked from among the just, And shall cast them into the furnace of fire: there shall be wailing and gnashing of teeth.' The most horrible version of this attitude to human destiny is probably Matthew xvi 9: 'Woe to the world because of offences! for it must needs be that offences come; but woe to that man by whom the offence cometh!' The offhandedness of the explanation here that the necessity of there being offences and (eternal) punishment for them is just part of the system, agreed by all concerned to be beyond alteration, surely reproduces with great fidelity the tone of voice of Jehovah.

It is disappointing to find this sort of thing in the mouth of such a forceful advocate of personal forgiveness and compassion: the Samaritan did not care whether the man he helped was wicked or just. There are, indeed, many moments in the Gospels at which there seems to be a conflict between, as it were, prescriptive authoritarianism and personal, instinctive liberalism. The summary injustices of God are half overlaid by the imaginative leniency of Jesus. Thus it is like Jesus to upbraid whomsoever is angry with his brother without a cause (Matthew v 22), but like the Almighty to threaten such a dire miscreant with hell fire. And the qualities extolled in the Beatitudes are those which Jesus made his own for ever, but the rewards promised those who practise them imply a selectivity that has more primitive connections. Mercy cannot meaningfully be promised the merciful as a special reward unless it is to be denied some other group.

Some of these difficulties can be alleviated by invoking a characteristic of Jesus that has perhaps been insufficiently remarked. His great talent for language, manifested in both formal and informal tones, was combined with an inherited stylistic tradition that laid heavy stress on parallelism and balance. The result is a strong tendency towards what we now understand by epigram, in which neatness and memorability may count for more than precision. In the case of the Beatitudes I detect an intention to glorify and activate various unspectacular virtues in terms that should, by their verbal arrangement, bring out God's allegedly scrupulous sense of justice towards those who did his will. The irony whereby overt justice involves covert injustice is appropriate to what I make of the Gospels in general, but it does not damage Jesus in my esteem. The demand on the religious teacher that he should be continuously memorable and meaningful together must be a heavy one, and I find it natural that one so agonizingly aware of the precariousness of his situation should have embodied his convictions in forms that did not limit or explain or qualify, but were aimed instead at being durable in oral transmission.

To recognize in Jesus a sometimes overriding inclination to the striking phrase helps to account for those sayings of his which, when their armour of familiarity has been peeled off, are disconcertingly obscure. 'Let the dead bury their dead' sounds like something one ought to be on the side of, until one realizes that a major point about the dead is that it is the living who must bury them, in all senses. 'I will make you fishers of men' has a fine clarion ring that is vulnerable to the question: 'You mean earn a living by selling batches of men in the market?' In that eerie (and theologically tricky) episode in which the tempter confronts Jesus in the wilderness, it is like Jesus to bring up 'Man shall not live by bread alone' out of Deuteronomy and impose on it his own stamp of permanent truth; but the tempter might fairly retort: 'I never said he should; my point is that he has to have bread to live. And this conversation is about you, not man.'

Try as one may to circumvent such puzzles, however, there remain formidable barriers, some of them accidental, between the Jesus of the

211

Gospels and the uncommitted inquirer. The faith-healing and miracle-working aspect, in particular, has shed most of its impressiveness and acquired instead, partly by chance, an aura of the modern crank or quack, on or outside the fringes of the Church and voluble with grossly superstitious (or grossly mechanistic) explanations. There are occasions when Jesus's motive for healing seems not to be compassion, as with the restoring of the blind man's sight at the opening of John ix. Asked if the blindness results from the man's sin or his parents', Jesus answers that the reason is nobody's sin, but 'that the works of God should be made manifest in him'. This is detestable. Some of the miracles that do not involve healing, such as the walking on the water, look like an arbitrary display of power, or an occasion for reprehending a disciple or two for lack of faith.

At other times the reader becomes aware that he is overhearing, without the chance of fully entering into, a long argument between Jesus and various conservative or established opponents about doctrine and practice. The image of Jesus as a bright young rabbinical intellectual is not a compelling one, especially since it seems to include the occasional substitution of debating points for straight answers. I think for instance of his evasion of the Sadducees' admittedly thorny question about the resurrection of the body (Matthew xxii 23 ff.), and of his outmanoeuvring, astute as it is, of the chief priests' demand to know by what authority he taught (Matthew xxi 23 ff.). But only once, as far as I can see, did he betray his principles for the sake of policy: he could not have known that this particular equivocation – 'Render unto Caesar the things that are Caesar's' – was to become the most disastrous in history.

Despite these and other flaws in the image, there is much in the evangelists' Jesus which draws a ready response. The development of his character in its successive versions, from Matthew's practical teacher and organizer, driving his disciples along by the force of his will, to John's extraordinary combination of the mystic and the warmly intuitional human being, reinforces certain unchanging traits. He appears – after he began his ministry, at any rate – to have needed no strict regimen of fasting, solitude or other inspirational technique; on the contrary, he plainly enjoyed conviviality, eating with people in their houses, changing the water at Cana not just into wine but into more than 120 gallons of the best available (John ii 6–10 – how many guests were there at that wedding?), seeing himself correctly as a different breed from John the Baptist with his locusts and wild honey: 'The Son of Man is come eating and drinking' (Luke vii 34 – a passage embodying one of the most delightful jokes in the whole of ancient literature). It was a last supper, not a collective session of fasting and prayer, from which Jesus went to his final ordeal. And there is something which seems to sum up a great deal in that request of the risen Christ (Luke xxiv 41): 'Have ye here any meat?' At any rate, he moves me here more than anywhere else, and if I envied Christians anything I would envy them a God who could feel hungry.

In rough proportion as he moves away from being divine Jesus invites approval and affection. It is right that (as portrayed by John) he should have much preferred some people to others – only a God could and should love everybody equally – and that the only tears he sheds, unless I have overlooked something, should be for the death of a friend. He loved children for themselves in a way that reinforces his theme that the good man must cultivate childlike qualities, and his use of traditional shepherd-and-flock imagery seems appropriate to one so instinctively protective and, like the lamb he made his emblem, so gentle. (I know he was tough as well.)

In so far as they can be separated, it is the character of Jesus, the image he presents to us, which is powerful, not his teaching. I note sadly that his set of simple, unambiguous instructions has turned out too difficult to be obeyed, not only by unbelievers but by professed believers too. I have never met a Christian who was detectable as such by any external sign of behaviour beyond that of attendance at church, etc. This is evidently a religion for sinners in a less creditable sense than the one so often professed by the Church. The present state of this Church, descended as it is from a uniquely dedicated foe of canting pietistic nonsense, gives occasion for irony.

And yet it may be that man's inability to respond to the message of Jesus points to a – perhaps inevitable – deficiency in that message. If we are trying to be good we need moral support at those moments when we choose between what is right and what is attractive, and here the sayings of Jesus may not be of much help. The very simplicity and downrightness of his teaching limits it. Thus we may agree that to love our enemies is both important and difficult, but few of us have many enemies or many chances to love the ones we have. Loving our friends,

213

behaving with love towards those we love, is just as important, and sometimes just as difficult. Jesus took it for granted that 'the good tree bringeth not forth corrupt fruit'. We recognize every day that unfortunately the situation is more complicated than that.

If we find the teaching of Jesus, whatever its urgency and depth, lacking in scope, we may find it relevant to observe that the circumstances of his career limited his first-hand knowledge of human experience, especially in its more uncomfortable aspects. I refer to such items as war, disease, starvation and madness, also to those subtler engines from Jehovah's armoury of maleficence, the pains incidentally accruing from sexual love, marriage and the begetting of children. As a result, there is intermittently visible a rather absurd disparity between what Jesus says to us, tells us is necessary, gets us ready for, and the striking panorama of horror with which we are actually confronted. It is not surprising that so few of us should have taken him to our hearts in the way he wanted: '. . . because iniquity shall abound, the love of many shall wax cold.'

1962

POSTSCRIPT 1970

The above piece was commissioned by the *Sunday Telegraph*, which printed alongside it a retort by Dr Donald Coggan, the Archbishop of York. As one reared in a Christian society, I was not even mildly surprised at his being shown in advance what I had written without having to show me what he had written. His retort, though moderate in tone, wasted some space by going on asking, in effect, who I thought I was. At two points he descended to the particular. I had been inaccurate, he said, in writing that Jesus had been unacquainted with the uncomfortable forms of human experience; on the contrary, he said, these had been all around him. And, he went on, Jesus refrained from giving straight answers to straight questions, because he wanted men to *think*, to love God with their *minds*.

I felt I had covered the first point adequately in what I wrote, by using the phrase 'first-hand' immediately before the phrase 'knowledge of human experience'. I cannot devise very much to say to the second point, which would seem to justify any old equivocation from the days of the Delphic oracle to those of the spiritualist medium. To solve a riddle or a puzzle is an intellectual exercise that presupposes being able to recognize the solution when found. Just wondering for an indefinite period what somebody might have meant is an activity without relish of salvation in it: all of which, now I come to think of it, raises the question why, if God wanted human beings to have religion, he did not simply give it to them, instead of arranging the world in one way and then sending somebody along to explain that really the whole set-up was quite different. This oddly side-long or possibly off-hand approach I find to be employed by all gods whatever.

At any rate, the Bishop's larger theme was that, having failed to peruse the fundamental documents of the faith and the writings of some of the greatest minds down the centuries and today, I had not earned the right to do all this rejecting. A correspondent answered this for me by observing that, if rejection was valid only after prolonged and intensive study, so too, presumably, was acceptance. At about that stage the controversy, such as it was, came to an end.

What, in retrospect, I find healthy, reasonable and appropriate about the Archbishop's contribution is that it attacked mine head-on, and in doing so made assertions about the Kingdom of God and Christ's embodiment of this in himself – not very precise concepts to many, perhaps, but no matter: they clearly meant something, and something important, to the Archbishop. There would be a different tale to tell, one may be sure, if almost any newspaper were to run such a debate today. A churchman of the 1970s would not be found rebuking my lack of faith but chiding my superstition. He would think it touching (or rather *sweet*) that I should spend so long disavowing belief in something that nobody (well, nobody *in touch*) has taken seriously for God knows how long.

An unbeliever, even a non-militant one like myself, who has grown up in what was then a Christian country makes fairly strong and specific demands on the Church – his Church. He might well be bored or angry if, as could hardly happen nowadays, she were to threaten him with hell fire, but he would rather that than that she should tell him that God is irrelevant. That is for *him* to say. It upsets his sense of the fitness of things to witness the Church fighting to be in the fore-front of her own demolition. How quickly, and with what a will, have her servants switched from the canting pietistic nonsense that had not yet died down in 1962 – and which I now rather miss – to the canting humanistic nonsense of the last few years.

I realize how much more I have in common with a believer of my own generation than either of us shares with the modern Christian: it was the most natural thing in the world to find myself recently supporting a traditionally minded Roman Catholic against one of a newer persuasion who was all for the sanctioning of the contraceptive pill. 'Adaptation to the needs of society', droned the latter in educationistical vein; 'moving with the times in order to survive . . .'

Like the university, which she still resembles in several ways, the Church must shut her mind firmly against the needs of society. This is not only her age-long duty, it is also her only chance of turning out in the end to have served the needs of society. If she is to survive, the one thing she must not do is move with the times. She must pursue or regain her role as a force for order and continuity, stay as she is or was until the times move back to her, still or once more preach, not indeed torments or sectarian hatred, but an all-powerful, all-loving God and his divine Son. Whether she likes it or not, she has her obligations to my sort of person as well as to her communicants.

MORE ABOUT PENGUINS
AND PELICANS

For further information about books available from Penguins please write to Dept EP, Penguin Books Ltd, Harmondsworth, Middlesex UB7 0DA.

In the U.S.A.: For a complete list of books available from Penguins in the United States write to Dept CS, Penguin Books, 625 Madison Avenue, New York, New York 10022.

In Canada: For a complete list of books available from Penguins in Canada write to Penguin Books Canada Ltd, 2801 John Street, Markham, Ontario L3R 1B4.

In Australia: For a complete list of books available from Penguins in Australia write to the Marketing Department, Penguin Books Australia Ltd, P.O. Box 257, Ringwood, Victoria 3134.

In New Zealand: For a complete list of books available from Penguins in New Zealand write to the Marketing Department, Penguin Books (NZ) Ltd, P.O. Box 4019, Auckland 10.

Kingsley Amis

RUSSIAN HIDE-AND-SEEK

Amis's brilliant and deadly new comedy, set in twenty-first century England ruled by the Russians. Looking for kicks, our hero, the dashing young cavalry officer Alexander Petrovsky moves into an affair with the insatiable, big-breasted wife of the Deputy Director of Security, and on to a dangerous flirtation with counter-revolutionary politics. In attempting to give England back to the English, he's unwittingly joined a game of Russian hide-and-seek. It's just like Russian roulette, except you play it in the dark and you shoot to kill – other people.

'Staggeringly successful' – Brian Aldiss

'Amis has emerged triumphant' – *Daily Mail*

'A shattering book – and its sombre message will remain with me for a long time' – *Daily Express*

and

THE ANTI-DEATH LEAGUE

GIRL, 20

JAKE'S THING

LUCKY JIM

MY ENEMY'S ENEMY

ONE FAT ENGLISHMAN

TAKE A GIRL LIKE YOU

COLLECTED POEMS 1944–1979

A PORTRAIT OF JANE AUSTEN
David Cecil

David Cecil's magnificent and highly enjoyable portrait of a writer who represents for us, as no other, the elegance, grace and wit of Georgian England.

'A masterpiece which ought to be in every educated home. Nobody could have done it better, nobody will be able to do it so well again. The book is a monument to subject and author' – Auberon Waugh in *Books and Bookmen*

THE MUTUAL FRIEND
Frederick Busch

'It's some time since history came so grippingly fictionalized as it does in Frederick Busch's latest novel. As a re-creation of Dickens's blackly possessed life and suicidal rampage towards death by Public Reading, *The Mutual Friend* coolly steals the limelight of even the very best recent historical novels' – *New Statesman*

THE PRIEST OF LOVE
A LIFE OF D. H. LAWRENCE
Harry T. Moore

From a career that began in an ugly mining village in the Midlands, Lawrence was to become what E. M. Forster called 'the greatest imaginative novelist of our generation.' Yet during his lifetime, and for years afterwards, his views were greeted with hostility, his works banned. By exposing the reality behind the myth, Harry T. Moore has created a vivid and everlasting portrait of Lawrence – as the prophet, the artist, but above all, as the man.

LOLITA
Vladimir Nabokov

Shot through with his mercurial wit, quicksilver prose and heady, intoxicating sensuality, Nabokov's novel of a middle-aged Englishman's passion for a honey-hued, delicately pubescent twelve-year-old American girl, has become one of the world's great love stories. It is published here for the first time in Penguin.

'No lover has thought of his beloved with so much tenderness, no woman has been so charmingly evoked, in such grace and delicacy, as Lolita' – Lionel Trilling

THE GHOST WRITER
Philip Roth

A celebrated blend of sympathy and pitilessness were the trademarks of E. I. Lonoff's work. And it was to this great Russian-Jewish author that Nathan Zuckerman turned for support and inspiration – only to find, when he visited Lonoff's rural retreat, that the presence of an enigmatic female houseguest disturbed and haunted his imagination. Savagely funny, ironical and wise, the author of *Portnoy's Complaint* exposes the artist as voyeur and poseur and explores the problems of unrequited lust.
'Brilliant, witty and extremely elegant' – Emma Tennant in the *Guardian*

BECH: A BOOK
John Updike

Henry Bech, American Jewish writer of international repute, has not written for five years and knows it only too well.

Lurching comically between mistresses, visiting Eastern Europe as a cultural representative, while attempting to recharge his creative batteries, Bech reveals the pathos of the emptied writer and the fear that must haunt every creative artist.

Thomas Love Peacock
NIGHTMARE ABBEY
CROTCHET CASTLE
Edited by Raymond Wright

Thomas Love Peacock is literature's perfect individualist. He has points in common with Aristophanes, Plato, Rabelais, Voltaire, and even Aldous Huxley, but resembles none of them. A romantic in his youth and a friend of Shelley, he happily made hay of the romantic movement in *Nightmare Abbey*, clamping Coleridge, Byron, and Shelley himself in a kind of painless pillory. And in *Crotchet Castle* he did no less for the political economists, pitting his gifts of exaggeration and ridicule against scientific progress and the March of Mind.

THREE GOTHIC NOVELS
With an Introduction by Mario Praz

The Gothic novel, that curious literary genre which flourished from about 1765 until 1825, revels in the horrible and the supernatural, in suspense and exotic settings. This volume presents three of the most celebrated Gothic novels: *The Castle of Otranto* was published pseudonymously in 1765, and in its blending of two kinds of romanticism, ancient and modern, it is a precursor of Romanticism. *Vathek* (1786), an oriental tale by an eccentric millionaire, exotically combines Gothic romanticism with the vivacity of *The Arabian Nights*. The story of *Frankenstein* (1818) and the monster he created is as spine-chilling today as it ever was; as in all Gothic novels, horror is the keynote.

John Buchan

GREENMANTLE

1915 was a crisis point in the First World War for England
and her allies. In the East a new prophet has been promised,
and the fanatical spirit of Islam threatens to be harnessed to
the might of the German war machine.

In this thrilling sequel to *The Thirty Nine Steps*, Richard
Hannay is dispatched on an undercover mission in pursuit of
the mysterious and elusive 'Greenmantle' through occupied
Europe into Constantinople. It was a mission that would
demand all Hanney's courage and resourcefulness.

and

THE ISLAND OF SHEEP
THE THREE HOSTAGES

Sir Arthur Conan Doyle

THE HOUND OF THE BASKERVILLES

The ancient legend of the hound of the Baskervilles had persisted in family history for generations. And it was Sir
Charles's mysterious death in the grounds of Baskerville Hall
that brought Sherlock Holmes to the scene of one of his most
famous and intriguing cases.

'He was running, Watson – running desperately, running for
his life, running until he burst his heart and fell dead upon
his face ...' What had it been, then, looming through the
darkness, that could have inspired such terror? A spectral
hound loosed from hell; or a creature of infinite patience and
cunning, with a smiling face and a murderous heart ...

Penguin publish all the Sherlock Holmes stories
in nine individual volumes, as well as
in a handsome compendium edition:

THE PENGUIN COMPLETE SHERLOCK
HOLMES